WARRIOR DIPLOMATS

WARRIOR DIPLOMATS

Civil Affairs Forces on the Front Lines

EDITED BY

Arnel P. David,
Sean A. Acosta, and Nicholas Krohley

Rapid Communications in Conflict and Security Series
General Editor: Geoffrey R.H. Burn

CAMBRIA
PRESS

Amherst, New York

Requests for permission should be directed to permissions@cambriapress.com, or mailed to: Cambria Press, University Corporate Centre, 100 Corporate Parkway, Suite 128, Amherst, New York 14226, U.S.A.

Library of Congress Cataloging-in-Publication Data

Names: David, Arnel, editor. | Krohley, Nicholas, editor. | Acosta, Sean A., editor.

Title: Warrior diplomats : civil affairs forces on the front lines / edited by Arnel P. David, Sean A. Acosta, and Nicholas Krohley.

Other titles: Civil affairs forces on the front lines

Description: Amherst, New York : Cambria Press, [2023] | Series: Rapid communications in conflict and security series | Includes bibliographical references and index. | Summary: "America kicked off the 21st century with a two-decade losing streak. In Iraq and Afghanistan, the United States failed to understand the societies in which it was fighting. Blind to local fundamentals, the military proved unable to achieve effects via futuristic technology and lethal force-while civilian-led development and governance initiatives delivered a negligible return on a staggering investment. Representing the collective experience and expertise of nineteen soldiers, marines, and scholar-practitioners, this book draws upon the lessons of recent past to chart a contrarian view for the future. How should the US military understand the current geopolitical environment? What are the essential capabilities to succeed therein? Cutting against the grain of contemporary military thought-which focuses overwhelmingly on so-called "near-peer" competitors and the technologies needed to confront them-this book argues for the importance of understanding the playing field of strategic competition"-- Provided by publisher.

Identifiers: LCCN 2022058758 (print) | LCCN 2022058759 (ebook) | ISBN 9781621966722 (library binding) | ISBN 9781621966746 (paperback) ISBN 9781621966821 (pdf) | ISBN 9781621966838 (epub)

Subjects: LCSH: United States--Armed Forces--Stability operations. | United States--Armed Forces--Civil functions. | United States--Foreign relations--21st century. | National security--United States. | United States--Military policy.

Classification: LCC UH723 .W37 2023 (print) | LCC UH723 (ebook) | DDC 355/.0320973--dc23/eng/20230103

LC record available at https://lccn.loc.gov/2022058758

LC ebook record available at https://lccn.loc.gov/2022058759

TABLE OF CONTENTS

LIST OF FIGURES

ACKNOWLEDGMENTS

The editors and chapter authors are extremely grateful to Brigadier General (retired) Christopher Stockel for his unwavering support and encouragement throughout the development of this book as well as The Civil Affairs Association.

The Civil Affairs Association is a code section 501(c)19 veterans' organization. The purpose established by the founders was for the association to be an advocate of a strong and ready US military that has a capable and adequate Civil Affairs force. The association was also envisioned as a military professional organization that would serve as a forum for professionals to present and exchange their ideas on Civil Affairs. This book serves this purpose and has received support from The Civil Affairs Association, but it does not reflect or represent the views of the association in any way.

A special thanks to Colonel Carl E. Cooper, Jr. (USMC), Director of the Joint Advanced Warfighting School, for supporting and sharing the early draft of the book with senior civilian and military leaders. Their feedback and subsequent endorsement has been invaluable.

Our warmest thanks go to Dr. Geoffrey R. H. Burn, General Editor for the Rapid Communications in Conflict and Security, and the team at Cambria Press. They have been extremely amiable and supportive throughout the writing process.

Finally, this book is dedicated to the men and women of the armed forces and the interagency who have served as warrior diplomats overseas to advance peace and security.

Warrior Diplomats

Introduction

Shall the Nation Again Find Itself Unprepared?

Arnel P. David, Sean A. Acosta, and Nicholas Krohley

All militaries fail, even the most powerful ones: the Romans were crushed at Cannae, Napoleon was routed from Russia, the Red Army was humiliated in Afghanistan, and the list goes on. In war, as in life, failure is inevitable.

Over the past two decades, the United States has endured its own staggering failures. In Iraq and Afghanistan, America has reaped only the most modest of geopolitical dividends from a $6.4 trillion-plus investment and some 53,000 casualties.[1] Failure of this magnitude begs the questions: what lessons must be learned, and how does the US military adapt? Failure can be redeemed, at least in part, if constructive changes are made in response.

Efforts to learn from military disasters typically focus on breakdowns in strategic vision and failures to adapt and modernize.[2] The expression "generals always fight the last war" is once again in vogue as the US pivots from a Global War on Terrorism to a new era of so-called strategic competition. In the face of a radically different threat environment, the experts tell us that strategies, tactics, and capabilities must be overhauled.[3]

To that end, the United States now has a Futures Command, and the United Kingdom has established a Futures Directorate. The US military's focus is on the horizon and beyond. Military strategists cast themselves as "futurists." Technology is ascendant, and the Fourth Industrial Revolution offers transformative new tools to the warfighter. The consensus is clear: rather than dwelling on precisely how and why the US failed in Iraq and Afghanistan, preparation for the next set of challenges should be prioritized.

This book takes a starkly different view. We, the editors of this volume, have each witnessed America's failures firsthand and argue that the US military's most urgent task is not to transcend its recent history and transform itself into something fundamentally different. Instead, the US military needs to remedy a critical weakness that doomed its campaigns in Iraq and Afghanistan, a weakness that will yield the same result in any future conflict. This weakness is the inability to understand—and therefore act on—the facts on the ground in areas of geopolitical importance.

The US military suffers from a systemic inability to understand and influence human beings: friends, foes, and bystanders alike. Without this basic capability, American military might and technological prowess are wasted, time and again. Failure to engage with the fundamental building blocks of humanity—culture, society, politics, economics, and religion—leaves US military strategies and plans untethered to reality with disastrous results.

The bloodstained lessons of America's recent past must be heeded so that weaknesses that have been exposed are corrected and skill sets that have been refined at great cost can be built upon. The multiplicity of ad hoc structures developed over the last twenty years (to meet operational requirements and improve strategic performance) needs to be examined for its merits. The structures that are still useful must feed into the balance of investment decisions. Those that are inadequate must be improved or replaced. The US military cannot afford to repeat the mistakes of the post–Vietnam War era when military leadership ran from its counterinsurgency debacle and back to the comfort of preparing for large-scale conventional combat against the Soviets. Nor can the US military simply "move on" based on the false belief that technological advances will solve these problems for us.

THE WARS THE US WISHES TO FIGHT

The US military's pivot to strategic competition has brought a twofold debate: how to frame this new strategic environment, and how to optimize American forces to operate therein? Regarding the first issue, there is broad consensus (which we, the editors, share) that the geopolitical landscape is defined by both the disaggregation of international systems and norms and the increasingly intense competition from challengers to American hegemony. China is rising, offering an alternative vision of the future. Russia seeks a return to past glories and the reconstitution of historic spheres of influence. Iran envisions a fundamentally different geopolitical order in the Middle East. Formidable regional powers like Turkey and India are charting their own paths toward the future. Meanwhile, the United States and its core allies defend a fragmenting global system that is rooted, ostensibly, in democracy and free markets. This is the new great game.

What does this competition actually look like? This question shapes the second element of the debate regarding the optimization of forces within this environment, concerning how the great game will be played. We, the editors, are deeply skeptical of conventional wisdom. In the United States and the United Kingdom, debates center on "offsets" and modernization efforts to prepare for head-to-head conflict with competitors.[4] Large-Scale Combat Operations has become a proper noun, with an acronym to match (LSCO). Hardly a press conference goes by without reference to the centrality of technological innovation and force modernization. Underpinning these discussions is an obsession with the physical clash of steel and delivery of ordnance. The next war will be fast and decisive. Fires and maneuver, and the technologies that enable them, will dictate the outcome. This is the sort of war in which the US thinks that it can reliably dominate its adversaries, in contrast to the messy and intractable "small wars" of recent decades.[5] This is the war that the US military *wishes to fight.*

What if conventional wisdom is wrong? What if America's geopolitical foes are aware of Western technological superiority and equally cognizant of the US military's ineptitude in the human domain of conflict? America's failures in Iraq and Afghanistan exposed the fact that the US military pays only passing attention to the human condition and the timeless passions of war. People's visceral emotions and their *will to fight* are fueled by their perceptions of injustice, opportunism, racism, reaction, vengeance, and terror. On these issues, the US military is consistently out of its depth—to the point that, after two decades of failure, it is leaving these behind and retreating to more comfortable ground.

Why does the US military think this will work? Why does it believe that futuristic kinetic power will achieve results in the new great game when it has demonstrably failed to do so in the past? Time and again, the US military has sought technological panaceas. Among modern Western militaries, this is a cultural compulsion, which is inextricably intertwined with the desire for decisive battle.[6] Yet, the annals of military history show that rapid and decisive outcomes are few and far between (particularly those against near-peer adversaries).[7]

Nations must obviously invest in technological development, but technology must be understood as a means to an end—not the end itself.[8] Critically, the pursuit of technological advantage must not come at the expense of capabilities to understand and influence the human domain of competition and conflict. The US military cannot possibly leverage technology and platforms without understanding the context in which they are to be utilized. Understanding must precede action, yet a lack of understanding remains a prime area of strategic weakness.

This book expounds on the primacy of ground truth and the need to align US strategic objectives with local realities. This straightforward (yet far from easy) task is a sine qua non for success in the new great game. Fulfilling it is the most urgent and most cost-effective step that the US military can take to improve its competitive position. At present, the inability to understand operational environments is the Achilles heel of the US military. For all the data and expensive technology the US military has, it still does not know *why* events are unfolding as they are. As a result, the US military does not know how to use the extraordinary tools at its disposal. Strategic policies and plans are crafted by individuals who are blind to fundamental contextual dynamics.

Large scale peer-to-peer combat is a real possibility, certainly more so than at any time since the end of the Cold War. Such a prospect demands preparation. Buzzwords of the moment, such as "Large-Scale Combat Operations" and "lethality" are circulating for good reason, and the US military needs to train accordingly. That said, although these efforts are necessary, they are by no means sufficient. It is far from evident that the new great game will be a head-to-head clash of titans.[9] The principal adversaries of the United States have clear track records of attacking on the margins, in subtle (and, at times, deniable) ways that short-circuit US technological prowess. Just as conventional forces like those of the United States, the United Kingdom, and Israel have increased their ability for precision strike and lethal fires, competitors have shifted away from direct confrontations to an indirect contest of wills. This contest plays out among people, as American foes leverage populations to constrain Western action and freedom of movement.[10]

America's adversaries (nation-states and nonstate actors alike) consistently overmatch the US military's frontline personnel in the human domain, leveraging a deeper understanding of the people among whom the military fights. The United States deploys young people to the corners of the earth for fleeting periods of time, where they are all too often bested by cunning foes who know the lay of the land and speak the local language. America's adversaries are older; they blend in and know how to manipulate people's emotions to influence their behavior. Western military advisors, aid workers, humanitarians, and diplomats consistently find themselves ill prepared and uncompetitive. The US government is perpetually the "away team," losing to rivals with a clear home field advantage.[11]

A Gap Between Soldiers and Diplomats

To win this fight, the US military must be able to understand, engage, and influence *people*. This must be done one-on-one, face-to-face, at the individual level as well as collectively at communal and institutional levels. Under certain circumstances, it must be done indirectly through local partners or via social media. At all times, it must be done with a clear understanding of the contextual dynamics that shape the human domain.

This is a complex undertaking, which requires a robust skill set. This is a challenge that calls for *warrior diplomats*: people who can operate in austere environments, manage the risks attendant with direct exposure to the communities inhabiting contested terrain, and who possess the requisite skills to untangle complex dynamics and build substantive local relationships.

Within the US military, this has become the preserve of Civil Affairs forces: whether negotiating with the Taliban in the hinterlands of Afghanistan or conducting civil society engagement in the far-flung jungles of the Southern Philippines, this small and special capability has adapted to meet the demands of the larger Joint Force and national security apparatus. That said, Civil Affairs continues to struggle for relevance, consistency, and direction. In a defense culture that privileges technology and combined arms maneuver, Civil Affairs forces are systematically marginalized and divested.[12]

This book attempts to change this dynamic in two ways: firstly, by making the case for Civil Affairs's critical value in the new great game, and secondly, by suggesting how Civil Affairs might optimize itself to excel on the playing field. Civil Affairs forces offer a granular understanding of people and societies. They are global scouts, providing the insight that enables informed decision-making by military and civilian leaders. They deliver the contextual knowledge that should precede (and, thereafter, inform) military action. They map and engage with human networks. They discern how individuals and communities fit within the operational environment. Not only can Civil Affairs forces provide military leaders and their civilian counterparts with an unmatched understanding of civil considerations, they also provide the Joint Force with a capability to engage and influence human networks without establishing a large military presence.

The term "warrior diplomat" has been coined in reference to Civil Affairs forces, and it is used in this way throughout this book. The term "warrior" evokes an ethos of and commitment to operational excellence. Warriors are willing to sacrifice all, taking risks to secure victory in peace and war. The term "diplomat" is used to describe how these professionals must operate overseas. Prudence and discretion are essential. The warrior diplomat is not a gunslinger. Tactical excellence is a prerequisite, but only as a means to an end. Put another way, the warrior side of the coin enables them to get to their work site—the diplomat side of the coin enables them to do their job.

An Evolution in Capability

The earliest references to Civil Affairs activities are found in accounts of General Winfield Scott's negotiations in the Black Hawk War and of the treatment of Mexican citizens in the Mexican-American War in the 1830s and 1840s. In this context, military leaders were mindful of the indigenous perspective and used this understanding to win wars and secure peace. A century later, World War II was, arguably, the peak of Civil Affairs's prominence in the US military, as Civil Affairs forces conducted military governance operations throughout Europe and North Africa as contested terrain transitioned from Nazi control.[13] This was pivotal in the Allies' ability to consolidate military gains into political outcomes in a post-combat environment.

Historical reference points are helpful to understand the evolution of Civil Affairs, but they must not serve as anchors that define this capability. Civil Affairs has evolved into something more dynamic and versatile. The United States is engaged in a multifront competition with numerous adversaries, wherein it must maintain global influence through military and diplomatic engagement, economic investments, and in the information environment. Civil Affairs personnel have a critical role to play in each of these efforts. The most important task is to understand civil considerations, identify friendly and neutral civil networks, and then engage those networks on behalf of the Department of Defense—a capability replicated by no other element of US armed forces.

The contemporary Civil Affairs role is far closer to that of the Corps of Discovery than the examples cited above relating to the Mexican-American War or World War II. Following the Louisiana Purchase in 1803, President Thomas Jefferson charged two military officers to lead an expedition through this newly acquired land. The mission was to map a route to the Pacific Ocean, open up trade with indigenous tribes, and study terrain, plants, and wildlife.[14] Though not technically Civil Affairs officers (as the branch had yet to be established), the historic mission of Captain Meriwether Lewis and Lieutenant William Clark captures the essence of modern Civil Affairs: conducting civil reconnaissance and mapping human networks for the purpose of engagement on behalf of the United States government.[15]

Embarking from St. Louis, Missouri, Lewis and Clark were charged with a unique set of responsibilities, nestled somewhere between those of a soldier and a diplomat. As they traveled westward toward the Pacific Ocean, the territory became unknown and rugged, with indigenous tribes known to violently attack outsiders encroaching on their land. President Jefferson knew this type of mission required military men capable not only of traveling in a small unit safely across the landscape but also of interacting with the indigenous tribes and conveying the interests of the government to tribal leaders. This mission required characters adept in both military and diplomatic matters. Possessing the aforementioned skills, the members of the Corps of Discovery were the original warrior diplomats.

Throughout their journey, the members of the expedition convinced numerous tribes to travel to Washington, DC, to meet with President Jefferson. These tribes included the Oto, Sioux, Nez Perce, Shoshone, Missouri, Mandan, and others. Some engagements lasted only a day, whereas others saw the team living among tribes for months at a time.[16] Expedition members kept meticulous notes, highlighting each tribe's culture and the negotiation techniques that yielded successful results. Furthermore, the expedition mapped the physical terrain, including plants, animals, and any other information about the environment deemed important by the mission.

Today, Civil Affairs forces map infrastructure, organizations, cultural dynamics, important people, and more. These insights are as valuable today to commanders and interagency partners as Lewis and Clark's reports were to Congress and the president. The Civil Affairs mission is thus far from new or novel. On the contrary, its roots reach deep in the history of the United States and its military. Some have forgotten its importance, however, and the capability has been relegated. As the

United State rebalances and refocuses within a new strategic paradigm, it is vital that the US military rediscovers the value of Civil Affairs—and that Civil Affairs itself is ready to rise to the challenge.

A GLOBAL NETWORK OF SENSORS

At the height of the wars in Iraq and Afghanistan, the US military coined the phrase "every soldier is a sensor."[17] Recognizing that information provided a potentially decisive advantage, the military moved to turn frontline soldiers into data collectors. The basic premise was sound, to the point of being a statement of the obvious. Quite literally coated in technology, US military personnel set about vacuuming up data points from the battlefield. But the endeavor quickly went wrong because they were not trained, equipped, or empowered to make sense of what they saw. Calibrated just to gather bits and bytes, the prevailing mentality was that analysis would be done by others, elsewhere.

This was a fatally flawed approach to understanding operational environments because it was based on two false premises: First, that analysts far removed from the front line could make sense of data points that had been stripped of context. Second, that the sheer quantity of data collected by this sensor network could overcome the limitations of quantitative analysis. Regarding analytical failures over the past two decades:

> The very bigness of our data imparts an illusion of understanding. If we have terabytes of data, after all, surely we *must* know what we are looking at? But data sets, no matter their size, can never answer the question "why?" Indeed, context-free data sets can be structured to say virtually anything—and this is where our shift toward quant [quantitative analysis] goes from being an analytical limitation to a terrifying strategic liability. In a highly politicized environment where *no one* in the room has an intuitive feel for ground truth, and where qualitative context is largely absent from the intelligence cycle, the field is left open for mistaken

assumptions, political manipulation, and old-fashioned careerist bullshitting.[18]

This is precisely what occurred in Afghanistan, where US forces were perennially said to be "turning the corner" during two decades of consistent failure.[19]

Surveying the current strategic environment, the "sensor" concept remains sound. Indeed, it is *essential.* But the US military has been calibrating the wrong sort of sensors. The US military does not need more ones and zeroes to process. It is already overwhelmed by the troves of data that are fed into its analytical systems. Instead, the US military must break from the trend of treating frontline personnel as robots, unable to interpret what they see. To master the playing field, the US military needs focused insights from human beings who can make sense of what is happening before their eyes.

Civil Affairs should be the US military's go-to informational source, one that delivers insights as opposed to mere data: a global network of human sensors that can explain *why* events are happening in the human domain and enable the development of strategies and plans that further national interests. This is an indispensable capability in the new great game and will impart a greater competitive advantage than any futuristic kinetic weapons platform—at a fraction of the cost.

CHAPTER OVERVIEWS

This book begins with analysis of the current strategic environment. Chapter 1, "The Strategic Environment and the New Great Game," explores how a disaggregating international system is reshaping the balance of competition. The authors, all officers who served in US Army Civil Affairs, survey a range of contemporary geopolitical issues, highlighting the importance of local detail and the need for warrior diplomats. Chapter 2, "Thriving in The Gray Zone: Competition in the Space Between Peace and War," examines the features of the so-called "gray zone." The author, a serving officer in the British Army with deep experience in irregular warfare, shows how ambiguities and uncertainties create both risks and opportunities, which must be mastered if the US, the UK, and their allies are going to win wars. Chapter 3, "The Human Domain," unpacks confusing aspects of military doctrine and explores the cognitive aspects of the human domain. The authors of this chapter have a mix of scholarly and operational experience in special fields, which helps buttress an argument for a theory for the human domain —and why it matters to the US military.

The focus then shifts to the value proposition of the warrior diplomat and how this capability can be optimized for success. Chapter 4, "Civil Reconnaissance: Understanding the Playing Field," written by serving officers and non-commissioned officers within the special operations component of US Army Civil Affairs, explains how civil reconnaissance adds crucial context to the understanding of operational environments. Chapter 5, "Canceling the Crosswalk: Re-framing Civil Considerations," explains the inadequacy of the processes and methods that the US military uses to understand civil considerations and proposes a radically different approach. The author, an advisor to American, British, and partner-nation militaries, offers a view of the results this new approach might bring. Chapter 6, "Networks of Influence and Action: Cross-Functional Teams in the Lake Chad Basin," tells the firsthand story of how a team of warrior diplomats identified, engaged, and cultivated a network of influence across international borders. This enabled the authors, serving officers in US Army Special Forces and the special operations element of US Army Civil Affairs, to achieve the sort of locally framed yet internationally resonant strategic effects that are needed in the new great game.

The final three chapters dig deeper into how different warrior diplomat capabilities function and how they could be improved. Chapter 7, "Three Tribes to One: Integrating Civil Affairs," makes the case for further integration and interoperability among component forces within US Army Civil Affairs. The authors, both Civil Affairs officers, argue that integration within Civil Affairs is necessary to optimize Civil Affairs as a Joint Force capability. Chapter 8, "Joint Information Fusion & Synergy: Opportunities for Collaboration with United States Marine Corps Civil Affairs," argues for closer collaboration between Army and Marine Corps Civil Affairs elements, nested within a "whole of government" approach to the information environment. The authors, both serving US Marine Corps Civil Affairs officers, detail the evolution of the Marine Corps' Civil Affairs capability. They highlight the need for the sustained health and development of Civil Affairs ahead of the next conflict, through closer working relationships between Department of State and Department of Defense entities and improved analytical proficiency. Chapter 9, "Building a Global Civil-Military Network," identifies opportunities for engagement between the United States' warrior diplomats and their Civil-Military Cooperation (CIMIC) counterparts worldwide. The author, a retired US Army Civil Affairs officer, outlines the numerous benefits that would result from the development of a global network of military partners with similar capabilities.

The conclusion weaves together the different themes and arguments laid out in this book. The central focus is on the fundamental realities of the new great game and the fact that the US military is ill-equipped to navigate the playing field. The US military is using the wrong tools, attempting to make sense of the world using staggeringly expensive technology, which is incapable of explaining *why* events unfold as they do.[20] At the same time, the US military is asking the wrong questions, approaching the strategic competition paradigm with a near-exclusive focus on competitors—when, in fact, careful attention needs to be paid to the playing field itself.

Civil Affairs has a critical role to play in addressing these issues. Civil Affairs forces are the US military's eyes, ears, and voice vis-à-vis the 90-plus percent of an operational environment that is not a direct opponent. At present, the marginality of Civil Affairs leaves the US military incapable of discerning civil dynamics that have profound strategic resonance.

The US military is failing to seek out contextual ground truth, and thus causal understanding and informed decision-making are impossible. This must be understood as a structural fault in the US military's intelligence architecture and in the information flows that shape its view of the world.

Resolving this dysfunction is no easy task. Ground truth is often contested and, at times, actively concealed. A blurry line must be walked between objective facts and subjective inference. Here, the US military is well outside its comfort zone, even within the special operations community. Put bluntly, it is not something that the US military entrusts to frontline personnel. That said, the willful disregard for the messy complexity of the human domain is untenable. We, the editors, believe that the US military cannot afford to *not* grapple with these challenges and that Civil Affairs is the capability best positioned to take this on.

The hard truth, however, is that Civil Affairs is not the weapon that it needs to be. Civil Affairs has yet to clearly articulate its value to the US military and to consistently deliver results. Nor is Civil Affairs presently trained, staffed, and equipped to adequately investigate and understand the human domain—not to mention any large-scale efforts toward engagement and influence. This is a result of the fact that US military leadership does not fully appreciate Civil Affairs's strategic potential, as well as of the aforementioned culture bent toward lethal action and traditional warfighting activities. This book attempts to change these dynamics: first, by establishing the need for warrior diplomats as global scouts in the human domain, and second, by offering suggestions and examples of how Civil Affairs forces might best fill that vital role.

NOTES

1. The full cost of the wars in Iraq and Afghanistan remains challenging to pinpoint. For reference, see Department of Defense, *Casualty Status* (Washington, DC: Department of Defense, 2023), https://www.defense. gov/casualty.pdf; and Neta C. Crawford, "United States Budgetary Costs and Obligations of Post-9/11 Wars through FY2020: $6.4 Trillion," The Frederick S. Pardee Center for the Study of the Longer-Range Future, (November, 13, 2019), https://watson.brown.edu/costsofwar/ files/cow/imce/papers/2019/US%20Budgetary%20Costs%20of%20Wars %20November%202019.pdf?utm_source=Daily%20on%20Defense%20(2 019%20TEMPLATE)_11/15/2019&utm_medium=email&utm_ campaign=WEX_Daily%20on%20Defense&rid=84648.

2. Many Department of Defense doctrinal documents carry this theme. A strong view in this direction can be seen from the Commandant of the US Marine Corps at Department of the Navy, *Commandant's Planning Guidance: 38th Commandant of the Marines* (Washington, DC: Department of the Navy, 2020), https://www.marines.mil/Portals/1/ Publications/Commandant's%20Planning%20Guidance_2019.pdf?ver=2 019-07-17-090732-937.

3. For example, see "US Secretary of Defense outlines vision for how America fights 'the next war,'" *The National*, May 1, 2021, https://www.thenationalnews.com/world/the-americas/us-secretary- of-defence-outlines-vision-for-how-america-fights-the-next-war-1.12 14567. Secretary of Defense Lloyd Austin comments, "the US must develop a new vision of defence that takes greater advantage of new technologies, including quantum computing, artificial intelligence, and edge computing."

4. Dmitry (Dima) Adamsky, "The Revolution in Military Affairs," in *Net Assessment and Military Strategy*, ed. Thomas G. Mahnken (Amherst, NY: Cambria Press 2020), 169–172.

5. Discussed in Russell Weigley, *The American Way of War* (Bloomington: Indiana University Press, 1977). For a description of an earlier, pre-indus- trial American way of war, see John Grenier, *The First Way of War: Amer- ican War Making on the Frontier, 1607–1814* (New York: Cambridge Uni- versity Press, 2005). On precision targeting and decisive battle see Max

Boot, *War Made New: Weapons, Warriors, and the Making of the Modern World* (New York: Gotham Press, 2007).

6. There are a number of scholars who make this point. See Robert Johnson, "Hard Truths, Uncomfortable Futures and the Perils of Group-Think: Rethinking Defence in the 21st Century," in *Agile Warrior 2018–2019 Annual Report* (Andover: British Army Capability Directorate, 2019), 21–29; and Antulio J. Echevarria II, *Toward an American Way of War* (Carlisle: US Army War College, Strategic Studies Institute, March 2004), 1.

7. H. R. McMaster, *Battlegrounds: The Fight to Defend the Free World,* (New York: Harper Collins, 2020).

8. Jonathan Caverly, Ethan Kapstein, and Srdjan Vucetic, "F-35 Sales are America's Belt and Road," *Foreign Policy,* July 12, 2019, https://foreignpolicy.com/2019/07/12/f-35-sales-are-americas-belt-and-road/.

9. Sean McFate, *The New Rules of War: Victory in the Age of Durable Disorder* (New York: William Morrow, 2019).

10. Charles T. Cleveland, Benjamin Jensen, Susan Bryant, and Arnel P. David, *Military Strategy in the 21st Century: People, Connectivity, and Competition* (Amherst, NY: Cambria Press, 2018).

11. For discussion of US military forces as the "away team" and the attendant disadvantages, see Patrick Hulme and Erik Gartzke, "The U.S. Military's Real Foe: The Tyranny of Distance," *19FortyFive,* January 25, 2021, https://www.19fortyfive.com/2021/01/the-u-s-militarys-real-foe-the-tyranny-of-distance/.

12. The dissolution of 85th Civil Affairs Brigade cut the entire active-duty Civil Affairs force in half, as detailed in Arnel P. David and Clay Daniels, "Strategic Misfire: The Army's Planned Reduction of Civil Affairs Forces," *Foreign Policy,* accessed August 5, 2020, https://foreignpolicy.com/2016/05/12/strategic-misfire-the-armys-planned-reduction-of-civil-affairs-forces/

13. Harry L. Coles and Albert K. Weinberg, *Civil Affairs: Soldiers Become Governors,* (Washington: Center of Military History, 1964), 730–738.

14. Stephen E. Ambrose, *Undaunted Courage* (New York: Simon and Schuster Paperbacks, 1996).

15. Shafi Saiduddin and Robert Schafer, "Civil Reconnaissance on the Frontier," *Eunomia Journal,* February 28, 2021, https://www.civilaffairsassoc.org/post/civil-reconnaissance-on-the-frontier

16. Stephen E. Ambrose, *Undaunted Courage* (New York: Simon and Schuster Paperbacks, 1996).

17. The initial concept briefing on "Every Soldier is a Sensor," or "ES2," from the Association of the United States Army in 2004, can be found here: https://www.ausa.org/sites/default/files/TBIP-2004-ES2-Every-Soldier-is-a-Sensor.pdf. For discussion of how this concept entered mainstream military training and recruiting in the years that followed, see Stew Magnuson, "The Army Wants to Make 'Every Soldier a Sensor,'" *National Defense Magazine*, May 1, 2007, https://www.nationaldefensemagazine.org/articles/2007/5/1/2007may-army-wants-to-make-every-soldier-a-sensor.

18. Nicholas Krohley, "The Intelligence Cycle is Broken. Here's How to Fix it," *Modern War Institute at West Point*, October 24, 2017, https://mwi.usma.edu/intelligence-cycle-broken-heres-fix/.

19. For example, see Paul McLeary, "The U.S. Has 'Turned the Corner' in Afghanistan, Top General Says," *Foreign Policy*, November 28, 2017.

20. For detailed discussion of the limits of data-driven analysis, see Judea Pearl, *The Book of Why: The New Science of Cause and Effect* (London: Penguin Books, 2020). For commentary on the limited potential of artificial intelligence, and the myriad misconceptions surrounding its utility, see Kate Crawford, *Atlas of AI: Power, Politics, and the Planetary Costs of Artificial Intelligence*, (New Haven: Yale University Press, 2021).

CHAPTER 1

THE STRATEGIC ENVIRONMENT AND THE NEW GREAT GAME

James Micciche, Kyle Staron, and Kevin Chapla

Across the literature on strategic competition, there is a pervasive and dangerous idea that the US has been here before.[1] That the current environment can be understood as a redux of the Cold War but with three competitors: America, Russia, and China. Cue the proxy wars, political crises, and arms races. The US was victorious once. The thinking is that if it follows the same plan, it can win again.

The US military is focused on conventional military power, enhanced weaponry, and force deployment. It views conflict through the lens of direct confrontation with another great power. As General Mark A. Milley, Chairman of the Joint Chiefs of Staff, has said, "units are getting back into the ability to shoot, move, communicate and maneuver against significant enemies."[2]

All of this is important, of course, in war. But the question remains of how to *compete.* The 2017 National Security Strategy heralded the return of "great power competition."[3] Yet, despite this strong statement (and the document directly naming Russia and China as revisionist rivals), the concept of competition has remained opaque and ill-defined.

Within a year of the 2017 *National Security Strategy*'s publication, the US Army announced a $57 billion equipment-based modernization program that established the military's prioritization of comparative overmatch in Large-Scale Combat Operations. However, it took nearly four years to publish a document defining the army's role in competition.[4] This offers clear evidence of the military's priorities and comfort zone. Meanwhile, America's principal rivals were honing their competitive strategies and refining their ability to win without fighting.

In the view of the authors, the United States is not engaged in the Cold War 2.0. The US does not inhabit a structured international system wherein great powers are clashing. Instead, the world is moving toward disintegration. International organizations, norms, and practices are unraveling. This disaggregation will make the world more chaotic, and leading global powers will struggle to exert control. In this environment, local grievances will take on global importance. Thus, a key capability in strategic competition is to understand societal dynamics at a granular, local level. From this understanding, the United States can make informed decisions vis-à-vis its competitive posture in the new great game.

In this chapter, the macro characteristics of America's current strategic environment will be examined. What does power look like in the middle of the twenty-first century? What are the overarching threats and emerging opportunities? If the Cold War blueprint is not suitable for the game the US is playing, what is the correct approach?

Having framed the overall environment, the chapter will look at regional dynamics to examine how strategic competition plays out in specific contexts. At the same time, it will survey region-specific trends that affect American interests. Highlighted throughout the chapter will be the reasons why warrior diplomats (i.e., Civil Affairs and other interagency capabilities) are essential to navigating the localized issues that resonate on the global stage. These issues become magnets for multidirectional geopolitical competition, where granular nuance is vital to strategic policy making. This is clearly evident today, from Syria to Libya to Somalia, where disparate and ever-shifting coalitions are waging multipronged offensives. It is equally vital in Eastern Europe, where Ukrainian and Russian forces' will to fight is of paramount importance on the battlefield, and the social, economic, and political consequences of war will reshape the regional geopolitical landscape for generations to come. In such environments, combat power is critical and technology can provide an edge—but local knowledge and relationships may prove decisive.

Contextual understanding is key to identifying and managing threats, challenges, and opportunities. Nowhere is that understanding more important than in geopolitics. Within the great game of strategic competition, knowing oneself, one's opponents, and the overall system is merely the baseline for projecting power and securing one's interests. Context in geopolitics, however, is far from static. Actions can have vast repercussions. A nation must anticipate not only the second- and third-order effects of its actions but those of rivals and allies as well. Such insights are extraordinarily difficult to gain due to the complexity and dynamism of the real world. But the very act of pursuing these generates value in the form of experience and refined instincts.

Even when nations enjoy marked systemic advantages, they may only be temporary. Power can vanish in a moment with technological, environmental, or even social shifts. To help overcome the "wicked problems" of international relations, academics and policymakers often create simplistic models better suited for "tame problems" with finite boundaries and singular solutions.[5] Scholars, for example, have described the world in geometric terms. In 1948, Hans Morgenthau, one of the founding scholars of international relations, described states as "billiard balls" with the tendency to crash into one another. In a chaotic international system, balls differed in size based on their overall power, or the sum of their capabilities and assets.[6] More recently, political commentator Thomas Friedman described the world as "flat."[7] Friedman used this metaphor to show how the world of the 2000s was interconnected more than ever before, after decades of hyper-globalization, migration, liberal trade policies, and offshoring.

Morgenthau's and Friedman's theories are diametrically opposed. One describes a world of disjointed entities in near-constant conflict. The other views the world as an ever-growing network of cooperative relationships. However, they both fall prey to a long-standing fault of the international relations discipline: the lack of focus on local detail.

A WORLD OF MANY—DISAGGREGATION

Disaggregation has been under way since the fall of the Soviet Union, via the fragmentation of large states into smaller ones. At the start of 2021, the US government recognized 195 sovereign states. This is more than twice the number of states that were recognized at the end of World War II.[8] The disaggregation of empires, colonial territories, and larger nations occurs through various processes, but they can be divided between those that were internally generated and those that were externally catalyzed.[9] The rebellion of the United States and its subsequent independence from England are an example of an internally generated disaggregation. Inversely, the myriad arbitrary borders drawn by colonial powers with insufficient regard for the subnational compositions of the polities they created are a classic example of external generation. External disaggregation like the Sykes-Picot Agreement's division of Southwest Asia into European zones of control following World War I, the 1947 partition of India and Pakistan, and the various colonial boundaries drawn across Africa have all led to unstable states mired in conflict, highlighting the power of subnational variables and *context*.

International organizations, agreements, alliances, and supranational entities are also disaggregating. The Union of Soviet Socialist Republics (USSR) broke apart into a dozen nations following the fall of the Berlin Wall. Despite growing throughout the 1990s and 2000s, the market size and population of the European Union decreased when the United Kingdom left in 2021.[10] In addition to being examples of supranational disaggregation, both the USSR and Brexit highlight the cascade effect of disaggregation and the power of the subnational unit, as many of the newly formed nations that emerged from the USSR remain mired in separatist movements—oftentimes supported by Moscow to advance Russian interests and regain influence over key strategic terrain or mineral deposits. Another example of disaggregation can be seen when the terms of the last World Trade Organization's (WTO) appellate judges expired, and the appointing body was unable to achieve consensus on replacements.[11] Although the WTO still physically exists in name, location, and membership, the lack of appointed and approved appellate judges prevents it from carrying out its oversight and regulatory responsibilities in settling and arbitrating trade disputes.

Nigeria is an example of disaggregation at the national level. The borders created by British cartographers included a diverse set of cultures that are spread across a wide range of identities, including religion, tribe, language, and even former imperial allegiance. This patchwork has long prevented the creation of a true national identity and has forced Nigerian politicians to expand from three states to the present number of thirty-six (plus a federal capital territory) to balance centers of power and better govern people with distinct cultural identities.[12] Even the most autocratic nations, such as China, Russia, and Saudi Arabia, are facing disaggregation, as subnational movements in Hong Kong, Chechnya, and Qatif vie for greater autonomy (or even independence), refusing to submit to centralized leadership and authority.

POWER AMONG POPULATIONS: OPERATING BELOW THE STATE

As disaggregation breaks the world into smaller and smaller pieces, consensus building has become increasingly difficult. In response, states aspiring for increased influence have undermined or circumvented existing norms and systems. One such approach is through lawfare, which involves restructuring the international system in one's favor and enabling economic predation and coercion along the way.[13] Jill Goldenziel offers the best explanation of the modern application of lawfare with her two-part definition of the concept: "1) the purposeful use of law taken toward a particular adversary with the goal of achieving a particular strategic, operational, or tactical objective, or 2) the purposeful use of law to bolster the legitimacy of one's own strategic, operational, or tactical objectives toward a particular adversary, or to weaken the legitimacy of a particular adversary's particular strategic, operational, or tactical objectives."[14] China, for example, has been utilizing its influence over international organizations to establish legal precedence for its territorial expansion into the South China Sea—justifying the actions of its maritime militia and framing freedom of navigation passages by the United States as acts of aggression.

The overt use of coercive force between states is highly restricted by three systemic factors: nuclear weapons, hyper-globalization, and the rise of the Information Age.[15] This concept was best articulated in a 2020 article on the future of American grand strategy by Daniel W. Drezner, Ronald R. Krebs, and Randall Schweller, who wrote: "Military power rarely achieves national goals or fixes problems anymore; interventions usually only make bad situations worse. The yawning outcome gap in clear outcomes between the first and the second Gulf wars makes this plain. Power simply isn't as fungible as it used to be."[16] These restrictions have compelled states to find alternative means to carry out their security strategy, such as the fostering of fragmentary forces within rival states, which has become a major trend. Examples include Iran empowering Shiʻa militias throughout the Levant and Iraq, the Kremlin manipulating

Russian-speaking minorities in Eastern Europe and Central Asia, and the Chinese Communist Party's United Front Work Department using the ten-million strong Chinese diaspora as an extension of the state.[17]

Furthermore, powerful nations that seek to upend the existing US-led international order use information operations to sow dissent among their rivals, fomenting instability and empowering fragmentary proxies. Russia, for example, has weaponized social media to incite American domestic political polarization and to exacerbate societal fault lines across Eastern Europe.[18] Subnational entities are thus increasingly powerful, and this dynamic is critical to understanding the current international system. The use of proxies, lawfare, and information operations are all examples of how nations operate without escalating to the level of armed conflict. This enables them to bypass America's comparative military superiority.

US military doctrine recognizes this challenge, despite prevailing emphasis on interstate conflict and traditional maneuver. The US Army's capstone doctrine *Operations* clearly and directly outlines the aforementioned situations:

> War is inextricably tied to the populations inhabiting the land domain...Understanding the human context that enables the enemy's will, which includes culture, economics, and history, is as important as understanding the enemy's military capabilities. Commanders cannot presume that superior military capability alone creates the desired effects on an enemy.[19]

Within the current international system, power, influence, and information all flow through substate actors.[20] Due to shifting geopolitical fundamentals, an adversary today may be an ally tomorrow and then a frenemy the day after. What was once a nation's strength can soon become a weakness. Most importantly, what worked to coerce or deter one state will not always work to deter, compel, or coerce another. As noted in chapter 2 of this book, this unpredictability places a premium on the speed at which states apply power and on the ability to understand a shifting geopolitical environment.

A NONPOLAR NETWORK: A THEORY OF NONPOLARITY

The US has enjoyed a privileged position in the international system for eighty years. From 1945 until 1989, the global order was bipolar, with power split between the US and the Soviet Union. Although each superpower maintained global alliances, the US and USSR carried out their foreign policies with their own direct interests in mind. In 1989, after the fall of the Berlin Wall and the start of the Soviet Union's dissolution, the US found itself in the position of sole superpower. Through the 1990s, the US sought to construct a "revised" world order, one centered on meeting humanitarian challenges in places like Somalia, Bosnia, and Kuwait and later described as the "Responsibility to Protect," or R2P doctrine.[21]

After the September 11th terrorist attacks, the United States used this unipolarity to prosecute the Global War on Terrorism. Over time, however, unilateral action undermined US prestige and influence and set the conditions for a nonpolar world. The United States cannot stand as the world's sole leader any longer, and no other state (or collection thereof) is willing or able to fill this void.[22]

In the view of the authors of this chapter, the geopolitical landscape of the mid-twenty-first century is neither flat nor populated by independent monolithic states, but rather can best be described as *dynamic*. The international system is in flux, with shifting alliances and unstable power dynamics.[23] The geopolitical status quo is like an unstable chemical compound, one in which the individual atoms constantly change form and bond with and separate from other atoms. Within the vast network of nations, power is exerted through connectivity and the strength of underpinning bonds. Much like atoms, the world has polarity: states and subnational units are drawn to or repelled from their counterparts.

This gives each nation more autonomy and agency. Nations aspiring to become great powers compete for the support of smaller nations in order to grow their overall influence. Smaller powers, for their part, actively manipulate larger powers in pursuit of advantage against local or regional rivals. To be successful, larger powers like the United States must understand the grievances and aspirations of smaller nations. This is not to say that the grievances and aspirations of these smaller states are geopolitically significant in and of themselves and that the US should adopt an intrusive, interventionist posture around the world. On the contrary, nuanced understanding of local realities will enable the judicious application of influence and, as needed, hard power. This is all the more important in a disaggregating international system where alliances are framed less around broadly shared ideals and more so around bilateral quid pro quo arrangements.

The use of force may also lose value in a strategic sense. National power built on military force is not fungible; once a nation decides to expend military power, that power is gone. The United States has lost international prestige and weakened its ability to influence events because its military has been bogged down in Iraq and Afghanistan without a commensurate return on this geopolitical investment. The US has merely *lost* power. Despite continuous indications that the US military could not kill and capture its way to victory, it tried exactly that.[24] The prevailing ideology posited that institutions would hold through armed conflict and that US military success would translate directly and immediately to political gains. However, in reality the US did not achieve sustainable gains and only wounded itself in the eyes of the world.[25]

The world is now facing crises that are too large and multifaceted to be solved by unilateral action or fragmentary alliances. From climate change to social media manipulation to intractable civil wars, the world has challenges that require coordinated solutions. But few viable frameworks exist through which such coordination might occur. The United Nations, the largest and most well-known international organization, has become a battleground for Chinese lawfare. The appointment of some of the least free and open societies to the human rights council degrades its credibility as an impartial arbiter. Lastly, given the complexity of the aforementioned challenges, it is shortsighted to maintain that a competitor is always an enemy. To navigate the challenges of a nonpolar world, the US may have to simultaneously compete and cooperate with the same country regarding different areas and topics.

THE STATE OF PLAY

The strategic environment in the near term will, of course, retain features of the recent past. The world has not changed overnight. However, global dynamics must now be approached through the paradigm of strategic competition. For example, after a large decline throughout the 1990s, the number of civil wars has increased dramatically over the last decade. The UN reports that there are more wars, more instances of intrastate violence, and more deaths this decade than in the early 2000s. The UN, for its part, has struggled to offer meaningful solutions. One of the given reasons for these increases is the internationalization of civil wars. International involvement in the Syrian conflict, for example, has prolonged the war and placed a solution far out of reach.[26]

Similarly, international terrorist groups will take advantage of local and regional grievances and disputes to grow their influence. The war in Mali serves as an example of this phenomenon. A local civil war, started by a disenfranchised ethnic group, has morphed into a regional war involving international terrorists and multilateral organizations. Lesser-known jihadist groups have been able to grow their influence by coming under the umbrella of Al-Qaeda or merging into the Islamic State's regional franchise.

In the near term, these local grievances provide an opening for a great power (or regional power) to sow chaos—or, conversely, foster stability.[27] Of course, proxy war has been a long-standing tool of foreign policy— but it required substantive manpower and logistics from the sponsor. Now, a sponsor can aid the proxy from afar and with greater cover with the informational tools just discussed and in chapter 3.

Asia

Despite a long-promised pivot to Asia, the United States has been peren-nially overtaken by events elsewhere, such as the rise of the Islamic State in the Middle East. As a result, China has had a freer hand to expand its presence—in terms of influence, economics, and physical control—in the region. At the heart of China's expansion is the strategic concept of three warfares, which utilizes public opinion warfare, psychological warfare, and lawfare to shape perceptions of the Chinese government, the US, and third-party governments.[28] As two of the three warfares exist primarily within the human domain, local context is paramount in identifying and mitigating malign efforts that are the modern-day equivalent of preparatory fires.[29]

Unlike the US, which views state-centric competition primarily through the lens of the military, China has weaponized its economy to create a series of debt-laden investment deals to expand its presence, power, and influence (while concurrently denying market access to others). Often, China extends their economic hand bilaterally, through what former National Security Advisor H. R. McMaster has described as a form of strategic corruption, explaining that "the new vanguard of the Chinese Communist Party is a delegation of bankers and party officials with duffel bags full of cash. Corruption enables a new form of colonial-like control that extends far beyond strategic shipping routes in the Indian Ocean and South China Sea, and elsewhere."[30] The ability of China to execute this strategy was only enhanced when the US left the Transpacific Partnership (TPP), forcing many smaller and middle-tier nations in the Indo-Pacific to negotiate with China bilaterally rather than collectively, which provides an exceptionally advantageous position for China.

Interestingly, the US seems to have taken cues from regional partners in crafting a strategy for the region. In a recently declassified Indo-Pacific strategic framework, American strategists and policymakers incorporated strategies and ideas from regional partners like Japan and Australia. The Australian Strategic Policy Institute wrote that "[then National Security

Advisor Robert] O'Brien properly notes this emerging convergence, and the common ground among the Indo-Pacific policies of the US, Australia, India, Japan, ASEAN, some key European partners and, increasingly, South Korea, New Zealand and Taiwan. This emerging consensus gives the lie which the Chinese claim the Indo-Pacific is some American or Australian invention that will 'dissipate like ocean foam.'"[31] It is worth reiterating that building international consensus reinforced American security rather than weakened it.

Long-standing US alliances in the Pacific have, so far, withstood the pressure of disaggregation and the relative deterioration of the rules-based order. However, absent meaningful restoration, aspiring powers and friendly nations alike may succumb to the allure of alternatives to US leadership, security, and economic partnership. Shoring up alliances and institutions will remain critical to US influence in Asia. To achieve this, and to counter Chinese encroachment, the US government will have to remain attentive to localized concerns and watchful of social, economic, and political fault lines that China might exploit. For example, the Chinese government does not publicly disclose its One Belt, One Road projects and often utilizes investments to restrict US access to key air and sea ports needed to project power and presence. The US developing local networks and understanding context would greatly diminish China's ability to obfuscate malign economic-related partnerships in key terrain. Furthermore, detailed local knowledge paired with credible governing partners is critical to combating and mitigating Chinese activity in the economic, diplomatic, and information domains.

Finally, discussion of the Indo-Pacific would be incomplete by only mentioning the challenge of China and not discussing the emerging opportunity of India. The world's largest democracy, and soon to be the world's most populous nation, India shares borders with two nuclear powers (both of which have attacked India multiple times in the past century). India now finds those two nations, Pakistan and China, working ever more closely together. Pakistan has provided China with an Indian

Ocean naval base in Gwadar, and China has infused Pakistan with large amounts of investment as a key node in the One Belt, One Road initiative.[32] The US has clearly seen the importance of India, as the DoD changed the acronym of the United States Indo-Pacific Command from PACOM to INDOPACOM in 2018. There have also been active efforts to reinvigorate and even expand the "Quad," a multilateral defensive alliance of the US, Japan, Australian, and India, the latter three being the most advanced and largest democracies in the Indo-Pacific. India has proven its military prowess consistently, defeating its long-standing rival and former aggregated colonial partner Pakistan in four wars. India now faces new threats to its northeastern border. This is a disputed border where both India and China have been conducting a series of aggressive maneuvers and military brinkmanship.[33]

Domestically, India is home to dozens of ethnic groups speaking hundreds of languages. Worryingly, despite its multiethnic democracy, India is undergoing a period of extreme identity-based polarization that could potentially threaten the long-standing plurality of its society; this complex web of local dynamics must be closely monitored and understood.[34] Regardless, India will need to be a key part in any US strategy in countering China in the region. With a large population, an increasingly advanced and developing economy, a key geographic position in the Indian Ocean, and a shared democratic tradition, India is an obvious and essential regional partner.

The Middle East
The past two decades in the Middle East have been fraught with military intervention and regime change, the failures of which prompted an eventual American retrenchment.[35] The ensuing instability has made the region a glaring example of disaggregation and chaotic turmoil. A host of nonstate, substate, state, and multinational actors are using the Middle East as a playing field to pursue political and ideological agendas. Regional actors like Turkey and Russia, and to a somewhat lesser extent China, have scrambled to fill the void left by the United

States, although none has yet demonstrated the willingness to assume a more prominent leadership role. The current condition of the Middle East may thus provide a glimpse into the future of a disaggregated world.

The destabilizing effects of the contemporary Saudi-Iran rivalry continue to drive regional geopolitical dynamics. The tenacity of the Saudi-Iran rivalry is vital to Riyadh's continued privileged position as a trusted US counterweight to Iranian aggression, while the royal family's legitimacy and authority is bolstered, in part, by its anti-Tehran rhetoric. This conditional relationship, described by Kim Ghattas as an "endless self-reinforcing loop of enmity," has no obvious end, and a solution will require deliberate statecraft and diplomacy from substantial multi-national coalitions.[36]

Simmering conflicts across the region remain open to intervention from a complex entanglement of regional and international allies. Substate conflicts in Libya and Syria, which began as relatively localized political and societal struggles, were exploited by Russia, Turkey, and several Gulf Arab states in pursuit of regional power. Truly understanding how local dynamics in these conflicts clash with the interests of ambitious state actors will allow the US to better predict opportunities as well as risks to national interests. Knowing which subnational conflicts are ripe to explode into wider transnational crises will create time and space to make informed policy decisions—but this foresight requires substantial investment in capabilities that live and operate at the local level.

Iran continues to meddle in internal affairs in countries across the Middle East through its proxies in Lebanon, Syria, Yemen, and Iraq, gaining pockets of support via the transfer of weapons and money. Iran funds and arms Shi'a militias in Iraq, supports Hezbollah in Lebanon, and bolsters the Assad regime in Syria.[37] The US and its partners cannot contain Iran's proxy actions without a deeper understanding of the local dynamics that the Islamic Republic exploits to achieve its political objectives.

A major result of the Saudi-Iranian regional rivalry is the ongoing civil war in Yemen. Although it is typically described as a conflict between a coalition of Sunni Gulf states intervening to defeat Iran-backed Shi'a rebels who overthrew the Yemeni government in 2015, the conflict is far more complicated. The now eight-year-old intrastate conflict represents disaggregation at multiple levels.[38] Exacerbating existing fault lines are various parties external to the conflict who use proxies to improve their regional geopolitical positions. The net effect is the existence of civil wars within civil wars. For example, the United Arab Emirates backed the Southern Transition Council (STC), declaring a state of emergency and threatening to overthrow the Republic of Yemen Government (ROYG) unless its demands were met. This act quickly led to the 2018 Battle of Aden, in which STC forces defeated Saudi-backed ROYG forces—in spite of the fact that the two armies had been fighting as allies against the Houthi-Saleh alliance for the previous three years.[39] Despite the best attempts of de facto coalition leader Saudi Arabia to avoid continued violence in the key port of Aden, the STC declared "self-rule" in 2020 due to a lack of southern representation at ongoing peace talks.[40]

On the other side of the civil war, the Houthis and elite forces loyal to former Yemeni president Ali Abdullah Saleh began open conflict with one another in 2017 because of the president's negotiating with external agents. This was despite two years of successful alliance and military success against government and coalition forces.[41] Further complicating the situation in Yemen are the myriad nonstate organizations present in the country. From NGOs and IGOs (intergovernmental organizations) providing aid to the world's worst humanitarian crisis to affiliates of both Al-Qaeda and the Islamic State using ungoverned space to advance influence, the competitive space features a complex, dynamic confluence of interests and actors.

Hanging over the Saudi-Iranian dynamic is an urgent need for the US to strengthen its leadership among regional players while simultaneously inventing a new approach to geopolitical competition made for a disaggregating world. Repairing US credibility and restoring meaningful partnerships will be difficult as the US-led international order faces unprecedented tests while foundational alliances have revealed signs of weakness and decay.[42] Such a monumental task amid the steady trend of disaggregation demands that the US reorient its regional presence toward diplomacy and engagement. This may also involve reorganization and some withdrawal or repurposing of American combat forces. Warrior diplomats, and similar interagency capabilities designed to understand the intricacies of local dynamics, will prove invaluable in enabling adaptation to this new reality.

Africa
Given its size, location, and abundance of resources, Africa has long been touted as the next strategic arena in geopolitics. Over the course of the last two decades, Chinese foreign policy has borne this out. From lucrative trade deals to extract rare-earth minerals to the inclusion of African nations in its One Belt, One Road initiative, China has placed a premium on access to African markets and influence over the continent.[43]

At first glance, this approach has been successful. African leaders have received infrastructure investments, steady exports of minerals, and a trade partner who asks no questions about human rights or quality of governance. However, as governance has improved in key African countries such as Ghana and Botswana, politicians and citizens alike are asking new questions about their relationship with China.[44] Why does China import workers for infrastructure and mining projects when local Africans are able to work and need jobs? Why is there no improvement in the local areas around Chinese operations? When Chinese investments enrich and entrench a narrow elite within a given country (via kickbacks and other trade practices forbidden by US law), how should the masses respond?

These local grievances have the ability to influence regional and global perceptions of strategic competition. The internationalization of local conflict in Africa has already been seen. The war in Mali now being seen as a counterterrorism campaign is just one example of this. At its outset in 2012, it was an ethnic conflict that was quickly hijacked by regional jihadist groups, who then pledged allegiance to international terror networks. Subsequently, the violence spread across borders. Africa's fault lines are also being exacerbated by climate factors. Over the last twenty years, conflict has broken out throughout the Sahel between nomadic and sedentary groups, principally over the availability of water.[45] As desertification spreads and the water table drops, control over each individual spring and water hole will be a matter of life or death for hundreds (if not thousands) of people.

Building good governance across Africa would further the United States' influence and undermine other competitors' aims on the continent. As it stands, the US military largely views "partnership" as building military capability to pursue terrorist networks. However, survey data shows that in the preponderance of cases, local government misdeeds were the final trigger pushing individuals toward extremism in Africa.[46] Most jihadist fighters are not ideologues; they were mistreated and disenfranchised by their own government and security forces and want recompense.[47]

However, America's approach to Africa cannot be framed entirely as a counter to Chinese expansion. As argued by the RAND Corporation: "Seeing Africans as Africans and not pawns in some great game paradoxically could go a long way toward strengthening the United States' position in its competition with other powers, especially if it translates into engagement with, and investment in, African economies and institutions in ways that are not limited to and transparently about countering Chinese moves."[48] Warrior diplomats and interagency practitioners of soft power are uniquely positioned to "see Africans as Africans" and provide an indispensable perspective to senior military leaders and policymakers in Washington.

Latin America

From the Monroe Doctrine to post–World War II military and political interventions, Latin America has been largely sidelined by foreign policy practitioners. When mentioned at all, it is most often relegated to conversations concerning counter-narcotics, drug trafficking, and immigration. Traumatized from America's history of military intervention and keen to offset American influence in the Western Hemisphere, some Latin American governments have turned to ambitious and commodity-needy states like China, presenting a perfect opportunity for the Asian colossus to provide economic alternatives that champion anti-interventionist ideals. As the Center for Security and International Studies notes, "[China] is an increasingly important source of demand for Latin American commodities (such as soy from Brazil), investment to provide needed jobs, and loans to help Latin American governments such as Ecuador and Argentina weather pandemic-induced fiscal crises."[49]

Although regional Chinese strategy is largely mercantilist in Latin America, military and security relationships are vital to protecting Chinese commercial interests (while also laying foundations for utility during a potential Sino-American military conflict). Likewise, Russia has been eager to make inroads in Latin America by stoking anti-American sentiments and empowering and backing American rivals like Venezuela and Nicaragua. Both Russia and China aim to leverage arms sales, military facility-use permissions, and sociopolitical capital to undermine American interests and institutions in the region.[50] Venezuela, in particular, remains a propitious geopolitical leverage point in the Western Hemisphere for both Russia and China, which have both publicly backed the regime and provided economic bailouts in exchange for privileged access to the Venezuelan petrol market.[51]

Signs of democratic backsliding in recent years, as well as a troubled history of regional US military intervention, have created an environment within which America must develop inventive, new approaches to security.[52] Despite the limitations of Russian and Chinese attempts to gain influence in Latin America, the US government has not developed methods to mobilize popular opinion on the ground in ways that support political outcomes. Properly positioned, warrior diplomats across Latin America could provide key insights and ground truths on how foreign adversaries' policies are playing out at the local level. Warrior diplomats are one of few tools in the American defense enterprise designed to detect the types of societal behavior at the local level that can be harnessed to further broader national security objectives.

Europe

Europe remains central to US foreign policy for a host of reasons. First, Europe is composed of many of the world's most mature democracies. The community of free societies has to be continuously nurtured; otherwise, democratic backsliding is a realistic possibility. Second, the European Union is the America's largest trading partner. Lastly, The North Atlantic Treaty Organization (NATO) alliance is critical to global security because it represents the largest military capability in the world by far. European bases and American troop presence are critical to logistics operations that are required by America's global deployment posture, especially in the Middle East and Africa.

The continued Russian campaign to sow discord throughout NATO will continue but should not be overestimated. In several instances, Russia has failed spectacularly. For instance, analysis showed that Russian interference in the 2017 French presidential campaign actually motivated people to vote to reelect President Emmanuel Macron. Some studies suggest that he would not have won the election if not for popular desire in France to undo the Russian interference.[53] Similarly, in Montenegro, Russia interfered in national elections that would decide if Montenegro would join NATO. After its information campaign was defeated, Russia attempted a coup. The plot was disrupted when Serbia, Russia's ostensible ally, tipped off the Montenegrin authorities.[54] In both cases, the Russians had a misguided concept of how target populations would respond to influence operations. Most recently, Russia's large-scale invasion of

Ukraine has offered the most poignant example to date of miscalculation in the human domain, wherein Russian leadership failed to anticipate the response of the Ukrainian military, the Ukrainian people, and the international community writ large.

Europe's economic situation will also fuel further disaggregation. The continent was already facing massive economic issues related to high unemployment and national debts. The COVID-19 pandemic has exacerbated that financial pinch. In turn, the countries that feel that pinch most keenly have begun to look at the European Union skeptically—while leading EU powers like Germany have grown structurally dependent on trade with China. Political movements similar to Brexit have appeared not only in Poland and Hungary but also Spain and Italy.[55] A key portion of this skepticism is the mistrust of the European Union's bureaucracy and institutions.

CONCLUSION

The world is facing mega trends that are too large for one entity—be it a military, agency, or country—to address. Disaggregation, the pandemic, and climate change all present opportunities and challenges in an increasingly chaotic world. Competition is embedded in each of these crises. However, power in the form of information can be built in local, subnational areas. The US military will need a granular understanding of ground truth in order to compete successfully.

The underlying theme of many of these macro-trends is that all politics is local. The trajectory of these mega trends will, in many respects, depend on how local populations respond to the advances of larger powers. Influence at a subnational level gives the US the ability to monitor, measure, and contain instability, chaos, and malfeasance.

Notes

1. Graham Allison, "The Thucydides Trap: Are the U.S. and China Headed for War?," *The Atlantic*, September 24, 2015, https://www.theatlantic.com/international/archive/2015/09/united-states-china-war-thucydides-trap/406756/. See also James Micciche, "Assessing the Fungibility of U.S.-Soviet Competitive Strategies," *Divergent Options*, March 22, 2021, https://divergentoptions.org/2021/03/22/assessing-the-fungibility-of-u-s-soviet-competitive-strategies/; and Sean McFate, "Ukraine's 'Back to the Future' Scenario: Deploying Troops is a Cold War Solution," *The Hill*, January 25, 2022, https://thehill.com/opinion/national-security/591094-ukraines-back-to-the-future-scenario-deploying-troops-is-a-cold-war.
2. Heather Graham-Ashley, "CSA Discusses Army's Growth, Modernization, Readiness during 2-Day Visit to Hood," *Fort Hood Sentinel*, July 19, 2018, http://www.forthoodsentinel.com/news/csa-discusses-army-s-growth-modernization-readiness-during-2-day-visit-to-hood/article_05c2a64a-8aaa-11e8-a32c-ebb36700efba.html.
3. White House, *National Security Strategy of the United States of America* (Washington, DC: White House, 2017).
4. James C. McConville, *Army Multi-Domain Transformation, Ready to Win in Competition and Conflict,* Chief of Staff Paper #1 (Washington, DC: Headquarters, Department of the Army, 2021), https://api.army.mil/e2/c/downloads/2021/03/23/eeac3d01/20210319-csa-paper-1-signed-print-version.pdf.
5. Horst W. J. Rittel and Melvin M. Webber, "Dilemmas in a General Theory of Planning," *Policy Sciences* 4, no. 2 (1973): 155–169, http://www.jstor.org/stable/4531523.
6. Hans J. Morgenthau and Kenneth Thompson, *Politics Among Nations: The Struggle for Power and Peace,* 6th ed. (New York: McGraw-Hill, 1985), 165.
7. Thomas L. Friedman, *The World Is Flat: A Brief History of the Globalized World in the Twenty-First Century,* 1st ed. (London: Lane Penguin Books, 2005).
8. "Independent States in the World," United States Department of State, January 29, 2021, https://www.state.gov/independent-states-in-the-world/.

9. These typologies are not mutually exclusive and in fact share a recip-rocal relationship, as external disaggregation has shown a propensity to lead to internal variations of the concept. South Sudan, the world's newest internationally recognized nation, was born of an intrastate con-flict caused partially by externally drawn postcolonial borders. South Sudan's disaggregation continued past its sovereignty, and the nation has been locked in deadly civil war fought between various subnational factions all vying for control of Juba.

10. "Brexit: What You Need to Know about the UK Leaving the EU," *BBC News*, December 30, 2020, https://www.bbc.com/news/uk-politics-328 10887.

11. Aditya Rathore and Ashutosh Bajpai, "The WTO Appellate Body Crisis: How We Got Here and What Lies Ahead?" *Jurist Legal News and Commentary*, April 14, 2020, https://www.jurist.org/commentary/2020/04/rathore-bajpai-wto-appellate-body-crisis/.

12. Adiele E. Afigbo, "Background to Nigerian Federalism: Federal Features in the Colonial State," *Publius: The Journal of Federalism* 21, no. 4 (January 1, 1991), 13–29, https://doi.org/10.1093/oxfordjournals.pubjof.a037965.

13. Charles J. Dunlap Jr., "Lawfare Today: A Perspective," *Yale Journal of International Affairs* 3 (Winter 2008), 146–154, https://scholarship.law.duke.edu/cgi/viewcontent.cgi?article=5892&context=faculty_scholarship.

14. Jill I. Goldenziel, "Law as a Battlefield: The U.S., China, and Global Esca-lation of Lawfare," *Cornell Law Review* 106 (2020): 1046.

15. Joseph S. Nye, "Power and Interdependence Revisited," ed. Robert O. Keohane, *International Organization* 41, no. 4 (1987), 725–753.

16. Daniel W. Drezner, Ronald R. Krebs, and Randall Schweller, "The End of Grand Strategy, America Must Think Small," *Foreign Affairs* (May/June 2020): 107.

17. Renée Diresta, Carly Miller, Vanessa Molter, John Pomfret, and Glenn Tiffert, *Telling China's Story: The Chinese Communist Party's Campaign to Shape Global Narratives* (Stanford: Stanford Internet Observatory, 2020), 10.

18. Catherine A. Theohary, *Information Warfare: Issues for Congress*, CRS Report No. RL 45142 (Washington, DC: Congressional Research Service, 2018), 9, https://crsreports.congress.gov/product/pdf/R/R45142/5.

19. Department of the Army, *Operations: ADP 3-0* (Washington, DC: Head-quarters, Department of the Army, 2019), 1–27.

20. Charles Cleveland, Benjamin M. Jensen, Arnel David, and Susan F. Bryant, *Military Strategy for the 21st Century: People, Connectivity, and Competition* (Amherst, NY: Cambria Press, 2018).

21. Gareth Evans and Mohamed Sahnoun, "The Responsibility to Protect," *Foreign Affairs,* (November/December 2002): 99–110.

22. Richard N. Haass, "The Age of Nonpolarity: What Will Follow U.S. Dominance," *Foreign Affairs* 87, no. 3 (2008): 44–56.

23. Michael J. Mazarr et al., *Understanding the Current International Order*, 2016, IX, https://www.rand.org/pubs/research_reports/RR1598.html.

24. Over 100,000 opposition fighters were killed between 2001 and 2018 in Iraq, Afghanistan, and Pakistan. Neta C. Crawford, "Human Cost of the Post-9/11 Wars: Lethality and the Need for Transparency," Costs of War, Watson Institute, Brown University, November 2018.

25. Nadia Schadlow, *War and the Art of Governance* (Washington, DC: Georgetown University Press, 2017), 15.

26. Sebastian von Einsiedel, *Civil War Trends and the Changing Nature of Armed Conflict* (United Nations University, March 2017), 2–6.

27. There is an extensive, evolving literature that explores how local dynamics fuel intrastate conflict. See Lars-Erik Cederman and Manuel Vogt, "Dynamics and Logics of Civil War," *Journal of Conflict Resolution* 61, no. 9 (2017): 1992–2016; Stathis N. Kalyvas "The Ontology of 'Political Violence': Action and Identity in Civil Wars," *Perspectives on Politics* 1, no. 3 (September 2003): 475–494; and James D. Fearon and David D. Laitin, "Ethnicity, Insurgency and Civil War," *American Political Science Review* 97, no. 1 (February 2003), 75–90.

28. Elsa Kania, "The PLA's Latest Strategic Thinking on the Three Warfares," *China Brief* 16, no. 13 (Jamestown, 2016), 10–13.

29. Military terminology describing intense and concentrated artillery fires before and during the initial stages of an attack to weaken and create gaps in enemy defenses and to limit the enemy's ability to react to the attacking force.

30. H. R. McMaster, "How China Sees the World," *The Atlantic,* May 19, 2020.

31. Rory Medcalf, "Declassification of secret document reveals US strategy in the Indo-Pacific," *The Diplomat,* Australian Strategic Policy Institute, January 13, 2021, https://www.aspistrategist.org.au/declassification-of-secret-document-reveals-real-us-strategy-in-the-indo-pacific/.

32. Gurmeet, Kanwal, "Pakistan's Gwadar Port: A New Naval Base in China's String of Pearls in the Indo-Pacific," in *CSIS Briefs* (Washington, DC: Center for Strategic & International Studies, 2018), 1–5.

33. Brahma Chellenay, "China's Unrestricted War on India," *Foreign Affairs,* April 2021, https://www.foreignaffairs.com/articles/china/2021-04-02/chinas-unrestricted-war-india.

34. Samanth Subramanian, "How Hindu supremacists are tearing India apart," *The Guardian,* February 20, 2020, https://www.theguardian.com/world/2020/feb/20/hindu-supremacists-nationalism-tearing-india-apart-modi-bjp-rss-jnu-attacks.

35. For a critique of US policy in the Middle East since the 9/11 attacks, see Andrew Bacevich, *America's War for the Greater Middle East* (New York: Random House, 2016).

36. Kim Ghattas, *Black Wave* (New York: Henry Holt and Company, 2020), 333.

37. For more discussion on Iranian influence in Iraqi affairs, see Tim Arango, James Risen, Farnaz Fassihi, Ronen Bergman, and Murtaza Hussain, "The Iran Cables: Secret Documents Show How Tehran Wields Power in Iraq," *The New York Times,* November 19, 2019, https://www.nytimes.com/interactive/2019/11/18/world/middleeast/iran-iraq-spy-cables.html. For a breakdown of Iranian-backed militias and its regional affiliates in the Middle East see Kali Robinson, "Iran's Regional Armed Network," *Council on Foreign Relations,* March 1, 2021, https://www.cfr.org/article/irans-regional-armed-network.

38. Charles Schmitz, "Understanding the Role of Tribes in Yemen," *Combating Terrorism Center (CTC) Sentinel* 4, no. 10 (October 2011), 17–22.

39. Raf Sanchez, "Yemen's government 'prepares to flee' as UAE-backed separatists seize control in Aden," *The Telegraph,* January 30, 2018, https://www.telegraph.co.uk/news/2018/01/30/yemens-government-prepares-flee-uae-backed-separatists-seize/.

40. Heather Lackner, "The Yemen Conflict: Southern Separatism in Action," *European Council on Foreign Relations,* May 8, 2020, https://ecfr.eu/article/commentary_the_yemen_conflict_southern_separatism_in_action/.

41. Saeed Kamali Dehghan, "Killing of Ali Abdullah Saleh Changes Dynmics of Yemen's Civil War," *The Guardian,* December 5, 2017, https://www.theguardian.com/world/2017/dec/05/ali-abdullah-saleh-killing-changes-dynamics-yemen-civil-war.

42. For discussion on how nationalist populism's rise, China's illiberal practices, and the undermining of multilateral institutions are challenging the liberal international order, see David A. Lake, Lisa L. Martin, and Thomas Risse, "Challenges to the Liberal Order: Reflections on Inter-

national Organization," *International Organization* 75, no. 2 (Cambridge University Press), 225–257.

43. Gustavo Ferreira, Jamie Critelli, and Wayne Johnson, "The Future of Rare Earth Elements in Africa in the Midst of a Debt Crisis," *Eunomia Journal*, August 15, 2020, https://www.civilaffairsassoc.org/post/the-future-of-rare-earth-elements-in-africa-in-the-midst-of-a-debt-crisis.

44. Hagan Sibiri, "The Emerging Phenomenon of Anti-Chinese Populism in Africa: Evidence from Zambia, Zimbabwe and Ghana," *Insight on Africa* 13, no. 1 (2021): 7–27.

45. For an assessment of how climate change is increasing competition for water accessibility and driving conflict in Africa's Sahel, see Robert Muggah, "In West Africa, Climate Change Equals Conflict," *Foreign Policy*, February 18, 2021, https://foreignpolicy.com/2021/02/18/west-africa-sahel-climate-change-global-warming-conflict-food-agriculture-fish-livestock/.

46. United Nations Development Programme, Regional Bureau for Africa, "Journey to Extremism in Africa: Drivers, Incentives, and the Tipping Point for Recruitment," 2017, 73.

47. Ibid., 5.

48. Michael Shurkin, "What Joe Biden's Africa Strategy Might Look Like," *The Rand Blog*, December 20, 2020,https://www.rand.org/blog/2020/12/what-joe-bidens-africa-strategy-might-look-like.html.

49. Evan Ellis, "The Latin America That Will Engage the New Administration," *Center for Strategic and International Studies*, December 14, 2020, https://www.csis.org/analysis/latin-america-will-engage-new-administration.

50. Rocio Cara Labrador, "Maduro's Allies: Who Backs the Venezuelan Regime?" *Council on Foreign Relations*, February 5, 2019, https://www.cfr.org/in-brief/maduros-allies-who-backs-venezuelan-regime.

51. Paul J. Angelo, "The Day After in Venezuela," *Council Special Report* no. 87 (Council on Foreign Relations, September 2020).

52. On democratic backsliding in Latin America, particularly in Venezuela and Nicaragua, see "The Global State of Democracy in 2019: Addressing the Ills, Reviving the Promise," *International Institute for Democracy and Electoral Assistance* (2019), 121.

53. H. R. McMaster, *Battlegrounds: The Fight to Defend the Free World* (New York: HarperCollins Publishers, 2020), 70.

54. Discussed further in *The Attempted Coup in Montenegro and Malign Russian Influence in Europe: Hearing Before The Committee On Armed*

Services United States Senate, One Hundred Fifteenth Congress, First Session, July 13, 2017, https://www.govinfo.gov/content/pkg/CHRG-11 5shrg34738/pdf/CHRG-115shrg34738.pdf.

55. McMaster, *Battlegrounds*, 60.

CHAPTER 2

THRIVING IN THE GRAY ZONE

COMPETITION IN THE SPACE
BETWEEN WAR AND PEACE

David Allen

> Since you know as well as we do that right, as the world goes, is only in question between equals in power, while the strong do what they can and the weak suffer what they must.
> —Thucydides, *History of the Peloponnesian War*[1]

In discussing the concept of the warrior diplomat, one should recall the dialogue related by Thucydides between the representatives of Athens and the island of Melos in the sixteenth year of the Peloponnesian War. One of the conflict's enduring ironies is how the Athenians use the language of the warrior since Sparta traditionally represents the archetypal warrior state, and Athens the diplomat state. In the Melian Dialogue, however, it is the Athenians who use the language of the warrior as they expose how to build up—and resolve to use—strategic advantage, which derives from power. The concept of strategic advantage lies at the heart of strategic competition.[2]

This chapter looks at how power and resolve define relative advantage, and how politically and socially constructed thresholds influence competition and conflict. Power, as well as the actions associated with how power is applied, sits at the heart of this discussion. The focus of this chapter is on what is termed "subthreshold" or "gray-zone" activities of interstate competition. These are the strategies employed by rival actors to pursue their interests—sometimes through force and other times through subtler means—without triggering an outright state of war. Specifically, this chapter examines the *opportunities* present within the gray zone for the creative employment of warrior diplomats. It does this conceptually; subsequent chapters add more detail to elaborate on warrior-diplomat capability.

The realities and challenges of gray-zone competition are central to contemporary military discourse. Two examples are *Competing*, the Marine Corps Doctrinal Publication (MCDP) 1–4, and "The Army in Military Competition" by the US Army's Chief of Staff.[3] These documents address how the Marine Corps and the US Army should operate in the competition space below the threshold of large-scale conflict. Avoiding a tortuous debate on what defines the gray zone, this chapter focuses on the conditions wherein state competition is not quite armed conflict but also not a quite a state of peace. There is a growing body of scholarship related to this activity, which has had a wide range of labels (from "new wars" to "hybrid warfare"), with many attempts to assign meaning and heuristics to this arena of competition.[4]

THE GRAY ZONE IN CONTEXT

In many ways, the gray zone defies definition. Some even deny its existence.[5] The *Cambridge English Dictionary* defines the gray zone as "activities by a state that are harmful to another state and are sometimes considered to be acts of war, but are not legally acts of war."[6] Such definitions seek to use the law to impose clarity. Reality, however, is more elusive—both the interpretations of what constitutes a "legal act of war" and of legality itself are disputed.[7] That said, far from being an obstacle, the very ambiguity of the gray zone suits players in strategic competition because such ambiguity creates opportunities for creative and agile action. The warrior diplomat is the ideal military instrument to identify opportunities within this ambiguity and to further strategic objectives without resorting to the application of violence.

Some of the gray zone's ostensible challenges should be viewed instead as *opportunities* to gain advantage without unnecessarily escalating to full war. For example, the inability to detect hostile action in the gray zone is often cited as a strategic threat. However, this framing overlooks America's ability to take advantage of this same dynamic. Frederick Spencer Chapman famously said that "the jungle is neutral"; so too is the gray zone.[8] The ability to send ambiguous signals creates opportunities to de-escalate and allows for changes in policy while saving face. In this sense, the gray zone offers paths to achieve Sun Tzu's ultimate goal of "winning without fighting."[9]

Figure 1. Conceptual illustration of operating in the gray zone.

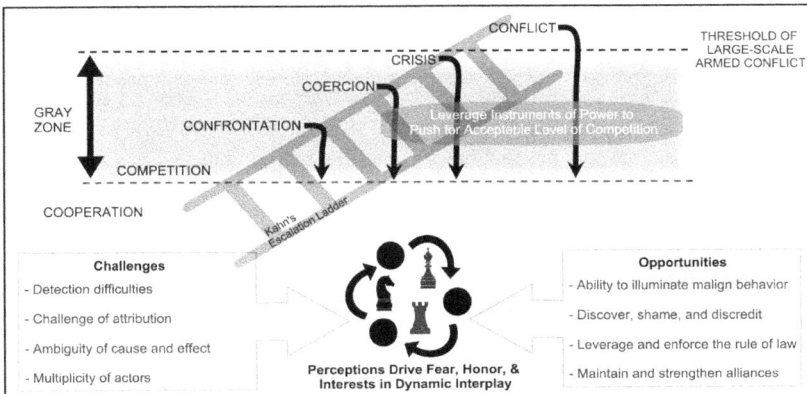

Source. David Allen and Arnel P. David.

Ambiguity provides opportunities that a system with perfectly defined rules would never generate.[10] Interstate competition, together with the complexities involved in gaining relative advantage in the gray zone, is one such field. In this arena, relative advantage is pursued in the corridors of power and likewise in the global commons.[11] For the purposes of this discussion, it is best to view the gray zone as a philosophy for the application of power rather than as a definable place. It is a dynamic interplay of actors working in a war of perceptions among states to influence people, societies, and governments (figure 1).

Carl von Clausewitz has written that war is driven by the policy of the state, the skill of the military, and the passion of the people.[12] When addressing this trinity, he concentrated on the first two categories, both of which relate to the concept of the warrior diplomat. However, it is the third aspect, the passions of engaged masses, that resonates most powerfully in gray-zone competition. The greatest challenge is the "primordial violence, hatred, and enmity as a blind natural force" that manifests itself in the human domain.[13] Neither the warrior nor the diplomat finds themselves optimized to operate in a space influenced by these pressures. Clausewitz, for his part, seems less interested in examining the nature of this primordial force.

In contrast, Leo Tolstoy's insights into human passions, as expressed in *War and Peace*, do much more to help one understand the gray zone.[14] Tolstoy did not see conflict as a scientific process, which could be understood through rational analysis. Instead, he emphasized the "blind force of nature" and the inevitability of chaos. The character of competition and conflict cannot necessarily be broken down into easily understandable components. There will always be unknowns that defy logic no matter how many categories and concepts one creates to comprehend the process. This creates ambiguity that can never be resolved, affecting all parties in a conflict. The counter-ISIS campaign in Syria, for example, saw Western forces both cooperating and competing with allies and adversaries in unpredictable ways, influenced by the different contexts and circumstances.[15]

In the context of the gray zone, this means that operations can never be proactively planned in every detail, as some elements will always resist analysis. Operational philosophy should, therefore, be focused on adaptability and agility.[16] Terms like "gray zone" and "hybrid warfare" are contemporary jargon, but the philosophy that underpins these ideas is not.[17] These terms represent a philosophical shorthand for how ambiguity, contrasting perceptions of history (and of reality itself), and the application of instruments of power interact in an ecosystem that no one state or actor can control.[18] The gray zone is not new, but what is different in the present are the technical, virtual, and structural means for activity to occur at such a higher rate.

Historical examples of the gray zone have resonance today. One example is Benjamin Armstrong's insights into the so-called Quasi-War between the United States and France from 1798 to 1800, which also involved Great Britain and a number of state-sponsored proxies and nonstate actors.[19] Numerous parties with complex motivations clashed in this conflict, using relatively low levels of violence to achieve political ends. The Quasi-War was a complex and fluctuating ecosystem of relationships, which saw erstwhile enemies such as the United States and Great Britain cooperating after the Jay Treaty of 1794 but then also confronting each other in November 1798 (for example, when British naval forces captured American civilians from the USS Baltimore and the merchant ships it was escorting).[20]

The Quasi-War highlighted several enduring truths of the gray zone. First, presence matters. To be influential and competitive, engagement is a constant imperative. Second, relationships may shift from cooperation to competition (and even escalate to conflict) when relative advantages change. Third, optimizing for the gray zone is difficult because the overall environment itself is difficult to define. This reality demands rapid adaptation to changing circumstances. In the Quasi-War noted earlier, the US Navy quickly developed small vessels such as the *USS Experiment* and *USS Enterprise* and used captured vessels as tenders. This enabled the US Navy to expand a low-end, low-cost capability that was optimized for the sort of counter-piracy operations that the United States found itself conducting. This adaptation is instructive today since there is no binary choice between state competition and irregular warfare—both will coexist, and actions in one will inevitably impact the field of play in the other. Indeed, irregular warfare is increasingly seen as an attractive vector of competition to control escalation. It follows, therefore, that irregular warfare is an integral feature of interstate competition in the gray zone.

INSTRUMENTS OF POWER IN THE GRAY ZONE

How can the warrior diplomat operate in the gray zone's ambiguity, unpredictability, and dynamism? Rather than bemoan its complexity, nations must embrace it. At the strategic, conceptual level, decision makers should seek out opportunities for creative action. As noted in the introduction, this can only occur if granular nuance is fed into the strategic planning process. Absent these inputs, such opportunities cannot be identified and acted on astutely. At the tactical, grassroots level, warrior diplomats must provide this nuance. As detailed in chapters 4 and 5, they must do so using focused investigative methods that establish causal understanding in complex environments.

Armed with an understanding of the playing field, the toolkit for operating in the gray zone becomes much more diverse. The US is not limited to the proverbial bag of "hammers" often associated with the application of military power. Instead, there is a wider range of precision instruments and blunt tools alike.

Before diving into the familiar acronyms of DIME (diplomatic, informational, military, and economic) and MPECI (military, political, economic, civilian, and informational) to classify the instruments of power, the nature of power itself should be examined. In their influential work on the

nature of power in international relations, Michael Barnett and Raymond
Duvall propose a definition of power as being "the production, in and
through social relations, of effects on actors that shape their capacity to
control their fate."[21] The authors are clear that there is a hierarchical logic
based on power. Power is not merely the capacity to produce relative
advantage but also the means of wielding that power in the context of
relationships. A state can possess direct power through the tools at its
disposal as a national government and indirectly through its ability to
influence institutional mechanisms in the international system. Therefore, ample opportunities exist below the threshold of armed conflict to
shape conditions to a nation's advantage through deterrence, coercion,
and inducement.[22] This can range from hard deterrence power such as
the NATO Enhanced Forward Presence in the Baltic States to the soft
cultural power influence of Hollywood in the United States.[23] Shaping
such conditions could provide the opportunity to achieve strategic goals
without resorting to armed conflict and could prove useful in the event
of armed conflict (e.g., basing rights and access).

   Most strategists are familiar with the concepts of "hard power" and
"soft power" and the production of coercive or attractive influence.[24] The
concept of "sharp power" is a more recent development.[25] Thought to be
positioned somewhere between hard and soft power, sharp power focuses
on the manipulative effect of shaping perceptions to gain advantage.
These concepts can be operationalized by applying the instruments of
power represented by DIME and MPECI. These instruments of power
can be applied as an integrated whole, with elements defying neat
compartments or stovepipes. Cross-cutting instruments such as cyber
and informational capabilities, for example, can be agents of soft, sharp,
or hard power. In this respect, the integrated application of soft, sharp,
and hard power is perfectly suited to the ambiguity and dynamism of
the gray zone. Former Secretary of Defense Robert Gates compared the
exercise of power to conducting a symphony with a full range of power
synchronized to achieve synergistic effects.[26] How can strategists perform
their overture if they have no framework in which to write the score?

ESCALATION THRESHOLDS AS FRAMEWORKS IN THE GRAY ZONE

Key to escalation is the concept of thresholds. Often associated with the concept of escalation dominance, the notion of escalation thresholds was examined most famously in Herman Kahn's "escalation ladder."[27] His concept defined forty-four rungs on a metaphorical ladder, with each rung being a threshold. The ladder was climbed to escalate and descended to de-escalate, with relative advantage held by the ability to dominate at each threshold. This concept of vertical escalation, which involves an intensification of effort via a particular instrument of power, is sound logic within an isolated system in which power is measured in only a single dimension (e.g., conventional or nuclear armament). It is less effective, however, in a situation where power can be applied across a wider array of instruments. Although one may strive to play a trumpet louder than an adversary, the adversary may decide to play percussion and strings.

The concept of horizontal escalation offers a different perspective, which has critical relevance in the gray zone.[28] Rather than viewing a challenge as a singular problem that must be addressed head-on, applying horizontal escalation means that decision makers address an issue at hand indirectly, using alternative methods. One example is the British response to the 2018 Novichok chemical weapon attack in Salisbury, which Prime Minister Theresa May publicly attributed to Russian agents, and after which Britain imposed asset freezes and a range of economic sanctions on Russia. This was followed by the expulsion of Russian diplomats from a further twenty-nine countries, in an unprecedented show of international solidarity. Such use of horizontal thresholds enabled the British government to impose costs and pursue retribution while avoiding a wider escalation. Importantly, while horizontal escalation is often considered in geographic terms (e.g., the Allies opened an offensive front in Gallipoli in an attempt to circumvent the stalemate on the Western Front in World War I), horizontal escalation in the gray zone is primarily conceived in terms of the type of activity pursued to impose costs to prevent vertical escalation. Horizontal escalation strives to strike a proportionate response.

Thresholds for action are not fixed in the gray zone. They are moveable and blurred, often by design. Conceptually, a threshold could be defined most simply as the lowest point at which a selected stimulus will cause a response. When applied to the use of instruments of power, this definition has four implications. First, the recipient of the applied power must receive a stimulus from its application. In basic terms, the target must realize that an instrument of power is being applied against it, and so the ability to detect such applications is an essential precursor to any further action. Second, even once detected, the recipient must be able to detect the source of the stimulus through attribution. Third, having linked the stimulus to the source, it must determine a means to react or counter it at an acceptable risk of escalation. Fourth, it must decide to act. By keeping these reaction points variable and obscured, gray-zone activities pose multiple dilemmas to an adversary.

In reality, the process does not end there. Options are generated, and actions are taken. The recent Solar Winds data breach, for example, was not immediately linked to Russian cyber capabilities.[29] It can take considerable time to establish such linkages, and the resulting delays can create space for further maneuver by America's adversaries. The power of horizontal escalation becomes clear.[30] An initiator seeks to move away from thresholds that seem to provoke a response before detection or attribution can compromise effectiveness.

At face value, this seems an entirely satisfactory way of conducting international relations. A choreographed game of set plays, alternating between offense and defense, which prevents undue intensification or escalation in any one dimension. Often characterized as a game of chess, the reality of this "game" is far more complex. On the one hand, there are never just two players. Even the Cold War, characterized as a bipolar clash of wills, saw far more agency from other powers than often acknowledged.

It is tempting to engineer a history of simple bipolarity throughout the period, but events such as the Vietnam War saw limited control of North Vietnamese policy by Russia and China, while the UK resisted sending troops in support of US policy (not to mention the challenges encountered by the United States in influencing the behavior of South Vietnam). Smaller powers, pursuing their own agendas, also damaged the Soviet-American détente in the 1970s: Egypt by attacking Israel in 1973; Cuba by intervening in Africa in 1975 to 1977; and Hafizullah Amin in Afghanistan, whose reported contacts with US officials helped trigger Soviet intervention in 1979.[31] This sort of activity is far from novel: Thucydides showed Corinth and Corcyra doing something similar to the Spartans and the Athenians in the Peloponnesian Wars.[32]

Concurrently, it is dangerously naive to assume that different countries are playing the same game and following the same rules. This is the fallacy of mirroring: the belief that an adversary sees the situation in the same way as oneself, with the assumption that one's actions will prompt a predictable or "logical" response.[33] This can make an initiator more confident in their approach to thresholds, which creates an illusion of control over escalation and de-escalation. Nikita Khrushchev's interventions in Berlin in 1958–1959 and 1961 were provoked by inaccurate warnings of collapse from East Germany's leader Walter Ulbricht. This misrepresented the actual state of US-Soviet relations, leading to increasing tensions that ultimately contributed to the Cuban Missile Crisis in 1962.[34]

Adding a further layer of complexity, Rebecca Hersman highlights how asymmetrical understanding creates the prospect of "wormhole escalation."[35] Defined in the context of escalation as a hypothetical connection between widely separated regions of space-time, wormhole escalation is when escalation in one threshold does not lead logically to the next but instantly triggers multiple thresholds in an unpredicted and uncontrolled manner. As Hersman stated: "wormholes are inherently, and indeed catastrophically, unstable. Whether in terms of space travel or escalation, they seem best avoided."

While clearly defined and mutually agreed thresholds seem to hold out the hope of adding order to chaos, reality is more complicated. The fact that thresholds are politically and socially constructed means that they can change and are rarely agreed upon or clearly defined. Red lines, as immutable thresholds never to be breached, make good political rhetoric. However, they risk becoming little more than meaningless catchphrases if not enforced. Even the most apparently clear-cut cases, such as the illegal use of chemical weapons, can be challenged (e.g., by the Syrian government, or the Russians' use of the Novichok nerve agent in Salisbury). In these cases, responses were muted and failed to match the rhetoric deployed over the use of such weapons in the past.

These situations have made the use of what David Kilcullen calls "liminal war" increasingly attractive.[36] Liminal war seeks to undermine an opponent's conventional military power by riding the edge of thresholds—doing just enough to frustrate an opponent and further one's interests but not enough to trigger an outright response. Guerrilla warfare—a useful means of competing with a far stronger opponent—is one such approach. Robert Taber calls guerilla warfare the "war of the flea."[37] A competitor suffers the dog's disadvantage of never getting to grips with the bites of multiple fleas and becomes exhausted. A classic means of doing this is through supplying arms to proxies, such as the Libyan government's supply of arms to the Provisional Irish Republican Army in Northern Ireland in the 1980s.[38] At the writing of this book, this kind of arms supplying from over twenty-five countries is happening on a large scale in Ukraine.[39]

Another perspective on thresholds offers a complementary vantage point. "Subthreshold," as a concept, has been referred to as the "rungs" on Herman Kahn's proverbial escalation ladder of armed conflict that remain below the level of outright armed conflict. Locating that particular "rung," however, can be challenging when considering what, exactly, armed conflict is. The International Committee of the Red Cross proposed that:

1. International armed conflicts exist whenever there is a resort to armed force between two or more States.

2. Non-international armed conflicts are protracted armed confrontations occurring between governmental armed forces and the forces of one or more armed groups, or between such groups arising on the territory of a State [party to the Geneva Conventions]. The armed confrontation must reach a minimum level of intensity and the parties involved in the conflict must show a minimum of organization.[40]

Although this may seem like a neat definition, it is not particularly useful in understanding what is meant by "below the threshold of armed conflict." This is partly due to varying interpretations of what constitutes armed force and a Western binary construct of armed conflict, which other actors see differently. Keir Giles wrote that Russia's definitions of "armed force" and "war" are not solely defined by armed violence and that other forms of war can exist.[41] This dichotomy is reflected in Western terminology, which sways between kinetic (lethal) and non-kinetic (non-lethal). Such discussion is usually presented in a context that links kinetic to lethal and non-kinetic to non-lethal, overlooking that virtual effects can have harmful consequences for targeted populations.[42] As highlighted in *Competing*:

Actors on the world stage are always trying to create a relative advantage for themselves and for their group. Sometimes this maneuvering leads to violence, but the use of violence to achieve goals is more often the exception than the rule. Instead, most actors use other means in their competitive interactions to achieve their goals. The competition continuum encompasses all of these efforts, including the use of violence.[43]

Peacekeeping operations in Mali would probably be considered subthreshold, but they can be highly lethal, especially for the civilian population. The gray zone, therefore, does not denote an absence of harm, even if it can signal an absence of intensity. The gray zone is not an area of inconsequential maneuvers. It can be as harmful as all-out armed conflict. It should, therefore, be approached with seriousness and care, not only because of the danger of escalation but also because of the harm that can exist within it.

So where does this leave the warrior diplomat? The military strategist likes to envision an end state or destination and work out steps to reach that destination. The heart of much operational planning is rooted in causality principles and often overly complicated pseudo-mathematical formulas.[44] Focused on crisis and conflict, many military strategists assume that an action will have a predictable effect that can map onto the next action, which, in this way, will inevitably reach a specified end state. This approach can manifest itself in the belief that breaking a network down into ever smaller pieces, or otherwise "disrupting" an enemy, will achieve a result.[45]

Tim Challans cites the French-Algerian War and the *Front de libération nationale* (FLN) as an example of how mapping a network in detail and breaking it down into fragments can create unintended effects.[46] Far from eradicating the FLN, French targeting fragmented it into new networks. Simultaneously, French actions fed the FLN's narrative of victimhood (especially once the torture used by the French to crack the network became widely known). This almost Machiavellian view, of the ends justifying the means, can create moral and ethical issues. It certainly did for French General Jacques Massu and his paratrooper "Centurions" of the 10th Parachute Division, where the widespread use of torture provided tactical advantage but created negative strategic effect on the outcome of the war. The efficient destruction of the FLN cells in Algiers created political blowback in France, which undermined French will to continue the war.

This highlights a key issue in the gray zone; it is an open, nonlinear system. Imagine an explorer sailing forth with no map or trade routes to follow. Action is probing and exploratory—what end state can be pursued? Is unconditional surrender or peaceful cooperation being sought? In the gray zone, there may not be decisive action, so what is the end goal? The gray zone is as much a test of comparative resolve to carry on as it is of the absolute strength of instruments of power.[47] It is far more of what Hans Delbrück calls *Ermattungsstrategie* (strategy of exhaustion) than a *Nierderwerfungstrategie* (strategy of annihilation).[48] The ongoing manipulation of gas supply from Russia to Europe as a means of policy constraint is an example of the economic instrument in action and an activity straight out of George F. Kennan's 1948 characterization of political warfare.[49]

EXPLOITING FEATURES IN THE GRAY ZONE

Faced with ambiguity, uncertainty, and complexity in the gray zone, warrior diplomats may feel overwhelmed. How can they make any sort of difference in this environment? How can they measure effects? Still, while pondering these questions, warrior diplomats should remember that the features that make the gray zone difficult to navigate also present opportunities and vulnerabilities for the adversary that can be exploited for advantage. The complexity of the environment drives smaller powers to seek alliances and partnerships, which provide a relative advantage regionally. Critically, foreign powers such as the United States and United Kingdom can neither identify emerging challenges and opportunities nor can they form the human relationships needed to act upon them without the forward presence and deliberate investigative efforts of warrior diplomats.

In the gray zone, the ability to build alliances for a common purpose is a powerful tool. Such tools are more powerful still if bound by common values and concepts of governance that are held together by mutual interests of states (rather than coercion or compulsion).[50] Strong alliances and institutions provide anchors in the storms that batter the explorer in turbulent seas. The power of alliances can also help build resolve and contain escalation. This can come through a more nuanced understanding of hostile thresholds; such understanding can be achieved through local understanding, cognitive diversity, and strategic empathy drawn from varied viewpoints. This diversity of view can help address what H. R. McMaster, quoting Morgenthau, terms "strategic narcissism."[51] This is the condition in which a state sees every situation through its own agency and exceptionalism, lacking strategic empathy and thus risking unintentional escalation. When required, the ability to mobilize a network of genuine allies pays dividends—as shown by the coordinated expulsion of Russian diplomats in the wake of the Salisbury poisoning.[52]

Having identified the value of alliances built on good governance and common values, what more can be done? Strategic empathy, built up through strong alliance networks, can be used to de-escalate tensions. Jason Healey and Robert Jervis, when discussing escalation in the use of cyber capabilities in the gray zone, recognize the value of a pressure release mechanism.[53] In this case, the breadth of actions across the power spectrum allows for horizontal escalation, which may actually defuse escalation from more threatening areas, especially where inadvertent wormhole escalation may occur.[54] The UK response to the 2018 Novichok case, aided by gray-zone operators such as citizen investigators of the Bellingcat group, is a good example of a "whole of society" response to an aggressive act.[55]

The warrior diplomat has a unique role to play in the gray zone. First, warrior diplomats have the ability to engage with all three aspects of Clausewitz's paradoxical trinity. There are limits, of course, to the breadth and depth of understanding that can be achieved by outsiders operating in contested environments. But this is not a compelling argument against the undertaking itself—on the contrary, it emphasizes the need for skill and professionalism. The ability to immerse in the human domain has great utility in building and holding together alliances. These alliances can deliver the strategic capability of empathy and build resolve through resilience. Second, warrior diplomats maintain a holistic understanding of the instruments of power. Routine engagement with hard, soft, or sharp power gives a far greater understanding of thresholds and the nature of apparent escalation. These engagements can prevent miscalculation and potentially dangerous vertical escalation.

CONCLUSIONS

> It came about step by step, incident by incident, emerging from an infinitely varied set of unimaginably different circumstances and was perceived in its entirety only when it had become a reality, a past event.
> —Leo Tolstoy on Napoleon's retreat from Moscow[56]

Lacking a precise definition, the gray zone between war and peace is an arena for *action*. Features of the international system can be instrumentalized for advantage. As shown from different perspectives, it is more of a mindset than a clearly defined operating space. This inherent ambiguity is reinforced by the fact that the thresholds themselves move, evolve, and mutate. They are, in and of themselves, political and social constructs. With a reflection on the symphony of power performed on a wide array of instruments, warrior diplomats can contribute to a virtuoso overture of applied power, integrating all the instruments at their disposal.

Having taken this varied route on the tempestuous sea of the gray zone, one should reflect on how to operate under such conditions. First, and above all, its complexity should be seen as an opportunity as much as a threat. The adversary often faces the same challenges, and systemic complexity can provide many ways to de-escalate and avoid armed conflict. Second, a competitive advantage accrues to whomever most effectively builds alliances and partnerships. Independent states will find that such a liminal strategy of the "war of the flea," where a thousand small events just below the threshold of detection and response is in the best case an irritant but in the worst case a substantial threat. Third, the states best able to understand and integrate their instruments of power are most likely the ones to gain a relative advantage. Partly, this will be through the identification and selection of the most effective instruments against the adversary. That said, this can also be achieved through the identification of their own and their partners' vulnerabilities to an adversary's instruments. Herein lies the dynamism of strategic competition—it hinges on fundamentally local concerns within smaller, weaker states. Fourth, immersion in the human domain (focus of the next chapter) can turn strategic narcissism into strategic empathy, which can enable the more effective orchestration of effects.

Finally, there will likely not be a big win" but rather a sequence of relative advantages—*for a while.* A culminating point or "victory" may be elusive, but avoiding large-scale armed conflict delivered through sustained resolve is, in itself, a laudable aim. With no clear definition and lacking simplicity, the gray zone is an arena of opportunity for the modern day warrior diplomat to thrive—but to take advantage of it, they must understand it.

NOTES

1. Robert B. Strassler, *The Landmark Thucydides* (New York: Simon and Schuster, 1996): 351–355.
2. Matthew Kroenig, *The Return of Great Power Competition* (New York: Oxford University Press, 2020), 31–35.
3. USMC MCDP, 1-4 *Competing* (Washington, DC: Dept of the Navy, 2020) and The Army in Military Competition Chief of Staff Paper #2 (Washington, DC: Dept of the Army, 2021).
4. See Mary Kaldor, *New & Old Wars: Organized Violence in a Global Era* (Stanford: Stanford University Press, 2001); and Michael J. Mazarr, *Mastering the Gray Zone: Understanding a Changing Era of Conflict* (Carlisle: Strategic Studies Institute, 2015).
5. Donald Stoker and Craig Whiteside, "Blurred Lines: Gray-Zone Conflict and Hybrid War—Two Failures of American Strategic Thinking," *Naval War College Review* 73, no. 1 (Winter 2020): 19–27.
6. *Cambridge English Dictionary*, s.v. "The Gray Zone," accessed January 29, 2022, https://dictionary.cambridge.org/dictionary/english/gray-zone.
7. Chapter 18 of US Code part 1 chapter 113 B defines the term "act of war" as meaning any act occurring in the course of "(A) declared war; (B) armed conflict, whether or not war has been declared, between two or more nations; or (C) armed conflict between military forces of any origin." This however focuses on war between state and the existence of nonstate actors adds further complications.
8. Frederick Spencer Chapman, *The Jungle is Neutral*, (London Chatto and Windus, 1949).
9. Sun Tzu used the concept of subduing the enemy without fighting as the acme of skill as part of chapter 3 on offensive strategy in Sun Tzu, *Sun Tzu The Art of War, Sun Tzu The Art of War*, trans. Samuel B. Griffith (London: Duncan Baird Publishers, 2005), 115 . Although extensively debated as to whether it was meant in the tactical context of the offensive or as a broader strategic concept, what is beyond doubt is that to achieve one's political ends without the risks associated with military means is certainly a skill.
10. Niccolò Machiavelli, *The Prince*, (London: Penguin,1961), 65–66.
11. Julian Corbett, *Some Principles of Maritime Strategy* (London: Adansonia Press,1911), 25–27.

12. Carl Von Clausewitz, *On War* (London: Everymans Library, 1993), 83–101.
13. Charles Cleveland, Benjamin Jensen, Susan Bryant, and Arnel David, *Military Strategy in the 21st Century* (Amherst, NY: Cambria Press, 2018), 10–13.
14. Leo Tolstoy, *War and Peace* (London: Penguin Classics, 2005), 1317–1358.
15. Sinan Hatahet, *The Limitations and Consequences of Remote Warfare in Syria*, in *Remote Warfare: Interdisciplinary Perspectives*, ed. Alistair McKay, Abigail Watson, and Megan Karlshoj-Pedersen (Bristol: E-International Relations, 2021) 173–187.
16. David Barno and Nora Benshael, *Adaptation Under Fire: How Militaries Change in Wartime* (New York: Oxford University Press, 2020).
17. Frank Hoffman, *Conflict in the 21st Century: The Rise of Hybrid Wars* (Arlington: Potomac Institute of Policy Studies, 2007).
18. Nations employ their diplomatic, military and economic instruments (or levers) of power, supported by their collective information resources to achieve strategic advantage. NATO Allied Joint Publication, AJP-01, *Allied Joint Doctrine* 2017, 3
19. Benjamin F. Armstrong, "'Things Done by Halves' Observations from Americas First Great Power Competition,." *Naval War College Review* 6 (Autumn 2020).
20. Affidavit of Lewis Trezevant and William Timmons, November 18, 1798, in *Naval Documents Related to the Quasi-War with France: Naval Operations, February 1797–December 1801*, ed. Dudley W. Knox (Washington, DC: U.S. Government Printing Office, 1935–1938) vol. 2, 26–27.
21. Michael Barnett and Raymond Duvall, *Power in Global Governance* (Cambridge: Cambridge University Press, 2004), 1–32.
22. Daniel Byman and Matthew Waxman, *The Dynamics of Coercion* (New York: Cambridge University Press, 2002), 50.
23. Emrah Aydemir, "Use of Hollywood as a Soft Power Tool in Foreign Policy Strategy of the United States of America," *International Journal of Humanities and Social Science Invention* 6, no. 11 (November 2017) 79–83.
24. For example, see Eliot Cohen, *The Big Stick: The limits of soft power and the necessity of military force* (New York: Perseus Books, 2018), 195–223 and Ajit Maan and Amar Cheema, *Soft Power on Hard Problems: Strategic Influence in Irregular Warfare* (London: Hamilton Books, 2017) 1–5.
25. Jacques deLisle, "Foreign Policy through Other Means: Hard Power, Soft Power, and China's Turn to Political Warfare to Influence the United States," *Orbis* 64 no. 2 (2020): 191

26. Robert Gates, *Exercise of Power* (New York: Alfred Knopf, 2020) 13–57.
27. Herman Kahn, *On Escalation* (New York: Routledge, 2009).
28. Forrest E. Morgan et al., *Dangerous Thresholds: Managing Escalation in the 21st Century* (Research Report, Santa Monica: RAND Corporation 2008).
29. Monika Evstatieva, "A 'Worst Nightmare' Cyberattack: The Untold Story Of The SolarWinds Hack," *NPR*, April 16, 2021.
30. Richard Smoke, *Controlling Escalation* (Cambridge, MA: Harvard University Press 1977).
31. Hal Brands and John Lewis Gaddis, "The New Cold War: America, China, and the Echoes of History," *Foreign Affairs* 100, no. 6 (November/ December 2021): 10–20.
32. Thucydides, *Thucydides: The War of the Peloponnesians and the Athenians*, ed. Jeremy Mynott, Cambridge Texts in the History of Political Thought (Cambridge: Cambridge University Press, 2013).
33. Charles Baroch, "The Mirror Image Fallacy: Understanding the Soviet Union," *The Backgrounder* (1982): 193.
34. United States Department of State, Historical Studies Division, *Crisis Over Berlin, American Policy Concerning the Soviet Threats to Berlin November 1958-December 1962*, pt. 1 (Washington, DC: Research Project 614-A, 1966).
35. Rebecca Hersman, "Wormhole Escalation in the New Nuclear Age," *Texas National Security Review* (2020): 1–20.
36. David Kilcullen, *The Dragons and The Snakes* (London: Hurst and Company, 2020), 29–30.
37. Robert Taber, *The War of the Flea* (Bungay. UK: Chaucer Press, 1969) 21–24.
38. Stanford University Mapping Militant Organizations: Provisional IRA (Provisional Irish Republican Army | Mapping Militant Organizations (stanford.edu)), https://www.web.stanford.edu/group/mappingmilitants/cgi-bin/groups/view/323.
39. Joseph Gedeon, "The weapons and military aid the world is giving Ukraine," *Politico,* March 22, 2022, https://www.politico.com/news/2022/03/22/ukraine-weapons-military-aid-00019104#:~:text=More%20than%202025%20countries%20have%20joined%20in%20delivering,Senior%20Airman%20Stephani%20Barge%2FU.S.%20Air%20Force%20via%20AP.
40. ICRC, *How is the Term "Armed Conflict" Defined in International Humanitarian Law* (Opinion Paper, Geneva: ICRC 2008).

41. Keir Giles, *Russia's 'New' Tools for Confronting the West: Continuity and Innovation in Moscow's Exercise of Power* (London: Chatham House, 2016).

42. David E. Sanger, *The Perfect Weapon: War, Sabotage and Fear in the Cyber Age* (London: Scribe, 2018), 167–168.

43. USMC MCDP, 1-4 *Competing* (Washington, DC: Dept of the Navy, 2020), foreword.

44. Phillip Meilinger, "The Origins of Effects Based Operations," *Joint Force Quarterly* 35 (2003): 116–122.

45. Tim Challan, "Tipping Sacred Cows: Moral Potential Through Operational Art," *Military Review* (2009): 19–29. Proponents of Systemic Operational Design (SOD) criticize effects-based operations for a flawed simplicity of cause and effect. Ofra Gracier, in an interview with Raphael Marcus, highlights that EBO in application by the IDF became precision strike focused. Raphael Marcus, *Israel's Long War with Hezbollah: Military Innovation and Adaptation under Fire* (Washington: Georgetown University Press, 2018), 169.

46. Tim Challans, "Tipping Sacred Cows: Moral Potential Through Operational Art," *Military Review* (2009) 19-29; Alistair Horne, *A Savage War of Peace: Algeria 1954–1962* (New York: New York Review Books 1977), 195–196.

47. Glenn Snyder and Paul Diesling, *Conflict among Nations* (Princeton: Princeton University Press, 1977).

48. Peter Paret, *Makers of Modern Strategy* (Princeton: Princeton University Press, 1986), 341–342.2

49. Hans Van Der Buchard, "EU's Borrell fires back at Putin by saying gas price surge is political," *Politico.eu*, October 18, 2021; George F. Kennan, *The Inauguration of Organized Political Warfare*, April 30, 1948 (History and Public Policy Program Digital Archive, National Archives and Records Administration, Record Group 59, Entry A1 558-B, Policy Planning Staff/Council, Subject Files, 1947-1962, Box 28).

50. Nadia Schadlow, *War and the Art of Governance* (Washington, DC: Georgetown University Press, 2017), 272–281.

51. H. R. McMaster, *Battlegrounds: The Fight to Defend the Free World* (London: William Collins, 2020), 15.

52. Julian Borger, Patrick Wintour, and Heather Stewart, "Western Allies Expel Scores of Russian Diplomats over Skripal Attack," *The Guardian*, March 27, 2018.

53. Jason Healey and Robert Jervis, "The Escalation Inversion and Other Oddities of Situational Cyber Stability," *Texas National Security Review* (2020): 1–20.
54. Christopher Whyte and Brian Mazanec, *Understanding Cyber Warfare: Politics, Policy and Strategy* (New York: Routledge, 2019).
55. Elliot Higgins, *We Are Bellingcat: An Intelligence Agency for the People* (London: Bloomsbury, 2021).
56. Leo Tolstoy, *War and Peace* (London: Penguin Classics, 2005), 1098.

CHAPTER 3

THE HUMAN DOMAIN

Aleks Nesic, Daniel Collini, and Arnel P. David

At the dawn of the twentieth century, the United States was in the midst of its first struggle to counter an Islamic insurgency. Under the command of then Brigadier General Leonard Wood in the distant islands of the Philippines' Sulu Archipelago, the US Army had little interest in understanding the local Moro people. Instead, with brute force, they delivered America's preferred way of war: overwhelming lethality and firepower to prevail by attrition.[1] The campaign culminated in a bloody massacre at the Battle of Bud Dajo on Jolo island, where nearly a thousand men, women, and children were slaughtered by barrages of artillery and automatic gunfire. In a photo of Leonard Wood, among soldiers overlooking piles of bodies, a dead woman holding her young child stood out.[2] The insurgency was temporarily suppressed, but this powerful image would linger in the social consciousness of the Filipino Moros for generations to come, fueling a desire to keep resisting and fighting.

Fast forward to 2008, when then Captain Arnel David and his four-soldier Special Operations Civil Affairs team were deployed to the same island of Jolo, where the famous massacre was still vividly remembered. Their team was part of the Joint Special Operations Task Force – Philippines, which had a mission to conduct counterterrorism and stability operations. This small team's approach was different than that of Leonard Wood and the US Army of the early 1900s. To understand the local dynamics of conflict (which had flared, once again, along religious lines), the team partnered with a Muslim imam. They developed an understanding of the complex sociopolitical issues that plagued governance on this small island, and through the imam's religious and cultural connections, they mapped a dizzying array of actors and groups operating in their new and unfamiliar environment. The most effective aspect of this team's approach was the relationships, trust, and legitimacy formed by working with local civil society groups alongside the Filipino military.[3] In the end, this small team, leveraging limited resources, was able to help the local government mobilize tens of thousands of people. Working together, they addressed waste management issues and environmental hazards, and they also orchestrated peace rallies that, at the end of the team's tour, prompted top commanders of the Abu Sayyaf terrorist group to seek reconciliation.

Collaborations of this sort are by no means unique. There are many such examples of comparable effects achieved by special operations forces in Colombia, Yemen, Somalia, Senegal, Tajikistan, and many other countries—but these stories are rarely shared, for a variety of reasons. Issues of classification and professional discretion are substantive factors, but unfortunately, it is most often due to a general lack of interest. These are messy, uncomfortable wars.[4] The long, costly, and recalcitrant interventions in places like Vietnam, Iraq, and Afghanistan have soured planners' and policymakers' conceptions of nation building, stability operations, and foreign entanglements. Nonetheless, these two stories of engagement in the southern Philippines illuminate an evolution in thinking that occurred during the past century as to how armies can use limited force and achieve strategically disproportionate effects with small groups of specially trained people.

The West needs to continue to evolve and preserve more of this type of unique capability: the warrior diplomat. Success in future foreign interventions will be achieved neither through a myopic focus on the enemy nor through the recurring tendency to focus on the clash of steel and delivery of ordnance. Put simply, success will require *people* who can understand and work with other *people*. Future interventions will place a greater premium on access, legitimacy, and influence, which may be equally important to—if not more important than—firepower.

Woven through contemporary debates over the changing character of modern war are different schools of thought that intersect but lack a central, cohering idea. One school of thought sees a return of great power competition and argues for an emphasis on lethality and warfighting competency. This narrow view of competition is challenged in chapter 1 and more broadly throughout this book. The other school of thought sees a change in the character of conflict and competition, where adversaries pursue their ends in the space between peace and war (as discussed in chapter 2).

Above all, and critical to stitching multiple paradigms together, is something that is eternal in all war and immutable: the human domain. For the purposes of this study, the human domain is defined as *the intersection of actors and interests, predominantly on land and in the virtual cyberspace, which comprise individuals, groups, organizations, and societies—peoplehood.* The human domain represents a web of networks that define power and interests in a hyper-connected world.

War is always a political act carried out by humans. Regardless of which school of thought gains the most currency in national security debates, the military needs the ability to understand, accurately interpret, and effectively influence other humans. A nation with forces on the ground early, working effectively with an indigenous populace and fostering relationships, can gain understanding. This understanding can never be comprehensive, and there are a host of formidable challenges attendant to untangling the complexity of the human domain, but the potential strategic advantage of superior contextual knowledge is vast.

This chapter advances in three parts. Part 1 starts with theory. The US military's current efforts to engage with the fundamentally *human* nature of conflict are marred by imprecise language and inconsistent terminology.[5] A sound theory can support one's thinking and is essential to support concept development. This chapter does not unpack a full theory for how to operate within the human domain but rather explains *why* the domain is needed and situates it in the broader construct of the global commons. Part 2 reviews the integration of academic scholarship and military experience to highlight ways in which engagement with scholarship can improve the efficacy of military operations. This is a cursory review of scholarship to highlight work worthy of deeper exploration for military practitioners. Part 3 closes the chapter by illuminating gaps in doctrine with regards to information and the way the military approaches influence operations.

Wars of the twentieth century are often characterized by head-to-head clashes between massive land forces and large naval groups, but today's war, more than ever, is marked by a struggle for influence among people and states. The twenty-first century advent of information technology and increased global connectedness is changing the character of competition, conflict, and confrontation. Creating strategic advantage in this century requires the understanding of and effective engagement with people, in order to access political, economic, and social networks, thereby achieving a position of relative advantage.[6] Russia's invasion of Ukraine in February 2022, which was initially heralded as validation of Western militaries' turn away from "messy" contextual dynamics and toward large scale force-on-force engagement, has instead showcased the centrality of the human domain: Russian leadership grossly misjudged how their forces would be received by ethnically and linguistically "Russian" Ukrainian citizens, and likewise Ukraine's will to resist. The latter has been vital not only to Ukraine's achievements on the battlefield but also to validating the continued supply of financial and military support by Western governments facing inflation, recession, and an energy crisis.

These dynamics are not limited to the physical confines of the land domain, which tend to focus on physical geography and terrain features. Nor do they sit alone, isolated in cyberspace. They represent a web of networks that define power and interests in a connected world. The state that best understands local context—and builds a network around relationships harnessing local capacity—is more likely to win the twenty-first-century "great game."[7]

The military's current approach to the human domain lacks depth and rigor.[8] Theory is absent. Methods and tradecraft are underdeveloped and often improvised. Thinking and theory have been largely outsourced to civilians and industry, neglecting the fact that theory is a core responsibility of military professionals—indeed, theory is foundational to concepts, doctrine, and strategy, just like it is in any other profession.[9] Doctors do not conduct surgery without understanding theories of medicine, and lawyers do not practice law without an understanding of the reasoning that underpins it. Concept development, strategy formulation, and theoretical exploration require academic study and intellectual engagement. At present, ill-defined concepts are being deployed without adequate grounding in a coherent theoretical framework, and this has resulted in strategic confusion and a litany of useless buzzwords. Theory must inform concept development and strategy; otherwise, execution and performance suffer.

Why a Theory for the Human Domain?

Theory is essential as a description of the elements of the environment, an indication of the workings and interaction of those elements, and a path to determine what winning looks like within defined policy parameters.[10] Theories also provide a logical structure from which practitioners derive predictions, and these predictions guide strategic choice.[11] In this century thus far, a cognitive dissonance exists with concepts and capabilities. There is a mismatch between the capabilities needed to perform effectively and those that are chosen for investment. This creates a cognitive tension, wherein military leaders align their behavior and beliefs to fit choices that have been made—irrespective of the wisdom of those choices. There is an inflated sense of confidence that these concepts will work, when in fact there has not been sufficient testing or exploration to unpack these concepts fully. For engagement among people across the spectrum of conflict and competition, a theory is needed for action in the human domain.

Physical aspects of the environment define all the traditional domains. The land domain is "the area of the Earth's surface ending at the high water mark and overlapping with the maritime domain in the landward segment of the littorals."[12] The maritime domain is similarly distinctly physical, denoting "the oceans, seas, bays, estuaries, islands, coastal areas, and the airspace above these, including the littorals"; the air domain is the "atmosphere, beginning at the Earth's surface, extending to the altitude where its effects upon operations become negligible."[13] As operations extended beyond the atmosphere, the domains expanded, resulting in a new space domain, "the environment corresponding to the space domain, where electromagnetic radiation, charged particles, and electric and magnetic fields are the dominant physical influences, and that encompasses the earth's ionosphere and magnetosphere, interplanetary space, and the solar atmosphere."[14] Because the Chairman of the Joint Chiefs of Staff found it helpful to "treat cyberspace as an operational domain to organize, train, and equip," planners added a cyber domain and began to align force structure and organizations.[15]

Figure 2. Illustration of domains.

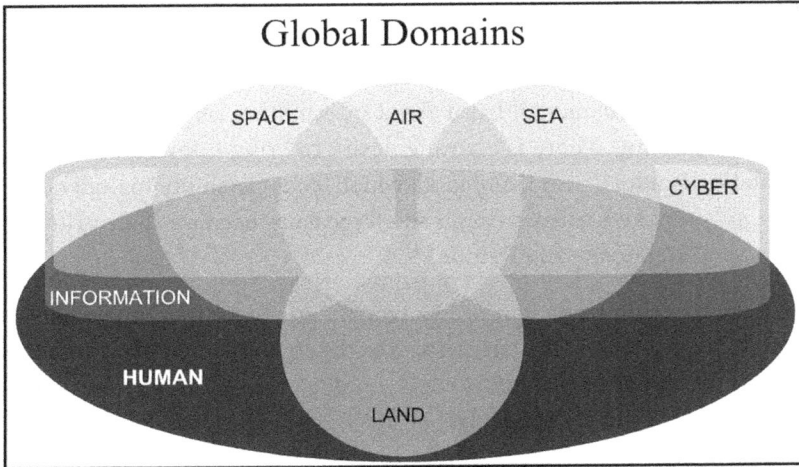

Source. Arnel David.

In 2017, another paradigm shift occurred when the Secretary of Defense established "Information" as the seventh Joint Function.[16] This addition of Information as a Joint Function brought increased emphasis on the information environment, but it misses a critical point about information. It is a human creation, it is complex and dynamic, it is global, and it is pivotal to understand the human domain to develop any meaningful messages. Therefore, by combining the various evolutionary features of doctrine, the following definition for the *information environment* is proposed because it clarifies and ties in the human component:

> The aggregate of sociocultural, cognitive, emotional, technical, environmental, historical, and physical features that shape how humans and automated systems understand, act upon, and are impacted by information.

Information and human behavior are inextricably intertwined. The relationship between people and information is key to understanding how the information environment shapes the operational environment.

They are not separate environments, with one prevailing over the other, but rather symbiotic ones. The symbiotic nature of this relationship is what enables the practitioner of information operations to pursue information advantage. They must also adequately understand the human domain. This fundamental truth about information is missed by current military thinking. There is a strong desire to bring information-related capabilities under Cyber Command, which lacks capability to understand foreign actors and entities (in no small measure because their principal languages are binary and Python).[17]

Dr. Herbert Lin from Stanford University attributes the Department of Defense's doctrinal confusion—as well as the entanglement of information operations, cyber operations, and psychological operations—to the lack of respect for military specialists in this field.[18] They are not part of the combat arts. The problem, argued by researchers, is rooted in institutional culture. The Department of Defense has been invested through the centuries into the mastery of the effects that govern physics—but not for the study of human behavior and the social sciences. This is troubling, given the investment in the human domain by competitors such as China and Russia.[19]

The continued struggle to define doctrinal terms exposes America's immaturity in the human domain. The current transformation of the information environment began over two decades ago. In 1998, the Joint Chiefs of Staff published Joint Publication (JP) 3–13 *Joint Doctrine for Information Operations*, which brought the first definitions of "information operations" and the "information environment."[20] It also outlined the need for "information superiority" and described offensive and defensive information operations as the two critical information operations, highlighting information's role in achieving advantage through "full spectrum dominance." It emphasized that operations in the "information domain" will become as important as those conducted in the "domains of land, sea, air, and space."[21] Since then, a surge of documents has continually emphasized the importance of information.

From defense reviews to planning guidance, information has been identified as important, but there has never been a clear understanding of the terminology to define this space. At present, there are six different definitions of the information environment in the Department of Defense Terminology Repository.[22] A similar issue exists with attempts to codify the human domain.

A variety of terms are used when discussing the human element of conflict and competition: "human terrain," "human aspect," "human factor," "human dimension," and the "human domain." The only official terms in the DoD's *Dictionary of Military and Associated Terms* that include "human" are "human intelligence" and "human factors."[23] Only "human terrain" and "human factors" are found in the *Terminology Repository.* The lack of standardized terminology creates systemic uncertainty and continued confusion. Put simply, these terms are unclear and at times specifically narrow, limiting the creative potential for broader conceptions of such important terms.

For example, the DoD narrowly bins human intelligence activity into a category designed specifically for intelligence professionals who manage human sources. It is often referred to, in short, as HUMINT (Human Intelligence). In Rob Johnson's seminal work on *Lawrence of Arabia on War*, he highlights how this enigmatic character, T. E. Lawrence, tirelessly worked on a form of "human intelligence," making it a personal obsession to assess people's character, psychology, and behavior.[24] Max Boot finds a similar instinctive quality in Edward Lansdale, a legendary figure who led a successful counterinsurgency in the Philippines against the Huk Rebellion. A clear talent in working among people, Landsdale explained that his skill was what he called "the art of friendly persuasion."[25] Current professional career development models are not designed to produce leaders like Lawrence and Lansdale.

The organizing concepts that served humanity for centuries appear increasingly antiquated.[26] Modern staff organizations, the byproduct of post-Napoleonic reforms and industrial-era concepts of bureaucratic management, continue to lead formations little changed since World War II.[27] Scholars and scientists at the Applied Research Laboratory for Intelligence and Security (ARLIS) warn that "neither the Department of Defense nor the interagency are postured or organized for success in the human domain and the information environment."[28]

Frontline personnel—military operators, development workers, peacebuilders, and diplomats—are operating on complex human terrain, where they are often overmatched by competitors with a superior understanding of the local populace, and who have far greater leeway to manipulate local dynamics to achieve effects. Without a unified theory in this age of persistent competition, the military will continue to struggle to educate, train, and equip soldiers for success. To begin developing a theory, the DoD must first recognize and define the human domain.

Coined by retired Lieutenant General Charles T. Cleveland, the "human domain" concept gained considerable traction during his tenure as the commanding general for US Army Special Operations Command (USASOC).[29] In 2013, the US Army, US Special Operations Command (USSOCOM), and the US Marine Corps commissioned a Strategic Landpower Task Force to research this human domain concept. The group defined this domain as the "totality of the physical, cultural, and social environments that influence human behavior to the extent that success of any military operation or campaign depends on the application of unique capabilities that are designed to fight and win population centric conflicts."[30] Although this was a useful start to exploring the concept, this initial outlook was viewed as a domain grab by USSOCOM for additional resources and funding, at a time of budget cuts and sequestration. The effort to define and scope this critical domain eventually faded away, and defense planners returned "back to the future," preparing for large-scale, high-end warfighting.[31]

ACADEMIC SCHOLARSHIP

To revitalize human domain thinking and better define the theory behind it, the military should stay closely tied in with academics to leverage the latest scholarship. Professional military education has improved over the years to introduce broader subjects to leaders, but more rigor and study is needed to bridge policy and strategy[32]—for as Winston Churchill put it, "at the summit, true strategy and politics are one."[33] Both civilian and military leaders require an understanding of politics and theory. To be sure, no military effort can overcome poor policy ends and a disconnected strategy.

Patricia Sullivan's research on war aims and political outcomes illuminates a new approach to this challenge. In reviewing military interventions since World War II, Sullivan finds that powerful states are less likely to achieve political aims that require target compliance. When major powers pursue coercive aims, weak actors are able to defeat stronger opponents nearly two-thirds of the time.[34] America's wars in Vietnam, Iraq, and Afghanistan are cases in point. This research created a new theoretical lens to examine war outcomes. The large body of past research focused on military strength and balance, whereas Sullivan provides a new typology on political objectives and their corresponding effectiveness.

Other scholarship studying large data sets from civil wars are yielding theoretical explanations useful for military and peacebuilding practitioners. Following the end of the Cold War, civil wars broke out in unprecedented numbers across Africa, South America, and Europe. The upsurge in civil conflicts led to an increased focus on the study of civil wars and on political violence more broadly, testing the definitional constraints and causal hypotheses developed in the last century.[35] It created a renewed focus on the field of peacebuilding and conflict, as scholars and practitioners sought to better understand which interventions failed and *why*.

In the early 2000s, multiple studies emerged examining the macro-level dynamics of civil wars: their length, their brutality, and the reasons why they start and end. These questions were analyzed via broad multi-decade datasets.[36] Some of the most prevalent theories about civil war onset presented explanatory correlations, such as the "greed and grievance" dichotomy, an econometric model that explains the causes of civil war as related to opportunity.[37]

Alternative theories posited that intrastate conflict could be better understood through analysis of identity issues as they relate to political instability. Many of the linear, deterministic theories of civil war have since been discredited due to an inability to replicate findings across studies. Cornerstone works such as Stathis N. Kalyvas's *The Logic of Violence in Civil War* demonstrate that preferences and identities can change during the course of a war, challenging deterministic theories.[38] Fotini Christia's work in *Alliance Formation in Civil Wars* disputes the notion that groups align or form because of shared identity considerations (e.g., ideology and religion).[39] Christia makes a compelling case that group choices are driven by relative power considerations to determine alliance formations, shifts, and fractures.

In the mid- to late-2000s, consensus developed around the importance of micro-level dynamics in explaining civil war outcomes, following a number of studies on the causes and variation of micro-level violence and the dynamics of participation, mobilization, and recruitment.[40] The importance of locally tailored, appropriately contextual peace programming is now championed more and more by practitioners. Any programming that aims to prevent, mitigate, or resolve conflict must be sensitive to the two-way interaction between activities and context. This is the only way to ensure that negative impacts are minimized in an intervention. Too often, both civilian and military leaders focus on macro-level dynamics rather than on the local drivers of violence and stability. Celestino Perez warns of this macro bias error contributing to strategic discontent.[41] Séverine Autesserre shares this concern with peacebuilding efforts and advocates for a bottom-up approach in which aid workers immerse themselves in the environment with grassroots organizations.[42] This is similar to the approach taken by the small Special Operations Civil Affairs team operating in the Philippines discussed at the beginning of this chapter.

All of this scholarship illustrates a core insight: interventions abroad should focus on the local level and do not need to be large. For interventions among the people, there is an inverse relationship with the size of the element and the effectiveness of the engagements. It does not take a Leviathan force to conduct small-scale missions, in which the political aims are limited and within reach.[43] Robert Kaplan argued that quality is more important than quantity; the composition of a force must be carefully planned out and "the smaller the unit, and the farther forward it is deployed among the indigenous population, the more it can accomplish."[44] General Cleveland observed this need to "go slow, go long, go small, and go local."[45]

Twentieth-century war saw massive land forces and large naval groups clashing on a global stage. In the twenty-first century, strategic advantage will emerge from how nations perform at the local level to develop relationships, trust, and legitimacy. To be successful in such struggles, the military profession must recognize and organize for its role in irregular conflicts and develop appropriate concepts that account for the need to gain a position of advantage in the human domain. Leading military powers like the United States must find ways to maneuver in an interconnected world of competing influence networks. Moreover, how a state attempts to influence matters, as does a key aspect of the human domain—the *human mind*—which demands more study and attention.

CONSCIOUSNESS: EMOTION AND COGNITION

Influence is central to competition and conflict alike. Information operations were once a core feature in the planning and execution of military operations. The art of influence, however, and the ability to message effectively, has waned over time—and will continue to atrophy because Western military forces are focused on combined arms maneuver and warfighting. Western nations require a course correction: the optimal paradigm for twenty-first-century competition is an influence campaign *backed by force,* as opposed to military campaigns backed by information operations (which, more often than not, do not adequately account for local context).[46] Nations such as China and Russia have already made this pivot, forming structures to operate with the human domain and to wield greater influence.[47]

The critical element of influence is neither the mechanism for information distribution nor the availability of social media platforms such as Twitter, Facebook, WhatsApp, et cetera. Instead, it is the message itself. Influence is achieved when a message affects its intended audience. The message can be overt or covert, violent or nonviolent, or some combination thereof. To be effective, it must be heard, seen, and acted upon by (and receive a reaction from) the target audience. For example, to demonstrate the intent to exert force, the US simply buzzed an airfield and shot a runway to demonstrate "extreme hostile intent," thereby preventing a military coup in the Philippines in 1989. It was an action backed by a strong verbal warning not to execute a coup. The message was received, and the Filipino military stood down.[48]

Looking to the present day, how can the contemporary information environment be leveraged by the US military and its allies, as they attempt to exert influence around the world? In order to understand the mechanics of influence, the military requires insight from the fields of neuroscience and psychology regarding the mechanics through which the brain processes information.[49] The study of emotion is at the center of scientific discoveries about the human condition. To understand how the mind works, consciously and subconsciously, one must understand emotion and recognize that "the mind represents an aspect of reality as primordial as the physical world."[50] To understand the complexity of the human mind and its relevance to military operations, one must look at the research comprehensively. Within Western military circles, there is an acute focus on cognition that dismisses or fails to account for emotion —the mental activity that predominantly drives cognition and human behavior. *Emotion* is the key variable to unlocking the full potential of influence operations in the human domain.

Significant differences exist between messaging the prefrontal cortex (where cognitive-rational and logical processes such as "thinking" occur) and the amygdala (where the brain registers and processes affects and emotions). Engagements with target audiences have continuously been in the prefrontal cortex and not the amygdala. Messaging in Afghanistan was a case in point. The coalition messaged the Afghan people to explain the logic of supporting the government, whereas the Taliban connected with the populace by playing on emotion, highlighting injustice and corruption.[51] A reliance on reason and logic (cognitive thinking processes) is the philosophical orientation of Western civilization. Arguably, emotion is the soft stuff that most military thinkers are either not comfortable talking about or do not fully understand. Hence, the more popular focus has been on the cognitive domain.

To that end, there have been attempts to establish "cognitive warfare" as an element of fifth-generation warfare. Most notably, Lieutenant General Vincent R. Stewart declared, "in the 21st century, war is about winning the information, the decision space either before or during the conflict. This is the deciding factor."[52] Others have attempted to define (and, subsequently, to operationalize) this cognitive warfare paradigm. Concepts such as "cognitive vulnerability" and "cognitive opening" refer to an audience already being predisposed and/or primed to receive and react to information.[53]

The focus on cognitive dimension prompted the notion of "cognitive security," as articulated by Rand Waltzman in his congressional testimony in 2017.[54] Waltzman emphasized the notion of "weaponized information," and the need to protect the population. Similarly, a 2019 RAND study concluded that influence and mass manipulation will inevitably lead to "virtual societal warfare."[55] The RAND study focused on the future of social manipulation efforts. The study clearly shows how information can be leveraged to shape individual and group behavior. However, it does not explain how the weaponization of information *actually* happens. Focusing only on cognitive aspects of behavior, these authors and studies neglect the critical element that drives much of human behavior: emotion.

In *The Logic of Failure* Dietrich Dörner finds "there is no thinking without emotion."[56] As stated previously, emotion (affect) is not emphasized in Western societal discourse. In consequence, many Western organizations struggle to fathom the vast psycho-emotional space of individuals and groups from other cultures, where affect is central to reasoning and narrative. This, in turn, subverts influence activities and messaging efforts. Human emotions and decision-making processes are complex. Yet, they must be understood if one is to influence them. Many competitor nations and nonstate actors are finding an asymmetric advantage against the West by improving in this field. Even some of the most authoritative voices from academia, think thanks, intelligence, and defense agencies continue to misunderstand the distinctions between cognitive and emotional dynamics.

Cognitive and emotional frameworks, as well as their complex interaction, are critically important. Developing a scientific understanding of the workings of the human mind is the first step toward recognizing and identifying *how* people feel, *what* they think, and *why* they do what they do. It is likewise important to develop the same level of understanding in order to assess the how, what, and why of adversaries.

Cognition-emotion frameworks and cognition-emotion interaction have received attention in recent clinical research and neurobiological studies. Researchers and scientists have demonstrated that cognitive and affective (emotional) processing are complexly interdependent.[57] It is estimated that approximately 80 percent of daily decisions are based on emotional processing, not on logic and reason. Furthermore, up to 100 percent of decisions are processed affectively when impacted by negative emotions such as hunger, anger, loneliness, and exhaustion.[58]

Research also shows how competitors have been able to access the emotional states of vulnerable populations, activating their emotional codes to influence, mobilize, radicalize, extremize, and ultimately weaponize them.[59] Adversaries' ability to influence, through a seemingly simple meme that evokes visceral emotional response in their target audience, is rarely contested or constrained.[60] US rivals are skilled at exploiting, disrupting, and destabilizing systems and communities. They are adept in crafting and disseminating information that can foster intra-communal dissent, mobilize popular support, and weaponize fault lines within society. At the same time, they advance their legitimacy and discredit their foes.

In engaging with other cultures, the military has repeatedly assumed a shared epistemology of ethics and principles. When they discover this is not the case, leaders either dismiss them as "irrational" or try to teach soldiers and statesmen superficial "cultural" differences that hardly scratch the surface. Frustrated by a failure to achieve results along these lines in Iraq and Afghanistan, the US Army has chosen to deprioritize the entire endeavor, as evidenced by the decision to close the University of Foreign Military and Cultural Studies.[61]

Conclusion

The opening of this book described a strategic landscape where power is diffusing and disaggregating. Local challenges and opportunities are thus a central feature of competition. In chapter 2, David Allen argues the gray zone should not be viewed as purely a zone of limitations and constraints but rather as an arena for creative action. This chapter set out to describe the need for theory to develop a framework for the human domain. The insights gleaned from the academy reveal scholarship not commonly read by military practitioners but that could prove valuable to those that need to operate among people. The chapter closes with a focus on consciousness—how people feel and think—and why there needs to be more balance when thinking about cognition and emotion.

Communicating effectively (with and across different societies) requires crafting a message that produces meaning. This requires knowing the audience's psychological, cognitive, and emotional operating systems —and recognition that emotions resonate *in context*. To succeed in the information environment and, ultimately, in the human domain, the US government must rethink its approach to understanding individuals and groups, their complex networks and psychological dynamics, their fears, terrors, and nightmares, and the fracturing of identities, families, and communities. A deeper and integrated understanding will improve influence efforts—and thereby strategic performance.

Notes

1. In Russell Weigley's seminal book *The American Way of War* (Bloomington: Indiana University Press, 1977), he describes a strategy of attrition and overwhelming force as seen in Ulysses S. Grant's emphasis on destroying the Army of Northern Virginia and the application of US airpower in the strategic bombing of Axis cities in World War II. See also Max Boot, "The New American Way of War," *Foreign Affairs* 82, no. 4 (July/ August 2003): 1, https://www.foreignaffairs.com/articles/united-states/2003-07-01/new-american-way-war.

2. James R. Arnold, *The Moro War: How America Battled a Muslim Insurgency in the Philippine Jungle, 1902–1913* (NY: Bloomsbury Press, 2011), 176.

3. Arnel P. David, "Civil Society Engagement in the Sulu Archipelago: Mobilizing Vibrant Networks to Win the Peace" (master's thesis, Command and General Staff College, 2013).

4. This description that these small wars were not large conventional but rather messy and "uncomfortable wars" comes from General John R. Galvin. See Daniel P. Bolger, "The Ghosts of Omdurman," *Parameters* 21 (Autumn 1991): 28–39; and Andrew F. Krepinevich, "Overhauling the Army for the Age of Irregular Warfare: The U.S. Military isn't Prepared to Wage Long Fights against the Islamic State and Other Enemies," *Wall Street Journal*, February 18, 2016, https://www.wsj.com/articles/overhauling-the-army-for-the-age-of-irregular-warfare-1455839486.

5. "Dr. Susan Bryant and Brigadier General (retired) Kim Field on The Pentagon Bureacracy and the Human Domain of War," interview by Nick Lopez and Kyle Atwell, *Irregular Warfare Podcast*, September 25, 2020, https://mwi.usma.edu/the-pentagon-bureaucracy-and-the-human-domain-of-war/.

6. Charles Cleveland, Susan Bryant, Arnel David, and Benjamin Jensen, *Military Strategy in the 21st Century: People, Connectivity, and Competition* (Amherst, NY: Cambria Press, 2018).

7. See discussion on the great game in chapter 1 which alludes to Peter Hopkirk, *The Great Game: The Struggle for Empire in Central Asia* (New York: Kodnasha International, 1992).

8. Arnel P. David, David Allen, Aleksandra Nesic, and Nicholas Krohley, "Why We Need A Modern Theory of Special Warfare to Thrive in the

Human Domain," *Wavell Room* (May 14, 2020): https://wavellroom.com/2 020/05/14/why-we-need-a-modern-theory-of-special-warfare-to-thrive-in-the-human-domain/.

9. Rachel Reynolds, "Strategy Verbs Theory: A Dysfunctional Relationship," *The Strategy Bridge* (February 2020): https://thestrategybridge.org/the-bridge/2020/2/25/strategy-verbs-theory-a-dysfunctional-relationship.

10. Joseph A. Gattuso Jr., "Warfare Theory," *Naval War College Review* 49, no. 4 (Autumn 1996): 112–123.

11. Andrew Hill and Stephen Gerras, "Systems of Denial: Strategic Resistance to Military Innovation," *Naval War College Review* 69, no.1 (2016): https://digital-commons.usnwc.edu/nwc-review/vol69/iss1/7.

12. Department of Defense, JP 1-02, *Dictionary of Military and Associated Terms* (Arlington: Department of Defense, 2016), 141.

13. Ibid., 150, 7.

14. Ibid., 224.

15. Department of Defense, *Department of Defense Strategy for Operating in Cyberspace* (Washington, DC: Department of Defense, 2011).

16. The seven Joint functions are intelligence, movement and maneuver, fires, information, protection, sustainment, and command & control. For adding of "information" see Office of the Secretary of Defense, "Information as a Joint Function" (official memorandum, Washington, DC: Department of Defense, 2017), https://www.rmda.army.mil/records-management/docs/SECDEF-Endorsement_Information_Joint%2 0Function_Clean.pdf. Office of the Secretary of Defense, "Information as a Joint Function" (official memorandum, Washington, DC: Department of Defense, 2017), https://www.rmda.army.mil/records-management/docs/SECDEF-Endorsement_Information_Joint%20Function_Clean.pdf.

17. Stephen Fogarty and Bryan N. Sparling, "Enabling the Army in an Era of Information Warfare," *The Cyber Defense Review* 5, no. 2 (Summer 2020): 17–26. The terms "binary" and "Python" refer to computer languages used by computer programmers.

18. Herbert Lin, "Doctrinal Confusion and Cultural Dysfunction in DoD: Regarding Information Operations, Cyber Operations, and Related Concepts," *The Cyber Defense Review* 5, no. 2 (Summer 2020).

19. Austin Branch, Ed Cardon, Devin Ellis, and Adam Russell, "We Ignore the Human Domain at Our Own Peril," *Modern War Institute*, June 14, 2021, https://mwi.usma.edu/we-ignore-the-human-domain-at-our-own-peril/.

20. Department of Defense. *Joint Doctrine for Information Operations*, JP 3-13 (Washington, DC: Joint Chiefs of Staff, 1998), https://www.c4i.org/jp3_13.pdf.

21. Department of Defense, "Joint Force 2000. America's Military: Preparing for Tomorrow," *Joint Force Quarterly* (2000), https://ndupress.ndu.edu/JFQ/.

22. The Terminology Repository of DOD Issuances is a DOD common access card (CAC) enabled database of over twenty-nine thousand terms and definitions from the Office of Secretary of Defense (OSD) and joint staff (JS).

23. Office of the Chairman of the Joint Chiefs of Staff, *DOD Dictionary of Military and Associated Terms* (Washington, DC: The Joint Staff, 2021).

24. Rob Johnson, *Lawrence of Arabia on War: The Campaign in the Desert 1916–18* (Oxford: Osprey Publishing, 2020), 21.

25. Max Boot, *The Road Not Taken: Edward Lansdale and the American Tragedy in Vietnam* (New York: Liveright Publishing Corporation, 2018), 632.

26. Kishore Mahbubani, *The Great Convergence: Asia, the West, and the Logic of One World* (New York: Public Affairs, 2013), 1–3.

27. Charles Cleveland, Susan Bryant, Arnel David, and Benjamin Jensen, *Military Strategy in the 21st Century: People, Connectivity, and Competition* (Amherst, NY: Cambria Press, 2018).

28. Austin Branch, Ed Cardon, Devin Ellis, and Adam Russell, "We Ignore the Human Domain at Our Own Peril," *Modern War Institute*, June 14, 2021, https://mwi.usma.edu/we-ignore-the-human-domain-at-our-own-peril/.

29. The idea of an overarching human domain was first introduced in a 2010 speech delivered in Amman, Jordan, by then commanding general for Special Operations Command – Central (SOCCENT), Major General Charles Cleveland. See Charles Cleveland, Susan Bryant, Arnel David, and Benjamin Jensen, *Military Strategy in the 21st Century: People, Connectivity, and Competition* (Amherst, NY: Cambria Press, 2018), 150.

30. Steven Metz, *Strategic Landpower Task Force Research Report* (Washington, DC: United States Army War College Press, 2013), https://www.hsdl.org/?view&did=745660.

31. Billy Fabian, "Back to the Future: Transforming the U.S. Army for High-Intensity Warfare in the 21st Century," *Center for a New American Security*, November 19, 2020.

32. Colin S. Gray, *The Strategy Bridge: Theory for Practice* (Oxford: University of Oxford Press, 2010).

33. Eliot A. Cohen, *Supreme Command: Soldiers, Statesmen, and Leadership in Wartime* (New York: Simon & Schuster), 159.
34. Patricia Sullivan, "War Aims and War Outcomes: Why Powerful States Lose Limited Wars," *Journal of Conflict Resolution* 51, no. 3 (June 2007): 496–524.
35. Keith Krause, "From Armed Conflict to Political Violence: Mapping & Explaining Conflict Trends," *MIT Press Journal* 145, no. 4 (Fall 2016): 113–126.
36. Paul Collier and Anke Hoeffler, "Greed and Grievance in Civil War," *Oxford Economic Papers* 56, no. 4 (2004): 563–595; and Nicholas Sambanis, "What is Civil War? Conceptual and Empirical Complexities of an Operational Definition," *The Journal of Conflict Resolution* 48, no. 6 (2004): 814–858.
37. James D. Fearon and David D. Laitin "Ethnicity, Insurgency, and Civil War," *The American Political Science Review* 97, no. 1 (2003): 75–90.
38. Stathis Kalyvas, *The Logic of Violence in Civil War* (Cambridge: Cambridge University Press, 2006).
39. Fotini Christia, *Alliance Formation in Civil Wars* (New York: Cambridge University Press, 2012).
40. Andreas Wimmer and Brian Min, "From Empire to Nation-State: Explaining Wars in the Modern World, 1816–2001," *American Sociological Review* 71, no. 6 (2006): 867–897; and Paul Staniland, "States, Insurgents, and Wartime Political Orders," *Perspectives on Politics* 10, no. 2 (2012): 243–264.
41. Celestino Perez, "Errors in Strategic Thinking: Anti-Politics and the Macro Bias," *Joint Force Quarterly* 81, no. 2 (April 2016).
42. Séverine Autesserre, *The Frontlines of Peace: An Insider's Guide to Changing the World* (Oxford: Oxford University Press, 2021).
43. Thomas Barnett, *The Pentagon's New Map: War and Peace in the Twenty-First Century* (New York: G. P. Putnam's Sons, 2004).
44. Robert Kaplan, *Imperial Grunts: On the Ground with American Military from Mongolia to the Philippines to Iraq and Beyond* (New York: Vintage Publishing, 2006).
45. Charles T. Cleveland, "Operating in Gray Zones," (speech, National Defense University, October 2015).
46. This concept of information and influence operations leading campaigns has been written about extensively; see Charles Cleveland, Susan Bryant, Arnel David, and Benjamin Jensen, *Military Strategy in the 21st Century: People, Connectivity, and Competition* (Amherst, NY: Cam-

bria Press, 2018); and P. W. Singer and Emerson T. Brooking, *Like War: The Weaponization of Social Media* (Boston: Houghton Mifflin Harcourt, 2018).

47. See Blagovest Tashev, Michael Purcell, and Brian McClaughlin, "Russia's Information Warfare: Exploring the Cognitive Dimension," *Marine Corps University Journal* 10, no. 2 (Fall 2019); and Larry M. Wortzel, *The Chinese People's Liberation Army and Information Warfare* (Carlisle: Strategic Studies Institute, March 2014).

48. Colin L. Powell, *My American Journey* (New York: Random House, 1995).

49. Lisa Feldman Barrett, Paula M. Niedenthal, and Piotr Winkielman, *Emotion and Consciousness* (New York: Guilford Press, 2005).

50. See report prepared by Mario Beauregard et al., "Manifesto for a Post-Materialist Science," *Open Sciences* (2014): https://www.opensciences.org/about/manifesto-for-a-post-materialist-science.

51. Sarah Chayes, *Thieves of State: Why Corruption Threatens Global Security* (New York: W. W. Norton & Company, Inc., 2015).

52. Kimberly Underwood, "Cognitive Warfare Will be the Deciding Factor in the Battle," *Signal*, August 15, 2017, https://www.afcea.org/content/cognitive-warfare-will-be-deciding-factor-battle.

53. Simona Trip, Carmen Hortensia Bora, Mihai Marian, Angelica Halmajan, and Marus Iaon Druggs, "Psychological Mechanisms Involved in Radicalization and Extremism. A Rational Emotive Behavioral Conceptualization," *Frontiers in Psychology 10* (2019): 437, https://doi.org/10.3389/fpsyg.2019.00437.

54. *The Weaponization of Information: The Need for Cognitive Security* (2017) (statement of Waltzman Rand), https://www.rand.org/content/dam/rand/pubs/testimonies/CT400/CT473/RAND_CT473.pdf.

55. Michael J. Mazarr, Ryan Bauer, Abigail Casey, Sarah Heintz, and Luke J. Matthews, *The Emerging Risk of Virtual Societal Warfare: Social Manipulation in a Changing Information Environment* (Santa Monica: RAND Corporation, 2019), https://www.rand.org/pubs/research_reports/RR2714.html.

56. Dietrich Dörner, *The Logic of Failure: Recognizing and Avoiding Error in Complex Situations* (New York: Metropolitan Books, 1996).

57. R. J. Dolan, "Emotion, cognition, and behavior," *Science* 298, no. 5596 (November 2002): 1191–1194, https://doi.org/10.1126/science.1076358.

58. Michael Levine, "Logic and Emotion: Delving into the Logical and Emotional Sides of the Human Brain," *Psychology Today*, July 12, 2012,

https://www.psychologytoday.com/gb/blog/the-divided-mind/201207/
logic-and-emotion.

59. Luiz Pessoa, "How Do Emotion and Motivation Direct Executive Control?"
    Trends in Cognitive Sciences 13, no. 4 (April 2009): 160–166, https://doi.
    org/10.1016/j.tics.2009.01.006.

60. Patrick J. Christian et al., "The Origins and Epidemiology of Violent
    Extremism & Radicalism," in *Countering Transregional Terrorism*, ed.
    Peter McCabe, National Counterterrorism Center, United States Spe-
    cial Operations Command (Tampa: Joint Special Operations University
    Press, 2018).

61. This is where the army developed a profound school of thought that
    enhances self-awareness, teaches groupthink mitigation, broods critical
    thinking, and fosters cultural empathy. Discussed in Lionel Beehner
    and John Spencer, "The Pentagon thinks urban warfare is obsolete.
    That's wrong," *The Washington Post*, November 20, 2020, https://www.
    washingtonpost.com/outlook/2020/11/20/afghanistan-iraq-pentagon-
    cuts-army-marines/.

CHAPTER 4

CIVIL RECONNAISSANCE

UNDERSTANDING THE PLAYING FIELD

Albert Oh, Guy Berry, Lucas Vaughan, and Sean A. Acosta

A 2018 congressional review of the US armed forces revealed that the American military was not prepared to face near-peer adversaries.[1] Senior military leaders responded with a renewed urgency to modernize. However, this modernization generally focused on platforms themselves rather than why they were needed in the first place. The word "innovation" became synonymous with artificial intelligence and machine learning, driving senior leaders to channel their efforts into technology instead of processes and methodologies.

Across the competition continuum, militaries must do three things: understand what is happening, decide what to do, and act to achieve an effect.[2] The military has focused much of its attention on developing tools oriented toward action. However, the first step in this process—gaining an understanding—is the most important. How can an appropriate solution be applied to a problem that is not understood?

The military has invested heavily in technological solutions to address the new context of strategic competition. Although technology may enhance an organization's ability to gather and sort data, human analysis is required to make sense of it. In the view of the authors of this chapter, the US military suffers from systemic faults in its efforts to develop understanding. Part of this can be attributed to the absence of coherent doctrine addressing the human domain (highlighted in chapter 3). The Joint Force thus struggles to engage with the more intangible aspects of the operational environment. This issue can also be traced to the military's overwhelming preference for quantifiable data and discomfort with qualitative insight. Budgetary allocations reflect this, as the military has embraced quant-based technological platforms as the backbone of its intelligence architecture.

Civil Affairs, the military's core cadre of warrior diplomats, has suffered as a result. In 2017, "senior leaders in the Army recognized the error in the decision to reduce active component CA capacity," but it was too little too late.[3] Funds were already moving into technologically oriented fields. For example, the Department of Defense requested a budget increase for new spending on autonomous systems technology from $1.38 billion in 2017 to $6.89 billion in 2018.[4] That same year, the Department of Defense disbanded the US Army's 85th Civil Affairs Brigade, and the Marine Corps deactivated the 2nd Civil Affairs Group the following year.[5] The active-duty Civil Affairs community was effectively cut in half, sending a clear message of how senior officers viewed the role of Civil Affairs in great power competition. While the autonomous systems were never meant to replace the Civil Affairs units, the disinvestment in Civil Affairs clearly highlights the fundamental misunderstanding of what capabilities provide the understanding US military commanders and diplomats need to maneuver against America's adversaries in politically sensitive environments.

Technology plays an essential *supplemental* role, but it is not a replacement for face-to-face human engagement. For example, strategic competition with China, Russia, and Iran requires a nuanced understanding of the civil networks and resources that comprise an operational environment. These networks consist of friendly, neutral, and malign actors—consisting of individuals, infrastructure, and organizations, both government aligned and private—and their relationships with one another. Mapping these individuals and groups is a complex undertaking. Add in the social nuances that depict the relationships between these nodes (political affiliations, financial connections, narratives and ideas, infrastructure, influences, etc.), and mapping becomes exponentially more challenging. Which populations are oppressed by malign actors, which resources are being exploited and removed to the detriment of local populations, and why is all of this happening?

The essence of civil reconnaissance, a skill set proprietary to Civil Affairs forces, lies in determining the linkage between humans and their positions within physical and societal infrastructure. Through overt, persistent engagement in regions vulnerable to instability, Civil Affairs forces help commanders visualize and describe relevant aspects of human geography. Through civil reconnaissance, commanders access much more deep-seated, nuanced details, such as population grievances and social movements.[6] Approached with diligence and careful analysis, an increased emphasis on information and influence over combat power allows the US and its partner nations to prevent adversaries from exploiting vulnerabilities. The evolution to a network-centric approach involves modeling data within the sociocultural landscape, engaging that network through viable programs or projects to fracture relationships with malign actors, and strengthening relationships with friendly nodes.[7] This approach toward identifying vulnerabilities demands a local lens to paint a clear picture of the relationships within a population and the narratives that influence them, not techno-centric scaffolding that may offer heaps of quantitative data with zero context.

The complexities of the twenty-first century security environment necessitate that the military expands beyond the trappings of land, sea, and air combat power to comprehend the civil component's levers, enablers, and motivators. Whereas traditional reconnaissance provides a commander with the enemy's location, civil reconnaissance explains *why* the enemy is there and, equally important, *why they are motivated to fight*.

This chapter focuses on one facet of the US military's current mandate to develop a nuanced, contextualized understanding of the playing field for strategic competition. The authors explore the inherit complexities of the human domain, military doctrine surrounding civil reconnaissance, the fundamentals of reconnaissance, and the value this capability offers the Joint Force.

REVISITING DOCTRINE

Traditionally, civil reconnaissance is not considered one of the five forms of reconnaissance, which are area, zone, route, in-force, and special. Despite its absence from maneuver doctrine, civil reconnaissance has become increasingly important. Doctrinally, civil reconnaissance is defined as:

> CA forces conduct [civil reconnaissance] across time and space in response to specific information requirements of the [operational environment]. This enhances the situational understanding and decision making of the supported commanders. [Civil reconnaissance] is a targeted, planned, and coordinated observation and evaluation of specific civil factors in the [operational environment]. [Civil reconnaissance] strives to consider the human, physical, and information dimensions of the [operational environment].

In layman's terms, civil reconnaissance provides an understanding of societies that can only be gathered from first-hand interaction. Civil reconnaissance is observing the impacts of illegal overfishing by Chinese flagged vessels on local coastal communities in Ecuador and then sharing this information with partner-nation governments, Department of State diplomats, and military commanders.[8] It is identifying the needs of the local populace in Manbij, Syria, after the Islamic State was ousted in 2016, so that commanders and the interagency community could accurately direct humanitarian aid and establish a local government.[9] It is assessing the localized dynamics of Russian influence across Eastern Europe so that the US government and its partners and allies can build societal resiliency and design resistance campaigns.

The value of civil reconnaissance to commanders and the interagency community has been demonstrated around the globe. Its relevance is undeniable. What is missing, however, is a clear-cut methodology for how to execute civil reconnaissance. To this end, the authors of this chapter contend that civil reconnaissance employs many of the same concepts that drive traditional, threat-oriented reconnaissance and security operations. Because doctrine is meant to clarify thought and achieve a common language across the Joint Force, one can look to extant reconnaissance doctrine as a framework for understanding maneuver in the human domain.

All soldiers are trained to understand two-dimensional map graphics to orient themselves and navigate their surroundings. Conversely, soldiers are also taught during basic combat training to translate their three-dimensional surroundings into an easily understandable two-dimensional sketch on a standard range card. This sector sketch is a product designed to facilitate the planning and controlling of direct and indirect fires. It also provides continuity of information from one soldier to the next. Through a series of geometric lines and shapes, a soldier assuming a fighting position can quickly ascertain what they can and cannot influence with their weapons system. It becomes readily apparent to a soldier where their left and right limits are, what terrain features exist in their assigned sector of fire, and how far they can see from their fighting position. Based on the lay of the land, a soldier can determine the most likely avenue of approach for an enemy and the features of the earth they may use to conceal their movement or defend as fighting positions.

This rapid form of terrain analysis is taught to the lowest-ranking soldier and can be scaled into more detailed overlays of terrain features, eventually feeding into a higher organizational view of maneuver capabilities on the ground. Terrain analysis is an essential part of intelligence preparation for the battlefield, a continuous process of information gathering and refinement in which a staff analyzes the geographic conditions of an operational environment and subsequently determines its effects on both friendly and adversary forces.[10]

Imagine this concept translated to a population. Instead of hills and valleys, a scout maps out the features of the human environment: a landscape of cultures, personalities, communities, and ideas. The link between cultural anthropology and warfare has been studied for decades, identifying societal grievances and primitive politics (tribal identity and resource management) as drivers of conflict.[11] Nonetheless, civilian considerations were eventually marginalized during the Global War on Terrorism, as population-centric approaches proved ineffective—and were replaced by kinetic lines of effort.[12]

The civil landscape of any operational environment should be actively reconnoitered and incorporated as a critical information requirement to commanders' decision cycles.[13] As the US military engages with a dynamic, complex global environment where the lines between war and peace are blurred, credence must be given to the levers that move the civil component. Although existing on a more subtle, intangible plane, these characteristics are paramount to understanding events as they unfold and affecting their trajectory. Influence requires substantive relationships and trust—which demand patient cultivation. As proclaimed by the US Special Operations Command, "you can't surge trust."[14]

Recent years have seen the prioritization of cyber warfare and electronic capabilities, depicting the information environment as a digital maneuver space that can be "dominated" or "conquered." Some have criticized decision cycles as being too slow to compete with America's adversaries, citing deficiencies in its technological capabilities as vulnerability in its ability to project power.[15] Although the advent of strategic competition has brought about recognition that the future of warfare will not resemble past conflicts, replacing human sensors with artificial intelligence is a misstep. Practitioners are swimming in a context-rich environment, and the automated sorting and synthesis of information dissolves nuanced social networks into quantitative data points. Though convenient for the military commander seeking to generate their own definition of mission success, this myopic drill has resulted in the "fetishization of data"—a burgeoning obsession to obtain those quantifiable inputs, enabled by rapidly evolving technology to harvest it.[16] A fresh perspective on maneuver within the human domain can offset the need to physically occupy or dominate "key terrain" with overwhelming firepower. What is the maximum area of influence of a select population? What is the maximum effective range of its influence platform? There may be little to no overlap with that population's physical sector of control, which is certainly not easily determined or resolved at the push of a button.[17] The answers to these questions are best determined through civil reconnaissance.

Resisting Maslow's Hammer

> I suppose it is tempting, if the only tool you have is a hammer, to treat everything as if it were a nail.
>
> Abraham Maslow

Two-dimensional maps and overlays suffice to depict the employment of maneuver and fires from land, sea, and air. However, enduring relationships based on trust, complex societal dynamics, and mutually supported objectives are not so easily represented to decision makers. The 2018 publication of the *Joint Concept for Integrated Campaigning* and the *Joint Concept for Operating in the Information Environment* highlighted the increasing impact of information and influence operations as "changing the character of modern warfare." That said, there was little explanation of the required capabilities of the future Joint Force beyond platitudes such as "the ability to determine the impact of" and "ability to understand the relevance of" the information environment.[18] Insofar as how one accesses the information environment to visualize and describe it to decision makers, the army field manual *Information Collection* connects the fundamentals of reconnaissance to operational planning methodologies but falls short of providing more than vague frameworks for how to organize a collection plan, much less address the complexities of the human domain.[19] "Civil considerations" are acknowledged but not adequately emphasized as a factor to consider within the planning process.[20]

The US military must acknowledge this gap between doctrinal tasking to develop understanding and the resources that tactical level units like Civil Affairs have at their disposal. The challenges of the past two decades have exposed the military's weakness in understanding and exploiting opportunities that develop along the seams between the physical and cognitive dimensions as well as at the touch points between adversaries and the societies in which the military confront them. Thinking back to the reconnaissance diagrams just discussed, one can see that the "human factors" of conflict which influence decision-making processes add another axis of maneuver across the traditional division of domains, as explained in the previous chapter.[21]

At the height of counterinsurgency operations in 2010, then soon-to-be CIA director John Brennan famously remarked, "we often need to use a scalpel and not a hammer" in navigating the fault lines of a population mired in conflict, lest unintended consequences turn "tactical success into strategic failure."[22] The allusion to the scalpel implies a need for precise engagements, with ample examination of a place's deeply rooted history, culture, and current events to forecast potential second- and third-order effects. It is precisely those delicate relationships between what is physically apparent and what is cognitively opaque that have bedeviled US military might in recent conflicts. But how is this understanding developed? And by whom?

Carter Malkasian's experiences in Afghanistan highlight this sentiment. America's tactical successes in Afghanistan never translated to the strategic success sought. Yes, the Taliban government was overthrown. Yes, Osama Bin Laden was eventually eliminated. But if the tactical successes the US experienced were so great, then why did America's exit twenty years later see the Taliban immediately retake control of the country? Malkasian argued that the US never understood why the Taliban fought.[23] The US focused on enemy composition, disposition, and capabilities instead of underlying motives. The former are necessary and vital in warfare—this is irrefutable. But casting aside why people fight, or worse yet, arrogantly thinking Western ideals and perspectives align with the rest of the world, will continue to produce results like those in Afghanistan. Insight into an adversary's motivation can only be provided by persistent, human interaction among those the US is attempting to help.

Within the scope of traditional military operational planning, the gravitation toward "Maslow's hammer" is understandable. America's approach to managing risk in warfare relies on a linear problem-solving methodology—components of the system that comprise the threat to the mission are packaged into neatly sorted inputs that can be reduced to smaller, targetable objectives to be eliminated or mitigated.[24] The military version of the scientific approach ultimately results in a machine-like, calculated game of reduction that strips interconnected, dynamic networks from the context that makes those networks relevant. Even the proposed approach of effects-based operations, meant to expand analysis of the operational environment past the traditional threat-centric perspective, was hastily crammed into a systems framework with step-by-step checklists and engineered to the point of obfuscation.[25] Put simply, the US military has yet to determine how the complexity and contextual *messiness* of the civil component can be integrated into core doctrinal and operational processes.

THE IRREGULARITY OF CIVIL AFFAIRS

Irregular warfare is gaining traction as a rising priority within the US military.[26] Civil Affairs's warrior diplomats have a pivotal role to play in irregular conflict: understanding the context of competition and conflict and developing relationships that can be leveraged toward deliberate ends. Civil reconnaissance is the essential first step to enabling understanding and facilitating effective engagement.

The purpose of all reconnaissance is to fill information gaps by confirming or denying facts and assumptions. To fill these gaps, the five doctrinal forms of reconnaissance can be scaled according to the desired information and level of detail. For example, a zone reconnaissance would look at the entirety of the Washington, DC, focusing on threat, terrain, infrastructure, and society; an area reconnaissance would focus on the National Mall and on gathering the same information as a zone reconnaissance; a route reconnaissance would involve driving the roads from the Capital Beltway to the National Mall.[27] A reconnaissance-in-force is solely enemy-focused and is used to determine weaknesses that can be exploited. Special reconnaissance is conducted in hostile, blocked, or politically sensitive environments to collect or verify information of strategic or operational significance. Although civil reconnaissance is not recognized as the sixth form of reconnaissance, the same fundamentals of reconnaissance, covered in the next section, still apply.

So, what is the difference between a Civil Affairs team conducting civil reconnaissance and US Army Scouts performing an area reconnaissance (which may include civil considerations)? What makes civil reconnaissance a unique and independent form of reconnaissance? Both are driven by a commander's critical/priority information requirements and specific information requests. Both clarify and enhance the common operating picture. Both facilitate a commander's decision-making and targeting processes. The differences are in the entities (executing either form) and the outputs generated. Every military unit, regardless of designation, conducts reconnaissance to confirm a leader's plan before execution. However, not every unit conducts civil reconnaissance.

Civil Affairs is the premier force for civil reconnaissance because it is a specified function of their branch based upon their specialized training, diplomacy, regional/cultural expertise, language capability, advisory skills, and level of autonomy.[28] These skills allow Civil Affairs teams to gather information, develop relationships, and conduct analysis to a depth that cannot be achieved by general purpose units. The enduring value of the relationships and networks developed through civil engagements, by conducting civil reconnaissance, are hard to measure and assess but remain crucial. An area safe and accessible one year can become consumed by a military coup or civil war, and enduring relationships can fracture as their levels of influence ebb and flow.

THE FUNDAMENTALS OF CIVIL RECONNAISSANCE

As outlined in *Scout Platoon*, the US Army scout platoon's training publication, the primary tools for reconnaissance are the human senses.[29] Likewise, a warrior diplomat's primary tools for civil reconnaissance are the human senses, supplemented by human emotions. These tools are used to interact with the human domain, wherein technological tools can be leveraged to accelerate or enhance investigative efforts. The language of traditional reconnaissance doctrine, meanwhile, is that of a combat unit reconnoitering and maneuvering against enemy elements. What is the language of civil reconnaissance? Particularly in a pre- or post-conflict environment, where the "enemy" may be distant, abstract, or absent entirely? The following section offers an answer to this question, with core reconnaissance commonalities highlighted in italics.

First, a Civil Affairs practitioner must *ensure continuous reconnaissance*, through perpetual engagement with a relevant population or individual. Commanders must *not keep reconnaissance assets in reserve*. Civil engagements and assessments must occur early and often and can be accomplished in person, telephonically, digitally, or by proxy through use of a partner force. Next, Civil Affairs must *orient on the reconnaissance objective*, which is determined by the commander's information collection plan, and *report information rapidly and accurately* to enhance the common operating picture. To make accurate decisions, a commander needs relevant information—time diminishes relevancy and is a precious resource that cannot be wasted.[30] The civil information gained (with subsequent processing, integration, evaluation, analysis, and interpretation by Civil Affairs) will clarify decision-making and targeting processes.

Subsequent reporting must accurately describe ground truth.[31] The analysis Civil Affairs provides in this reporting must be logical and highlight the reason why the civil information is important to commanders and US government entities. Finally, gaining and maintaining contact early and often to develop the situation/relationship rapidly is paramount. The relationships to be developed and maintained will be with US Embassy Country Teams, partner forces, clans and their elders, ministers, commissioners, militia leaders, and other key stakeholders to *retain freedom of maneuver*. This will allow the access, placement, and movement required within the operational environment to identify the vulnerabilities, enablers, and motivators that might enable the exertion of influence over certain individuals or groups.

THE THREE TYPES OF INFRASTRUCTURE

As with the fundamentals of reconnaissance, the US military's current understanding of infrastructure must also be refined. Civil Affairs practitioners must target their efforts in each step of preparing the operational environment. This is a significant challenge, as the human domain encompasses both the physical and societal structures within the civil component.[32] Although Norman Lihou and Marisol Nieves define the human domain as the "physical, cultural, and social environments as it relates to the sphere of human activity within an area of interest," they neglect the narratives and ideas that define a population's identity.[33] However,

Lihou and Nieves advance the idea of "Human Network Analysis and Engagement," in which friendly, neutral, and threat networks all exist as "complex adaptive systems," subject to a wide array of internal and external influences.[34] This echoes a marked shift in the military's understanding of the operational environment, moving away from a quantitative, threat-focused intelligence cycle to one that is rich in context with granular, qualitative detail—in other words, information that is more representative of reality on the ground.[35]

To better illustrate interactive networks, imagine the de facto leader for a relevant population, the individual who controls the narrative terrain and has the power to change this population's behavior through influence. That individual's influence is not derived from the raw number of their relationships (quantities of links and nodes). Rather, it is the strength of those links, the feedback from those nodes, and the level of influence commanded by each subsequent node (three hundred unpopular Facebook friends versus three hundred top social media influencers).[36] This individual represents *critical human infrastructure.* Their criticality is due to their relative centrality to the greater network in terms of influence power—in social network analysis terms, the eigenvector.[37]

Unlike reconnaissance operations over physical terrain, identification of this critical human infrastructure may not be readily apparent through traditional means of observation. This is the primary challenge facing foreign policy practitioners, highlighting the true value proposition of civil reconnaissance. How are efforts and resources driven toward identifying, engaging, and influencing critical human and social infrastructure?

To expand upon the concept of interactive networks as they relate to the targeting process, consider a power substation. It is a piece of critical physical infrastructure that could be rendered inoperable by damaging or destroying the apparatus itself. However, without the human infrastructure for maintenance, control, and administration, the station becomes as inert as if the machinery had been destroyed outright. To affect the station's capabilities, one needs to determine who is in control.

Who is able to push the button that would shut power off to specific parts of a city? Who is able to restore that power? What would happen if there were civil unrest and a mass walkout of employees, leaving no one to maintain the components? People operate the power grid, and their aspirations or grievances can be used to degrade, disrupt, or destroy its electrical production. In whatever capacity or role they fill, those individuals have been identified as the eigenvectors that can drive, influence, and change the behavior of a network among the hierarchies of infrastructure.

As with physical infrastructure, what are political organizations, fraternities, and tribal councils, to name but a few, without the human infrastructure to fill those positions? The societal infrastructure is a mechanism that can shape a narrative to influence a relevant population. Scholars find that "morality resides in groups rather than in individuals."[38] The networks that make up societies and their interconnectedness, spatial flows, and leaders are key information. Aside from the normal focus on threat networks and a persistent stare at the enemy, what organizations map out this type of information?

The questions posited previously are not all-inclusive—they are to show the nature of why relationships are built with key stakeholders. A commander's critical information requirements, priority information requirements, and specific information requests will drive civil reconnaissance. The purpose is to identify the key dynamics within that relevant population, and its key stakeholders.

To highlight the previous points, a Civil Affairs team was deployed to Somalia in support of Operation Octave Shield in 2017.[39] The team conducted joint, integrated civil reconnaissance patrols multiple times per week with their Somali Special Operations—the Danab Brigade—and Marine Special Operations Team trainers/mentors.[40] Within these advise/assist/accompany patrols, the Civil Affairs team was designated as the Joint Force Commander for Civil Affairs/Civil-Military Operations. The patrol would conduct civil engagements to develop relationships with pastoral nomads, for example, as they migrated their camel herds around a military base in the Somali hinterlands housing both US and Somali soldiers. They were also designed as a testing ground for Danab's first Civil-Affairs-trained Civil-Military officer.

By engaging with the nomads, the team and its Danab civil-military counterpart were able to map regional clan demographics and migration patterns. Al-Shabaab, an Al-Qaeda-linked transnational militia, would use the nomads for cover and concealment. This allowed al-Shabaab to maintain freedom of maneuver around the base and report on US and Somali forces. Of the vulnerabilities identified, the patrol began administering medications to the camel herds and nomads alike through veterinary and medical civic action programs. Providing these essential services legitimized Danab with the nomads, projecting a usually absent federal presence to a rural area that had not experienced a government above the local clan level within the past 30 years.

Additionally, the influence gained by Danab translated into the nomads providing information on al-Shabaab agents within their caravans, locations of watering holes that were used by the nomads and al-Shabaab, and regular sites used by the nomads to remain overnight. This information enhanced the common operating picture for the entire region and aided the targeting process to optimize effort and resources. It also prevented civilian casualties from inaccurate identification of suspected al-Shabaab formations.[41] Through the information provided by the nomadic population, the team and its Danab Civil-Military counterpart were able to distinguish between the predominant clans and sub-clans in that specific region and those that were interlopers. This allowed Danab to detain suspected al-Shabaab agents for questioning, decreasing the capabilities of al-Shabaab's early warning network and providing detailed information on the enemy's logistical nodes.

An Old Practice in A Modern Era

In the technology-laden world of the twenty-first century, commanders are overwhelmed with information. Futuristic tools funnel reams of data into antiquated systems. The resulting data sets describe the operational environment in terms of statistics, numbers, and locations. Yet, they ignore the unquantifiable motivations and relationships driving America's adversaries and allies, and they fail to explain the on-the-ground reality. Civil reconnaissance addresses these intangible variables, bringing an informative narrative to the operational environment, one that accounts for the constantly evolving culture, history, and ideas that drive the humans occupying that environment. No aircraft, drone, or cyberspace sensor can capture this. It takes interaction among humans, rooted in trust and developed overtime.

The United States' warrior diplomats remain marginal and secondary in the current strategic environment.[42] Niche capabilities like Civil Affairs may appear outmatched against an adversarial government's massive financial, political, and conventional military resources. But they are one of few instruments willing and able to deliver critical insights and access. They are the face of outreach and engagement with local government officials and community stakeholders, exemplifying America's commitment to partnerships abroad. They provide a granular understanding of local politics, culture, religion, and economics, which shape the playing field for strategic competition. They are frontline sensors, calibrated to identify and investigate the impacts of exploitative political and economic practices taken by America's adversaries. They cannot deliver a *comprehensive* view of the human domain of conflict or competition—nor should they be asked or expected to. Their purpose is to engage with the complexity, dynamism, and messiness of the real world and to provide as much clarity of understanding and insight as is possible. It is not a "silver bullet" or an easy path toward actionable insight, but it is nonetheless a vitally important undertaking.

Combining technology with human senses, warrior diplomats can interact with the human domain to identify and develop networks of influence and action. They remain the only capability within the US government willing and postured to gather contextual ground truth and provide analysis to senior US commanders and decision-makers. Civil reconnaissance offers both civil and military leaders the tools to understand, direct, and shape the constantly evolving operational environment. The next chapter dives deeper into what to do with the information collected from civil reconnaissance and highlights a glaring gap in analytical frameworks used by defense.

NOTES

1. David Ochmanek et al., *U.S. Military Capabilities and Forces for a Dangerous World*, RR-1782-1-RC (Santa Monica, CA: RAND, 2017), https://www.rand.org/pubs/research_reports/RR1782-1.html.
2. Christian Brose, *The Kill Chain: Defending America in the Future of High-Tech Warfare* (Boston: Hachette Books, 2020).
3. Joseph J. Malizia, Jr., *Understanding the Risks Created by Reducing Civil Affairs Capacity* (Carlisle: United States Army War College, 2017), 1, https://publications.armywarcollege.edu/wp-content/uploads/2022/11/3459.pdf.
4. Jon Harper, "Spending on Drones Projected to Soar," *National Defense*, December 7, 2017, https://www.nationaldefensemagazine.org/articles/2017/12/7/spending-on-unmanned-systems-is-ramping-up.
5. Arnel P. David and Clay Daniels, "Strategic Misfire: The Army's Planned Reduction of Civil Affairs Forces," https://foreignpolicy.com/2016/05/12/strategic-misfire-the-armys-planned-reduction-of-civil-affairs-forces/.
6. Department of Defense, *Joint Concept for Human Aspects of Military Operations* (Washington, DC: Joint Chiefs of Staff, 2016), ii, https://www.jcs.mil.
7. Department of the Army, *Network Engagement*, ATP 5-0.6 (Washington, DC: Department of the Army, 2017), ch. 1, 1, https://armypubs.army.mil.
8. Santiago Previde, "South America Overlooks Chinese Illegal Fishing at Its Own Peril," *The National Interest* (November 2021): https://nationalinterest.org/feature/south-america-overlooks-chinese-illegal-fishing-its-own-peril-195731.
9. Peter S. Brau, "Using Civil Affairs to Implement Stabilization Activities in Nonpermissive Environments," *Army University Press* (February 2019): https://www.armyupress.army.mil/Journals/Military-Review/Online-Exclusive/2019-OLE/Feb/Civil-Authority/.
10. Department of the Army, *Intelligence Preparation of the Battlefield*, ATP 2-01.3 (Washington, DC: Department of the Army 2019), ch. 4, 1, https://armypubs.army.mil.
11. Bronislaw Malinowski, "An Anthropological Analysis of War," *American Journal of Sociology* 46, no. 4 (January 1941): 537.

12. Richard D. Hooker, Jr. and Joseph J. Collins, *Lessons Encountered: Learning From the Long War* (Washington, DC: National Defense University Press, 2015), 21–74.

13. US Joint Chiefs of Staff, *Joint Planning*, JP 5-0 (Washington, DC: US Joint Chiefs of Staff, 2020).

14. US Special Operations Command, "Special Operations Forces 2020," (Tampa: Government Printing Office, 2020).

15. Christian Brose, *The Kill Chain: Defending America in the Future of High-Tech Warfare* (Boston: Hachette Books, 2020).

16. Nicholas Krohley, "The Intelligence Cycle is Broken. Here's How to Fix It," *Modern War Institute at West Point,* October 24, 2017, https://mwi.usma.edu/intelligence-cycle-broken-heres-fix/.

17. Charles L. Moore, Jr. et al., *Maneuver and Engagement in the Narrative Space*, SMA Report (Washington, DC: Strategic Multilayer Assessment, 2016), 13, http://nsiteam.com/social/wp-content/uploads/2015/12/Maneuver-in-the-Narrative-Space_Final_Jan2016.pdf.

18. Department of Defense, *Joint Concept for Integrated Campaigning* (Washington, DC: US Joint Chiefs of Staff, 2018), 16, https://www.jcs.mil.

19. Department of the Army, *Information Collection*, FM 3-55 (Washington, DC: Department of the Army, 2013), 2–14, https://armypubs.army.mil.

20. Department of the Army, *Intelligence*, FM 2-0 (Washington, DC: Department of the Army, 2018), 2–14, https://armypubs.army.mil.

21. JP 2-0, *Joint Intelligence*, defines "human factors" as the physical, cultural, psychological, and behavioral attributes of an individual or group that influence perceptions, understanding, and interactions.

22. John Brennan, *Securing the Homeland by Renewing America's Strengths, Resilience, and Values* (Washington, DC: Center for Strategic and International Studies, 2010), https://obamawhitehouse.archives.gov/the-press-office/remarks-assistant-president-homeland-security-and-counterterrorism-john-brennan-csi.

23. Carter Malkasian, *The American War in Afghanistan: A History* (New York: Oxford Press, 2021).

24. Robert D. Lamb and Melissa R. Gregg, "The Dual-System Problem in Complex Conflicts," Strategic Studies Institute, US Army War College, http://www.jstor.com/stable/resrep20101.7.

25. John T. Correll, "The Assault on EBO," *Air Force Magazine,* January 2013, 53.

26. The Department of Defense has prioritized the institutionalization and operationalization of irregular warfare (IW) with the addition of an IW Annex in October 2020 to the 2018 *National Defense Strategy*.

27. Department of the Army, *Reconnaissance and Security Operations*, FM 3-98 (Washington, DC: Department of the Army, 2015), https://armypubs.army.mil, 5–6.

28. Department of the Army, *Civil Affairs Operations*, FM 3-57 (Washington, DC: Department of the Army, 2021), iv, https://armypubs.army.mil.

29. Department of the Army, *Scout Platoon*, ATP 3-20.98 (Washington, DC: Department of the Army, 2019), ch. 3, 2, https://armypubs.army.mil.

30. Ibid., ch. 3, 3.

31. Ibid., ch. 3, 3.

32. JP 2-01.3, *Joint Intelligence Preparation of the Operational Environment*, provides guidance on where a practitioner of civil reconnaissance must focus their efforts to prepare the operational environment. The level of detail articulated within each chapter, for each step, provides intricate lists of *where* the physical, societal, and human infrastructure resides within the civil component and cognitive domain.

33. Norman Lihou and Marisol Nieves, "Conceptualizing Human Domain Management: Human Network Analysis and Engagement (HNAE) Operations," *Small Wars Journal*, April 4, 2014, https://smallwarsjournal.com/jrnl/art/conceptualizing-human-domain-management.

34. Ibid.

35. Department of Defense, *Joint Concept for Human Aspects of Military Operations*, (Washington, DC: Joint Chiefs of Staff, 2016), 12, https://www.jcs.mil. https://nsiteam.com/social/wp-content/uploads/2017/01/20161019-Joint-Concept-for-Human-Aspects-of-Military-Operations-Signed-by-VCJCS.pdf.

36. Jennifer Golbeck, *Analyzing the Social Web* (Waltham: Morgan Kaufman, 2013), 25.

37. An eigenvector is the influence of a central node within a network that can be regarded as a single-point of failure or success, if that node were to be degraded or bolstered, that would affect the entirety of the network.

38. Nicholas A. Christakis and James H. Fowler, *Connected: How Your Friends' Friends' Friends Affect Everything You Feel, Think, and Do* (New York: Back Bay Books, 2009).

39. Nick Turse and Sean D. Naylor, "Revealed: The U.S. Military's 36 Code-named Operations in Africa," *yahoo!news*, April 17, 2019, https://www.

yahoo.com/now/revealed-the-us-militarys-36-codenamed-operations-in-africa-090000841.html.

40. Mark Mazzetti, Jeffrey Gettleman, and Eric Schmitt, "In Somalia, U.S. Escalates a Shadow War," *New York Times,* October 16, 2016, https://www.nytimes.com/2016/10/16/world/africa/obama-somalia-secret-war.html.

41. "Somalia says U.S. airstrike killed civilians not al-Shabab," *BBC News,* September 29, 2016, https://www.bbc.com/news/world-africa-37514149. Patrols such as these began shortly after a US drone strike in Galkayo, Somalia where the misidentification of an allied militia as al-Shabaab was targeted and resulted in ten members killed. The catastrophic loss of rapport between the US, their partner force, and the population was exploited by al-Shabaab to reignite the civil war of opposing clans between North and South Galkayo, which had been relatively quiescent following a UN-backed ceasefire in April of 2016.

42. The creation of the US Cyber Command in 2017 as a unified combatant command was a clear statement of intent from the military. With this promotion, the military cyber community gained increased funding, oversight, and a direct line to the Secretary of Defense. There has been no commensurate activity in regard to the role of the military in generating an understanding of the contextual features of operational environments.

CHAPTER 5

CANCELLING THE CROSSWALK

REFRAMING CIVIL CONSIDERATIONS

Nicholas Krohley

America's post-9/11 wars sparked a rediscovery of the fundamental human element of conflict. Faced with faltering campaigns in Afghanistan, Iraq, and elsewhere where the application of force abetted by cutting-edge technology was failing to deliver results, the US military recalibrated. The result was an avalanche of "new" thinking and capabilities. The US Army's field manual FM 3-24 *Counterinsurgency* lays out a population-centric vision for military operations.[1] The Human Terrain System sought to harness academic expertise, with emphasis on ethnographic methods.[2] Village Stability Operations took a localized, bottom-up approach to security, development, and governance.[3] Female Engagement Teams provided a specialized resource to engage with "the invisible fifty-percent" of civilian communities on the battlefield.[4]

Each of these endeavors shared a common imperative: to understand, navigate, and influence the people among whom the US military fights. Military leadership amplified this message, giving rise to mantras like "the human terrain is the decisive terrain" and "the population is the center of gravity."

Each of these endeavors also shared a common fate: systemic under-performance and eventual marginalization. The mantras of counterinsur-gency were compelling theory, but they translated poorly into tactical and operational action (not to mention a glaring absence of strategic results).

This chapter identifies a critical root cause of this underperformance and the US military's inability to pivot from theory to action in the human domain. It then explains why this problem persists to the present day, subverting efforts to understand, engage, and shape civil dynamics. In conclusion, the chapter offers a solution that would transform the military's approach to understanding and operationalizing civil consid-erations.

THE PIVOT FROM THEORY TO ACTION

The counterinsurgency era's doctrinal appreciation for civil considera-tions and their connectivity to enemy-centric intelligence were clearly articulated. Documents like FM 3-24 *Counterinsurgency* touted social, economic, political, and cultural dynamics as integral features of intelli-gence. "Successful conduct of COIN operations depends on thoroughly understanding the society and culture within which they are being conducted," the authors noted, before offering an extensive list of societal dynamics that merit examination.[5] The counterinsurgent must under-stand "the nature and nuances of the conflict," the "motivation, strengths, and weaknesses of the enemy," and "knowledge of the roles of other actors" on the battlefield.[6] The enemy, meanwhile, must be "isolated" from its sources of popular and material support.[7]

> Counterinsurgency (COIN) is an intelligence-driven endeavor. The function of intelligence in COIN is to facilitate understanding of the operational environment, with emphasis on the populace, host nation, and insurgents...Intelligence in COIN is about people.

U.S. forces must understand the people of the host nation, the insurgents, and the host-nation (HN) government. Commanders and planners require insight into cultures, perceptions, values, beliefs, interests and decision-making processes of individuals and groups. These requirements are the basis for collection and analytical efforts.[8]

As a result, the authors continued, *Intelligence Preparation of the Battlefield* "places greater emphasis on civil considerations," and military forces were encouraged to draw upon "the knowledge of nonintelligence personnel and external experts" and to encourage the bottom-up flow of intelligence reporting.[9] The document's guidelines for "comprehensive insurgency analysis" focused heavily on civil considerations, particularly related to the enemy's connectivity with civilian communities:

Figure 3. Comprehensive insurgency analysis tasks.

- Indentify insurgent strategic, operational, and tactical goals, objectives, and imperatives.
- Identify motivations, fears, concerns, and perceptions that shape the actions of insurgents and their supporters
- Idenitfy grievances, fears, and concerns that the insurgents exploit
- Determine how culture, interests, and history inform insurgent and host-nation decision making
- Understand links among political, religious, tribal, criminal, and other social networks
- Determine how social networks, key leaders, and groups intereact with insurgent networks
- Determine the structure and function of insurgent organizations
- Indentify key insurgent activities and leaders.
- Understand popular and insurgent perceptions of the host-nation, insurgency, and counterinsurgents—and how these affect the insurgency.

Source. Department of the Army, 2006, *Counterinsurgency.* FM 3-24. Washington, DC: Department of the Army, https://fas.org/irp/doddir/army/fm3-24fd.pdf, see chapter 3, 32.

For all its emphasis on the importance of civil considerations, however, FM 3-24 *Counterinsurgency* offered little in the way of tools and skills to investigate them.[10] In contrast to the robust methods and established processes of enemy-centric intelligence analysis, those tasked to understand civil dynamics faced a doctrinal void.[11] On a Monday morning in Mosul or Musa Qala, what exactly were military personnel supposed to *do*? Assuming they discovered something, what should they do with it? The questions of how exactly this should be done, of where one should start, and what steps should be followed, were never adequately addressed.

Because theoretical imperatives were not accompanied by practical methods, the investigation of civil dynamics defaulted to operational art.[12] The success stories of the past two decades have, therefore, been a testament to the instincts and talent of individuals who pursued this work. Men and women served with honor and skill in support of these efforts, and individual- and unit-level successes showcased the potential impact of such capabilities and lines of effort. That said, civil-oriented capabilities have proven inconsistent (at best) in their operational impacts and have remained a marginal element of US military power. The Human Terrain System was ignominiously decommissioned.[13] Village Stability Operations failed to achieve scalable impacts.[14] Female Engagement Teams proved to be more of a public relations gimmick than a strategic weapon.[15] Time and again, contextual reporting on civil considerations begged the question: *so what?* Such failures, in light of the importance ascribed to civil considerations by leaders and "thought leaders" alike, expose a systemic problem within the enterprise.

CANCELLING THE CROSSWALK

The previous discussion referenced a "doctrinal void" for the practitioners of civil reconnaissance, human terrain analysis, and other such efforts to understand civil considerations. This was somewhat disingenuous. Doctrine does, in fact, offer an analytical framework: the ASCOPE/PMESII crosswalk. This framework, explained in the text below and hereafter referred to as "the crosswalk," is everywhere. It was the chosen approach to understanding civil considerations in the 2006 edition of FM

3-24 *Counterinsurgency.* It retains that function in its 2014 successor, FM 3-24 *Insurgencies and Countering Insurgencies,* as well as in more recent documents such as 2017's ATP 5-0.6 *Network Engagement,* 2018's JP 3-57 *Civil-Military Operations,* 2019's ATP 2-01.3 *Intelligence Preparation of the Battlefield* and FM 3-57 *Civil Affairs Operations,* and the USMC's 2020 *MCCMOS Circular: Civil Reconnaissance.*[16]

The crosswalk has metastasized throughout the US military, becoming *the* approach to understanding civil considerations. Contagion has spread beyond America's borders as well, among close partners such as the United Kingdom, Canada, and NATO. Its ubiquity notwithstanding, the crosswalk is utterly unfit for purpose.[17] Put directly, the crosswalk's unsuitability for the investigation and analysis of civil considerations is the most insidious source of inconsistency, marginalization, and systemic failure in America's efforts to understand (and, thereafter, to shape) operational environments.

ASCOPE is an acronym meaning "areas, structures, capabilities, organizations, people, and events." These categories are meant to encompass the full spectrum of potential civil considerations. They are the things soldiers may encounter. PMESII is another acronym that stands for "political, military, economic, social, information, and infrastructure." These categories represent potential operational variables. They are the categories soldiers use to classify what they may encounter. When laid out on an X-Y axis, a matrix or "crosswalk" is created, into which analysts input, for example, what is known about the areas, structures, capabilities, organizations, people, and events that relate to politics in a given area, and then to militaries, and then to economics, and so on.

Figure 4. PMESII/ASCOPE crosswalk.

	P Political	M Military	E Economic	S Social	I Information	I Infrastructure
A Areas	Areas - Political (District Boundary, Party affiliation areas)	Areas - Military (Coalition / LN bases, historic ambush/IED sites)	Areas - Economic (bazaars, shops, markets)	Areas - Social (parks and other meeting areas)	Areas –Information (Radio/TV/newspapers /where people gather for word-of-mouth)	Areas – Infrastructure (Irrigation networks, water tables, medical coverage)
S Structures	Structures - Political (town halls, government offices)	Structures - Military / Police (police HQ, Military HHQ locations)	Structures - Economic (banks, markets, storage facilities)	Structures - Social (Churches, restaurants, bars, etc.)	Structures - Information (Cell / Radio / TV towers, print shops)	Structures - Infrastructure (roads, bridges, power lines, walls, dams)
C Capabilities	Capabilities - Political (Dispute resolution, Insurgent capabilities)	Capabilities - Military (security posture, strengths and weaknesses)	Capabilities - Economic (access to banks, ability to withstand natural disasters)	Capabilities - Social (Strength of local & national ties)	Capabilities - Info (Literacy rate, availability of media / phone service)	Capabilities - Infrastructure (Ability to build / maintain roads, walls, dams)
O Organizations	Organizations - Political (Political parties and other power brokers, UN,)	Organizations - Military (What units of military, police, insurgent are present)	Organizations - Economic (Banks, large land holders, big businesses)	Organizations - Social (tribes, clans, families, youth groups, NGOs / IGOs)	Organizations - Info (NEWS groups, influential people who pass word)	Organizations - Infrastructure (Government ministries, construction companies)
P People	People - Political (Governors, councils, elders)	People - Military (Leaders from coalition, LN and insurgent forces)	People - Economic (Bankers, landholders, merchants)	People - Social (Religious leaders, influential families)	People - Info (Media owners, mullahs, heads of powerful families)	People - Infrastructure (Builders, contractors, development councils)
E Events	Events - Political (elections, council meetings)	Events - Military (lethal/nonlethal events, loss of leadership, operations, anniversaries)	Events - Economic (drought, harvest, business open/close)	Events - Social (holidays, weddings, religious days)	Events - Info (IO campaigns, project openings, CIVCAS events)	Events - Infrastructure (road / bridge construction, well digging, scheduled maintenance)

Source. MCCMOS digital archive, https://www.trngcmd.marines.mil/
Portals/207/Marine%20CIM%2014%20Aug%202019.pdf.

The crosswalk has a certain appeal. It is clean and organized. It presents boxes, which are to be methodically filled, until a chart is complete. It is scalable, insofar as the crosswalk can be used for a single village or for an entire country. Equipped with basic research tools, anyone can create a crosswalk for any operational environment. The "essential variables" can be identified and categorized. The analyst in question plays the role of a librarian, filing away bits of knowledge, box by box.

It could be argued that the crosswalk offers a serviceable taxonomy for the *presentation* of civil considerations. Someone with deep knowledge of a particular geography could use this framework to deliver information in a digestible manner. However, doctrine does not recommend the crosswalk as a mere presentation tool. It is the chosen analytical methodology for investigating civil dynamics. This is catastrophic, for several interconnected reasons.

The crosswalk's "fill-in-the-blanks" approach leads, necessarily, to the collection of civil information *without intent*. The most critical challenge in the assessment of civil dynamics is knowing where to start and deciding which questions to ask. Operating in complex, ever-changing environments, practitioners are confronted by a swirling sea of information. Only a small fraction of the potential civil considerations within a given area will hold relevance in a particular moment. The blanket collection of civil information, without any clear objective as to its purpose, is a reprehensible waste of time. The military may not be "boiling the ocean," per se, but collectors are trawling aimlessly, while analysts and information managers are drowning in meaningless data.[18]

As a practitioner catalogs, for example, the areas, structures, capabilities, organizations, people, and events that might relate to economic considerations in a given area, they have absolutely no way of assessing how this information might matter in an operational context. They will have been provided with the commander's intent (an aspirational statement of priorities and desired end-states), but this guidance tells them nothing about how to make sense of the facts on the ground. They know nothing about how or why specific economic or social considerations might present threats or opportunities. They are populating a chart for the sake of populating a chart. They have no way to appreciate or prioritize the significance of the inputs.

As a result, practitioners are inundated with data of uncertain value.[19] The crosswalk explains nothing. It can only categorize. The chart's creator can identify, for example, notable individuals and organizations within an economic system. But nothing in the crosswalk, or in the analytical process that feeds it, enables an analyst to understand why these individuals and organizations might matter in a specific situation. Any actionable insights emerging from a crosswalk-enabled analytical process will, therefore, be a function of the analyst's personal talent, initiative, and intuition. This is operational art compensating for doctrinal malpractice.

Finally, a completed crosswalk suggests that an analytical endpoint has been reached. But what can one actually do with this product, apart from identifying generalized information gaps of uncertain significance? The crosswalk is not an actionable product. Indeed, the fact that the foundational analytical approach to civil considerations does not generate actionable outputs should be sufficient grounds for its eradication from doctrine and training. After a crosswalk is produced, what happens next?

WHO CARES?

What relevance does this discussion have in the post-post-9/11 era? The Global War on Terrorism is over. Counterinsurgency is anathema. Domestically, there is growing pressure to retire the US military from the business of solving (or exacerbating) other people's problems in distant lands. Meanwhile, technology is ascendant. Data-driven insights are offered at the push of a button. Artificial intelligence and machine-learning tools sift, sort, and structure unfathomable quantities of data. Social media analysis is touted as a risk-free, cost-effective, and scalable replacement for old-fashioned groundwork. What need does the US government have for Civil Affairs's value proposition of understanding and influencing foreign societies through face-to-face engagement?

Notwithstanding current hype over so-called "great power competition," there is good reason to expect that, for those tasked with understanding operational environments, the decades to come will have much in common with America's recent past. Granted, large-scale occupation, in the style of Iraq and Afghanistan, is a remote prospect. As noted elsewhere in this book, large-scale conventional war with a country like Iran, Russia, or China is conceivable—but far from imminent or inevitable.[20] What is certain, however, is that the US military will remain consistently engaged in low-intensity conflict and strategic competition across multiple theaters for the foreseeable future. This is the inescapable day-to-day reality of America's current strategic environment.

This reality has been described using an array of overlapping jargon: the US is in a new era of irregular warfare; it is engaged in persistent competition below the threshold of war; it is maneuvering through a gray zone where distinctions between war and peace are blurred; and it must adapt to the new realities of unconventional and proxy conflict.[21] In all of these contexts, strategic priorities are typically framed around interstate rivalry. The US is countering Russian influence in the Black Sea region, or it is competing with the Chinese for influence and resources in sub-Saharan Africa. Strategic perspective is clearly "big picture" oriented. Yet, success in these endeavors (not to mention long-running counterterrorism and stabilization campaigns in the Sahel, the Levant, and elsewhere) will require a granular understanding of the *exact* same types of societal fault lines and contextual dynamics that bedeviled campaigns in Iraq and Afghanistan. As noted in chapter 1, today's great game is rooted in local context.

Counterinsurgency may be dead and buried, but many core information requirements remain strikingly similar. In the current geopolitical landscape, there are few plausible scenarios in which America's rivals would comprise more than ten- to fifteen-percent of a given operational environment. That leaves Civil Affairs, with the mandate to explore, understand, explain, engage, and shape the civil environment, as the US military's primary tool for addressing the remaining eighty five- to ninety-percent.

An instrument of this importance cannot allow itself to be inconsistent. Nor can it allow itself to be marginal. The fact that key stakeholders within the Department of Defense view Civil Affairs as being both inconsistent and marginal should be cause for introspection and a call to arms. Civil Affairs's warrior diplomats should be an essential, go-to instrument of American power. No other elements of the military are equipped (or inclined) to address civil considerations. Nor can conventional diplomats take on this challenge; they are isolated from ground truth by systemic risk aversion within the Department of State. This is particularly true in conflict zones, where US embassies are veritable prisons.

Finally, irrespective of the current tech-centric zeitgeist, technological innovation cannot fill this gap. The ability to assess events as they unfold, and to anticipate their trajectories, requires causal understanding. Technology can help find patterns and trends, but correlation is simply not good enough. It is insufficient to recognize that things are happening. Practitioners must decipher *why*.

No combination of hardware and software can deliver actionable situational understanding. Indeed, the innovations of the Fourth Industrial Revolution, from artificial intelligence to machine learning, have analysts swimming in oceans of data and able to detect patterns and establish connections in the subtlest ripples of current. For those in the business of hunting men, these are transformational weapons. They have much less to offer, however, to those tasked with understanding civil dynamics. The fundamental limitations of quantitative, data-driven analysis remain. As argued elsewhere:

> Quantitative data is reductive. On the battlefield, we can quantify and measure an extraordinary range of things, from incidences of violence to the price of bread to the movement of displaced people. Yet once we quantify something, stripping away its contextual meaning and turning it into a data point, it loses all of its explanatory power. A quantitative data set cannot tell us anything about the significance of changing rates of violence, price fluctuations, or patterns of migration. Is an uptick in violence the result of the enemy's growing strength? Is it tied to a rogue commander who has broken with the enemy's central leadership? Is it the final death throes of an insurgent movement that has lost local support? The data cannot tell us...data sets, no matter their size [or the sophistication of the tools used to process them], can never answer the question "why?"[22]

The military has no choice but to rely on people to make sense of operational environments. This holds equally true both in peacetime and in war. From the South China Sea, to Eastern Europe, to Central America, Civil Affairs must fulfill a critical mission: identifying key civil considerations, and offering courses of action to shape social, economic, and political dynamics to America's advantage.

Becoming Essential

The Civil Affairs community has embraced civil reconnaissance as a defining capability.[23] Statements of intent regarding the importance of this mission must now be matched with analytical and operational methods that deliver consistent results.

FM 3-57 *Civil Affairs Operations,* revised in 2019 and again in 2021, shares much in common with the 2007 edition of FM 3-24 *Counterinsurgency.* It is a thoughtful, articulate document, which spells out the importance of understanding civil considerations. It advocates Civil Affairs's utility in a broad range of military contexts. Civil reconnaissance features prominently as a core Civil Affairs activity. However, the document fails to complete the pivot from theory to action for two main reasons: First, like its counterinsurgency-focused predecessor, FM 3-57 *Civil Affairs Operations* spends far more time talking *about* civil considerations than it does instructing the reader in how they should be investigated. Second, the ASCOPE/PMESII crosswalk remains the framework for civil reconnaissance and the analysis of civil dynamics.

For Civil Affairs to assert itself as an essential military capability, the crosswalk must be erased from doctrine and training as an investigative framework.[24] Without a fit-for-purpose assessment methodology, Civil Affairs will remain dangerously over reliant on operational art. Individual teams will shine, as a function of raw talent within the community, but the wider endeavor will remain inconsistent. Furthermore, without a standardized service that generates recognizable, actionable products, commanders will remain uncertain of the Civil Affairs's value proposition.

THINKING DIFFERENTLY: VECTOR-BASED CIVIL RECONNAISSANCE

What might a new approach look like? How could Civil Affairs position itself to thrive as a provider of focused insights into the human domain? The answer does not lie in a new set of acronyms. Civil Affairs does not need a new macro-level taxonomy or new analytical boxes to tick. The problem is not the crosswalk itself but the analytical premise behind it. Civil reconnaissance cannot be conducted as a fill-in-the-blanks exercise. Instead, practitioners require a genuine investigative methodology: a framework within which the collectors, analysts, and integrators of civil information act as detectives, blending the processes of intelligence work with the methods of the social sciences to conduct targeted, deliberate investigation.[25]

Doctrine demands a holistic and comprehensive view of the operational environment. For example, ATP 2-01.3 *Intelligence Preparation of the Battlefield* opens with the declaration that this process "describes the totality of relevant aspects of the [operational environment] that may impact friendly, threat, and neutral forces."[26] The desire for a complete understanding of civil considerations is understandable. However, the breadth, depth, and dynamism of the real world make this impossible.[27] How could one capture anything approaching a comprehensive view of the societies in which the US military operates? Why do many in the military think this is possible? Even at the village or neighborhood level, this would be a staggering undertaking. Moreover, the vast bulk of the reporting would be un-actionable, if not wholly irrelevant.

This exposes the dilemma that makes civil reconnaissance uniquely challenging as a subset of the wider reconnaissance discipline. A traditional reconnaissance element can map every bridge on the battlefield or determine the exact disposition of enemy forces within a given area. Comprehensive knowledge is a realistic objective. The practitioner of civil reconnaissance is similarly tasked by doctrine: to provide commanders with comprehensive, actionable knowledge of civil dynamics. In this case, however, the practitioner faces an environment with infinite, ever-shifting features. This simply cannot be done. The question posed to the practitioner, therefore, both operationally and doctrinally, cannot be how the US establishes a comprehensive understanding of civil considerations. Instead, it must be how it establishes a focused, actionable understanding of the right civil considerations.

The practitioner, inevitably, must prioritize. This can be done informally, through the exercise of operational art. This is the unacknowledged status quo today within Civil Affairs, just as it was within civil-oriented capabilities during the counterinsurgency era. Due to the crosswalk's limitations, practitioners are forced to decide for themselves what should be prioritized within each box, and likewise which issues merit further examination. The pitfalls of this approach and the consequences of systemic inconsistency and ad hoc improvisation have already been discussed.

Instead, prioritization should occur through a structured process and method, which provides practitioners (and, by extension, their customers) with *the best possible view* of the human domain. The idea that practitioners must start with a high-level view of everything, and then gradually drill down, is a dangerous mistake. Civil Affairs needs an assessment methodology that rapidly and reliably zeroes in on what matters. The crosswalk does not even attempt to do this.

Civil reconnaissance requires the mindset of a detective. When a crime is committed, does a detective begin by interviewing everyone in a given city? In pursuit of a comprehensive view of the issue at hand, does the detective attempt an all-encompassing study of everything and everyone? Of course not. Utilizing proven criteria (e.g., motive and opportunity), the detective narrows the field immediately. Conducting civil reconnaissance via the crosswalk is like trying to solve a murder using the phonebook.

The field of view must be narrowed, from the outset, using a bottom-up analytical approach.[28] Analysts should start small, with a granular investigation of specific, targeted issues. The urge for "comprehensive" analysis must be tempered by the sheer impossibility of the task but assuaged by the knowledge that interconnectivity within the human domain will enable us to draw expansive insights from focused analysis. Put another way, the fact that social, economic, political, and cultural systems all interlink with one another means that a deep dive study of something "small" will inevitably illuminate broader features of the landscape.

This can be achieved through a vector-based approach to civil reconnaissance. Such a process would commence with the selection of discrete vectors that are active within an operational environment. These vectors could be human networks: organized groups that are maneuvering across the human terrain toward their own specific ends, provoking varied reactions from elements of the populace.[29] Alternatively, they could be phenomena: trends or events like disease outbreaks, resource scarcity, or natural disasters that trigger social, economic, cultural, and political responses.

Through a structured, step-by-step analytical process, practitioners would use these vectors as a guide through the operational environment. Civil Affairs conducts civil reconnaissance to help commanders understand, navigate, and influence the human domain. Why not structure the endeavor around close study of how others have maneuvered through that same terrain?

First, the practitioner would select a set of vectors and examine how and why they function. These vectors would be chosen for their ability to illuminate pre-identified priorities, which would be drawn from the commander's intent, strategic imperatives, and the military's own background knowledge. Second, the practitioner would map each vector's trajectory through—and/or their root structure within—civil society, identifying precisely where, when, how, and why they affect (and are affected by) specific civil dynamics. Third, the practitioner would use this understanding of each vector's relationship with civil society as a jumping-off point for the focused examination of key social, economic, political, and cultural dynamics. Such an approach, detailed further next, would fundamentally recast civil reconnaissance as an investigative activity and drive the consistent production of focused, actionable reporting.

CIVIL AFFAIRS AND INTELLIGENCE

Two qualifications are necessary after introducing the vector-based concept: First, this is not encroaching into the realm of military intelligence. Depending on circumstance, and delineations between active duty and reserve component mandates within the Civil Affairs community, civil reconnaissance may or may not be building toward lethal outcomes. Similarly, practitioners may be operating at varied levels of classification. Regardless, civil reconnaissance is the process of operationalizing common knowledge about social, economic, political, and cultural dynamics. The answers to questions about these dynamics are broadly known among the civilian population of a given area and can be readily obtained through overt, deliberate means. Moreover, even when hostile networks are used as exploratory vectors (a course of action that should be taken whenever possible), these vectors are not the ultimate objects of analysis. Rather, they are a means to an end, as they enable focused exploration.

This alignment of civil reconnaissance as a complementary discipline to enemy-centric intelligence (indeed, as an outgrowth thereof in instances where hostile networks like the Islamic State, Wagner Group, or Boko Haram are used as vectors) would bring a host of benefits. Most critically, it would create an integrated understanding of enemies and competitors *in context*, as outgrowths of the operational environment. At present, enemy-centric intelligence and the attendant lethal targeting process are siloed from the analysis of civil considerations and non-lethal course of action development. This is a recipe for dysfunction and a misallocation of resources. It is a critical root cause, for example, of the US government's woeful return on investment for development and reconstruction spending over the past two decades, and likewise of the strategic futility of its whack-a-mole approach to lethal effects-based targeting.[30] By building a coherent, integrated understanding of adversaries within the societies in which the military confronts them, the US would open the door to truly integrated planning and campaign design.

Second, this endeavor is—absolutely—an intelligence function.[31] Civil reconnaissance *must* generate actionable intelligence about civil considerations. To say otherwise, or to assert that civil reconnaissance does not produce intelligence, is simultaneously incorrect and poisonous to Civil Affairs's relevance. "We do not produce intelligence" is the hill that the Human Terrain System chose to die on. If Civil Affairs repeats this argument, it risks a similar fate. This is a statement that provokes immediate disengagement among commanders, who are in desperate need of precisely this sort of intelligence.

Instead, the practitioners of civil reconnaissance should offer a simple distinction: *we are generating actionable intelligence about civil considerations in the operational environment, using overt, deliberate collection methods.* That is a one-sentence elevator pitch that would immediately clarify the Civil Affairs value proposition, de-escalate any possible turf war with military intelligence, and capture the attention of commanders.

Concern that Civil Affairs professionals might lose access to foreign societies if tainted by association with "intelligence" is misplaced. The vector-based approach to civil reconnaissance would remain focused on civil considerations. The content of questions the military asks and the conduct of its investigations would preserve Civil Affairs's position as an overt, collaborative partner with local counterparts. In instances that required the insights of traditional, enemy-centric intelligence related to a particular vector, information requests could be passed to military intelligence professionals via Civil Affairs's own internal intelligence officers. There is no risk of Civil Affairs veering "out of its lane." On the contrary, it would be enabling integrated, multidisciplinary analysis within the intelligence cycle.

Finally, the notion that foreign nationals make a meaningful distinction between Civil Affairs and other elements of the US military is wildly overstated within the Civil Affairs community. Inside of the US government bubble, profound distinctions are drawn between Civil Affairs and its direct action and intelligence-oriented counterparts. From the outside looking in, however, foreign nationals distinguish subtle shades of gray, at best.[32] Does the US military *really* think that its local counterparts see Civil Affairs as an aid organization or as something distinct from its kinetically minded brethren?

THE ANALYTICAL PROCESS

Consider what a vector-based civil reconnaissance campaign might look like to investigate the Islamic Republic of Iran. Investigative vectors could include the Islamic Revolutionary Guard Corps (the IRGC, which is a dominant entity within Iran's military and intelligence apparatus), the remnants of the opposition Green Movement that has campaigned on political liberalization in successive elections, and COVID-19. The first line of inquiry would provide immediate insight into dynamics of civil-military relations, the government's societal power base, and Iran's political economy. The second vector would illuminate domestic politics, incorporating social, economic, religious, and class-based factors. The third would initially highlight issues related to public health, governance, and Iran's social contract. Taken together, these vectors would offer diverse yet complementary and interlocking insights into Iran's human terrain. Their simultaneous exploration would set the US on a path toward a granular, nuanced, and actionable understanding of the civil considerations that *matter*.

Step 1: Vector Analysis

Practitioners would begin by developing a deeper understanding of the vectors themselves. This provides essential context, which will enable them to understand the vectors' interplay with the civil dynamics that are

Civil Affairs's ultimate priority. For networks like the IRGC and the Green Movement, practitioners build from traditional human network analysis. How are the networks organized? Are they centralized or decentralized, hierarchical or modular, et cetera.? How does their structure create strengths or weaknesses? Was this structure a deliberate choice or born of adaptive necessity? What is the network trying to achieve and why? How does ideology shape the network's activity, and how does ideology shape its engagement with external parties? What binds the network together (e.g., ideology, financial incentives, kinship, etc.), and how does this affect its posture and strength within Iran?

For a phenomenon like COVID-19, the focus is not on the disease itself, but on the second- and third-order effects that it triggers. To that end, practitioners would begin with analysis of its impact on Iranian society. How has COVID-19 moved through Iran? What demographic and geographic cohorts have been most or least affected? Is the phenomenon accelerating, stable, or abating? Is there a consensus on how these trends will evolve in the near to medium term?

Step 2: Connectivity Assessment
From these initial assessments of the vectors themselves, practitioners would broaden the focus to the vectors' touch points in the operational environment. How have the networks in question gained a foothold in civil society? What societal responses have been provoked by the chosen phenomena? To continue the Iran example, precisely when, where, how, and why have the IRGC and the Green Movement sunk roots into various segments of Iran's social, economic, political, and cultural systems? With respect to COVID-19, how have the second- and third-order effects of the virus exposed, exacerbated, or created fault lines in the human terrain? How have responses to these vectors by specific segments of the Iranian population (socioeconomically, ethnically, demographically, geographically, et cetera) illuminated pivotal civil considerations?

Step 3: Green Layer Analysis

Having broadened the analytical lens from the chosen vectors to include when, where, how, and why they have impacted or engaged with specific elements of the human domain, practitioners now have a roadmap for onward exploration. Returning to the Iran example, practitioners could use the root structures of the IRGC and the Green Movement, and their view of the localized second- and third-order effects of COVID-19, as focused analytical pathways to further investigate civil dynamics.

How, for example, did the IRGC sink its roots into certain segments of Iran's political economy? How did the key players therein respond? What narratives (nationalist, theological, transactional, et cetera) sustain the IRGC's position in Iranian society, and how are they received by different segments of civil society? What does this tell us about the IRGC's strengths and weaknesses, and how social and economic levers might be used against it? How do the domestic operations of the IRGC, and the societal responses they provoke, illuminate key features of Iranian society?

What explains the Green Movement's ability to mobilize support from certain corners of Iranian society, but not others? What segments of Iranian society have been leveraged *against* the Green Movement, and with what sort of incentives and narratives? What can these dynamics teach us about fault lines in contemporary Iran? How have the inherent qualities of the Green Movement and the societal position of its supporters shaped its ability to resist official suppression? How has the explosion of social media since the movement's initial rise altered these dynamics? What does this tell us about the fundamentals of Iranian civil society? How might all of this inform Western-backed civil engagement initiatives or the development of irregular warfare strategies?

What narratives have been used by groups that are particularly disaffected with the government's response to COVID-19? How have those narratives resonated across the wider populace, and how has the government responded? Concurrently, how have official narratives allocated blame for the pandemic's impact on Iran? What insights can the pandemic offer into the condition of civil society and its mobilization behind (or opposition to) the Iranian government?

Questions such as these, and many others, would flow naturally from the structured analytical process outlined above. They could be answered through overt, deliberate investigation, with a clear view toward operationalization and course of action development. This bottom-up, micro-to-macro approach would culminate in coherent strategic analysis —with the distinction that the entire effort would be rooted in granularity, focused exclusively on relevant issues, and devoid of wasted effort.

Snapshot: Russia in the Black Sea Region

With a view toward other geopolitical priorities and operational contexts, consider a civil reconnaissance campaign to understand Russian influence in the Black Sea region. Analytical vectors could include the Russian Orthodox Church and its local affiliates, Russophile and Russophobe political parties, and oligarchic business empires that grew from the Soviet Union's collapse. How might this approach enable deep exploration into the civil considerations that Russia has exploited in the region? How might the practitioners of civil reconnaissance generate actionable insights and prospective courses of action to build societal resiliency and orchestrate civil resistance, further economic reform and anti-corruption efforts, and encourage westward alignment? How would such an effort compare to the insights generated via the ASCOPE/PMESII crosswalk?

Snapshot: China in the Global South

Alternatively, consider an effort to understand Chinese influence in Mozambique or Venezuela, via the exploratory vectors of Chinese state-backed extractive companies, climate change and attendant resource scarcity, and the debt-trap diplomacy that accompanies the One Belt, One Road initiative. How would the study of these vectors contextualize China's successes and setbacks, as a function of localized civic responses to Chinese actions? How might such an understanding enable the US government to craft a coherent, whole-of-government strategy to leverage local priorities and grievances against the Chinese?

Snapshot: The Islamic State Worldwide

Finally, consider a global campaign to map the root structure of the Islamic State, which would illuminate where, when, how, and why the network has succeeded or failed to mobilize local support from Mali to Mindanao to Molenbeek—and which would compare and contrast the localized civil considerations and narratives that have proved pivotal to its operations. How might the resulting insights feed an integrated lethal and non-lethal targeting campaign against that root structure, which would combine direct action against the network's key leadership with a more nuanced outreach, messaging, and engagement effort to disrupt the Islamic State's local alliances and build societal resilience? How would Civil Affairs's pivotal role in such an interdisciplinary, interagency campaign reframe perceptions of the branch?

SIGNATURE DELIVERABLES AND INTEGRATED ACTION

A vector-based approach to civil reconnaissance would generate a suite of actionable products, several of which could become "signature deliverables" for Civil Affairs. The most compelling of these, and likely the most valuable in Civil Affairs's effort to become an essential instrument of military power, would be root maps.

Root maps would identify where, when, how, and why an adversary (e.g., the Russians or Chinese governments, the Islamic State, or the IRGC and its MENA-wide proxies) have sunk roots into civil society within particular geographies, for the purpose of influence or operational action. These products would broaden the lens of traditional enemy-centric intelligence to capture an adversary's connectivity to the playing field for conflict and competition. Reporting would document precisely where, when, and how the adversary in question has mobilized support or exerted influence in a given operational environment. This would enable the targeting not only of opposing military forces but also their roots in the human terrain. The end result would be a sophisticated campaign to degrade an adversary and simultaneously disrupt its lines of local support. Such a product falls squarely in the remit of civil reconnaissance and would guarantee Civil Affairs a seat at the high table within the Joint Force.

The root-map deliverable would have the further effect of structuring Civil Affairs's onward investigation of civil dynamics. Building from the root map deliverable, Civil Affairs could also produce concise reporting on the underlying dynamics that have enabled adversaries to establish footholds on key terrain. What localized social, economic, and political issues, for example, have created fertile soil for Chinese influence across Southeast Asia or for Russian influence in the Caucasus? From this understanding, what courses of action might weaken or disrupt America's foes' roots in these geographies?

Similarly, the phenomenon-based vector analysis would generate focused reporting on how specific segments of civil society are responding to stimuli (e.g., COVID-19, drought, food insecurity, et cetera), with a clear view as to how strategic rivals are exploiting the resulting disruptions. How is climate change enabling the Islamic State to expand outward from core strongholds in the Sahel region? How did the European Union's faltering response to COVID-19 create conditions for Russia and China to pursue bilateral engagement with individual member states on issues like 5G technology? Such products would have strong relevance in interagency environments, particularly in collaboration with the Department of State.

These products would be fed into the US government's various decision-making processes and used as reference points to guide targeting, influence, engagement, and messaging activities. An integrated view of competitors, allies, and transformative phenomena *in context* would be a powerful catalyst for whole-of-government action, with Civil Affairs as a leading subject matter expert.

ACHIEVING CIVIL KNOWLEDGE INTEGRATION

At present, the management of civil information within the US military is a hopeless endeavor. Having erected mountains of data with no clear view as to America's ultimate objectives, the military relies on technology to sift, sort, and segment. This is done in the false hope of overcoming the structural limitations of quantitative analysis. The underlying problem has remained unaddressed: the military has far too much civil information clogging its databases, and it has been collected without intent.

The vector-based approach outlined above would immediately resolve key challenges facing the civil information management discipline, as well as the wider question of "what is to be done" with civil information. This is particularly important in light of Civil Affairs's doctrinal shift from "civil information management" to "civil knowledge integration," which reflects recognition that Civil Affairs's value is not a byproduct of database maintenance but of enabling commanders to make informed decisions.

Much like the Civil Affairs's embrace of civil reconnaissance, the transition to civil knowledge integration is a critical step in the right direction. However, the same challenge remains: it is one thing to articulate a statement of intent but quite another to deliver results. This is where the vector-based approach to civil reconnaissance would yield powerful secondary impacts. By focusing the military's view of civil dynamics and structuring its investigative process, Civil Affairs could establish a civil information framework based on three central pillars: Vector Profiles and Connectivity Assessments; Geographically Bound Thematic Reporting; and Comparative Analysis: Transnational Vectors in Context.

Pillar 1: Vector Profiles and Connectivity Assessments

Pillar 1 would be a database of vector profiles and their corresponding connectivity assessments. Documents could be cross-referenced geographically (by country or Geographic Combatant Command) and thematically (e.g., all vector-based assessments globally of COVID-19, Al-Qaeda, food insecurity, or Chinese extractive companies). As Civil Affairs institutionalizes the vector-based approach, this database would be populated with a growing list of focused, actionable reports.

Open the Iraq file, for example, and one might find network profiles of the Islamic State, Kata'ib Hezbollah, the Sadr Movement, the "October Revolution" protestors, and Marsh Arab smuggling networks—with detailed discussion of where, when, how, and why each network has sunk its roots into specific segments of Iraqi society. Additionally, one might find structured reporting on the second- and third-order effects of phenomena like COVID-19, water scarcity, and methamphetamine abuse.

These documents would be authored primarily by deployed units and would be based on fieldwork. As Civil Affairs elements cycle through deployments, additional vectors would be added, and preexisting vector profiles could be updated (perhaps in a wiki-style system or through straightforward archival management processes). Over time, this bottom-up, micro-to-macro approach to civil reconnaissance would generate an increasing depth and breadth of insight. This database would serve as an invaluable repository of knowledge for interagency collaboration, strategic and operational planning, and pre-deployment training within the Civil Affairs community (and among supported elements of the US military as well). It would also stand as a powerful advertisement for the value of the Civil Affairs community.

Pillar 2: Geographically Bound Thematic Reporting

The second pillar would be a database for Geographic Combatant Command- and country-based thematic documents, which dig deep into features of the human domain. With structured references to the vector profiles and connectivity assessments of Pillar 1, these files would further expound on critical social, economic, political, and cultural dynamics within a given area. These documents could be authored by deployed teams and based upon fieldwork, or by non-deployed Civil Affairs personnel in support, training, academic, or transitional roles.

Open the Mexico folder, for example, and one might find reporting on patterns of legal and illegal migration and the drivers thereof, agricultural productivity dynamics and their relation to the narcotics trade, and the unraveling of the two-parent family and the attendant growth of gang culture in specific areas of the country. Open the Ukraine file, and one might find documents addressing the elusive search for a coherent national identity, the toxicity of social media in public discourse, and the unifying potential of veterans entering politics. Similar to Pillar 1, this database would be continuously expanded and updated with the accumulating insights of Civil Affairs personnel. These would be short, punchy, action-oriented issue papers with a clear "so what" that ties back to Pillar 1 analysis.

Pillar 3: Comparative Analysis: Transnational Vectors in Context

Many of the military's vectors will span multiple geographies, in a manner that goes beyond the purview of a deployed Civil Affairs element. No single unit can offer a holistic view of the People's Liberation Army, the Islamic State, or Wagner Group. The same limitation applies to phenomena like COVID-19, climate change, and rural-to-urban migration. The first two pillars of this system would catalog troves of information about each of these vectors and their touch points in local society, drawn primarily from the insights of deployed teams within limited geographic areas.

Pillar 3 would aggregate these raw materials, enabling powerful strategic analysis. This could come in the form of actionable reporting in support of Geographic Combatant Commands, as strategic policy documents for interagency audiences, or as MA and PhD theses. Reporting could compare and contrast the "when, where, why, and how" of different vectors, and generate crosscutting insights into specific concerns or suggest particular courses of action.

Imagine a deep-dive comparative analysis of the Islamic State's successes and failures in mobilizing support on a village-by-village, neighborhood-by-neighborhood basis in areas of Mali, Syria, and the Philippines. Or of how specific societal impacts of COVID-19 in New Zealand, South Africa, and Pakistan have created opportunities for Chinese debt-trap diplomacy. These would be rigorous, policy-shaping documents that would draw heavily from the field reporting of deployed Civil Affairs elements.

THE WAY AHEAD

The Civil Affairs community has embraced civil reconnaissance. It is widely accepted as one of the core activities that will define Civil Affairs. But the pivot from intent to result has not been secured. The Civil Affairs community is on uncertain ground. The United States Marine Corps nearly disbanded its entire capability in 2020. The 83rd Civil Affairs Battalion has been described (by one of its own) as "liminal" and placed upon an administrative path toward dissolution.[33] The Reserve Component's Civil Affairs & Psychological Operations Command remains perennially "misunderstood," with its immediate customers and other key stakeholders within the Department of Defense unclear as to what, exactly, conventional Civil Affairs forces (and their PSYOP [psychological operations] brethren) provide to the Joint Force.

It is time for a sense of urgency. Civil reconnaissance is a pathway not merely to relevance for Civil Affairs but to *essential* status. Now is the time to adapt training and doctrine in order to harness the talent within the Civil Affairs community. The crosswalk, and its attendant analytical mindset, must be ripped out entirely and replaced with new ways of thinking. Absent that, no amount of force modernization will achieve results. Adopting a vector-based approach to civil reconnaissance would redefine the discipline. The resulting outputs could redefine Civil Affairs.

NOTES

1. Department of the Army, *Counterinsurgency*, FM 3-24 (Washington, DC: Department of the Army), https://fas.org/irp/doddir/army/fm3-24fd.pdf.
2. For an overview of the now-decommissioned Human Terrain System, see Christopher Sims, *The Human Terrain System: Operationally Relevant Social Science Research in Iraq and Afghanistan* (US Army War College Press, 2015), https://press.armywarcollege.edu/monographs/6.
3. For discussion of the Village Stability Operations concept, see Alex Deep, "Village Stability Operations and the Application of Special Warfare Across the Contemporary Global Operating Environment," *Small Wars Journal*, April 7, 2014, https://smallwarsjournal.com/jrnl/art/village-stability-operations-and-the-application-of-special-warfare-across-the-contemporary.
4. For discussion of the Female Engagement Team concept, see Janet Holliday, "Female Engagement Teams: The Need to Standardize Training and Employment," *Military Review* (March–April 2012): 90–94, https://www.armyupress.army.mil/Portals/7/military-review/Archives/English/MilitaryReview_20120430_art014.pdf.
5. *Counterinsurgency*, ch. 1, 22.
6. Ibid., ch. 1, 23.
7. Ibid., ch. 1, 23.
8. Ibid., ch. 3, 1.
9. Ibid., ch. 3, 2, 25.
10. The preface concedes this point, stating that "the primary audience for this manual is leaders and planners at the battalion level and above." *Counterinsurgency*, vii. The absence of practical methods in the document stands in stark contrast to ATP 5-0.6, *Network Engagement*, for example, which has entire sections dedicated to specific methodological approaches to understanding networks. See Department of the Army, *Network Engagement*, ATP 5-0.6 (Washington, DC: Department of the Army), https://armypubs.army.mil/epubs/DR_pubs/DR_a/pdf/web/ARN3696_ATP%205-0x6%20FINAL%20WEB.pdf.
11. For a valuable counterpoint on how enemy-centric intelligence has become bogged down in a "tyranny of process," see Addison Lamb, "Intelligence and the Tyranny of Process," *Modern War Institute at West Point*, April 27, 2021, https://mwi.usma.edu/intelligence-and-the-

tyranny-of-process/. There is a balance that must be struck between the need for systemic consistency and the need to enable intellectual curiosity. In Lamb's view, military intelligence has lost its edge due to an overabundance of process and procedure, which stifles critical thinking.

12. For a discussion of operational art as one of "the most noteworthy and controversial concepts in modern military thought," see Wilson C. Blythe, Jr., "A History of Operational Art," *Military Review* (November–December 2018): 37–49, https://www.armyupress.army.mil/Journals/Military-Review/English-Edition-Archives/November-December-2018/Blythe-Operational-Art/. Blythe describes operational art as the (somewhat opaque and subjective) process through which strategic objectives are translated into tactical actions in complex and dynamic situations, wherein strategic leadership is unable to account for all potential variables.

13. Brian R. Price, "Human Terrain at the Crossroads," *Joint Forces Quarterly* (Q4 2017): https://ndupress.ndu.edu/Publications/Article/1325979/human-terrain-at-the-crossroads/

14. Mark Moyar, *Village Stability Operations and the Afghan Local Police* (Tampa: Joint Special Operations University Press, 2014). Moyar presents a positive view of the concept but notes the obstacles encountered in scalability and transfer to Afghan responsibility.

15. Synne Laastad Dyvik, "Women as 'Practitioners' and 'Targets': Gender and Counterinsurgency in Afghanistan," *International Journal of Feminist Politics* 16, no. 3 (2014), https://doi.org/10.1080/14616742.2013.779139.

16. See Department of the Army, *Insurgencies and Countering Insurgencies*, FM 3-24 (Washington, DC: Department of the Army), https://armypubs.army.mil/epubs/DR_pubs/DR_a/pdf/web/fm3_24.pdf; Department of the Army, *Network Engagement*; Joint Chiefs of Staff, *Civil-Military Operations*, JP 3-57 (Washington, DC: Joint Chiefs of Staff), https://www.jcs.mil/Portals/36/Documents/Doctrine/pubs/jp3_57.pdf; Department of the Army, *Intelligence Preparation of the Battlefield*, ATP 2-01.3 (Washington, DC: Department of the Army), https://armypubs.army.mil/epubs/DR_pubs/DR_a/ARN31379-ATP_2-01.3-001-WEB-4.pdf; Department of the Army, *Civil Affairs Operations*, FM 3-57 (Washington, DC: Department of the Army), https://armypubs.army.mil/epubs/DR_pubs/DR_a/pdf/web/ARN16448_FM%203-57%20FINAL%20WEB.pdf; US Marine Corps, *Civil Reconnaissance*, MCCMOS Circular (Quantico, VA: US Marine Corps Civil-Military Operations School), https://www.trngcmd.marines.mil/Portals/207/Docs/wtbn/MCCMOS/Civil%20Reconnaissance%20Circular.

pdf?ver=2020-06-08-083635-060. Frustration with the ASCOPE/PMESII crosswalk is widespread within the Civil Affairs community, but a suitable replacement has not been created. For example, see Scott Stanford, "Enemies Wanted: No Experience Necessary - The Army's Addiction to Enemies Inhibits Analysis of the Operational Environment," *Small Wars Journal*, April 1, 2015, https://smallwarsjournal.com/jrnl/art/enemies-wanted-no-experience-necessary-the-army's-addiction-to-enemies-inhibits-analysis-of. Stanford astutely observes that "done perfectly, the ASCOPE/PMESII-PT crosswalk does not help to anticipate population reactions. It does not lead the planner to understand *why* a certain condition or perception exists, which is a prerequisite to course of action development."

17. Frustration with the ASCOPE/PMESII crosswalk is widespread within the Civil Affairs community, but a suitable replacement has not been created. For example, see Scott Stanford, "Enemies Wanted: No Experience Necessary - The Army's Addiction to Enemies Inhibits Analysis of the Operational Environment," *Small Wars Journal*, April 1, 2015, https://smallwarsjournal.com/jrnl/art/enemies-wanted-no-experience-necessary-the-army's-addiction-to-enemies-inhibits-analysis-of. Stanford astutely observes that "done perfectly, the ASCOPE/PMESII-PT crosswalk does not help to anticipate population reactions. It does not lead the planner to understand *why* a certain condition or perception exists, which is a prerequisite to course of action development."

18. "Boiling the ocean" is jargon from management consulting, referring to instances where an overly broad scope of work leads analysts to perform large amounts of superfluous labor. The issue with the crosswalk is not that it fails to *sufficiently* narrow one's focus but that it makes no attempt to do so, whatsoever.

19. Also emphasized in Stanford, "Enemies Wanted," who notes that "a useful tool would also help highlight what information about culture, history, politics, and other factors the staff *does not* need to know. In a time-constrained environment with planners who are neither trained nor inclined to distill these factors into operational inputs, this is as important as anything else."

20. Debates over the US military's likely near- to medium-term operational environment, as well as the probability of large-scale combat operations, are beyond the scope of this chapter. In the author's view, conflict with strategic rivals such as China, Russia, or Iran is far more likely to play out via proxy warfare and/or low intensity conflict than in open, large-scale

conventional clashes. That said, civil considerations would remain critical in open confrontation with a "near-peer" rival. Firstly, such a conflict would likely sprawl into the previously described proxy/irregular warfare dynamic across multiple theaters. It is inconceivable that head-to-head war with Russia, Iran, or China would not involve multiple fronts and the extensive use of irregular tactics by proxy forces. Secondly, civil considerations would also prove pivotal in any conceivable large-scale conventional conflict in a theater like the Black Sea region, the South China Sea, or the Persian Gulf. From pre-conflict shaping operations, to mid-conflict civil-military relations, to post-conflict stabilization, civil considerations would be absolutely critical.

21. For a representative discussion, see Kevin Bilms, "What's in a Name? Reimagining Irregular Warfare Activities For Competition," *War on the Rocks*, January 15, 2021, https://warontherocks.com/2021/01/whats-in-a-name-reimagining-irregular-warfare-activities-for-competition/.

22. Nicholas Krohley, "The Intelligence Cycle is Broken. Here's How to Fix it," *Modern War Institute at West Point*, October 25, 2017, https://mwi.usma.edu/intelligence-cycle-broken-heres-fix/.

23. For discussion of tactical level Civil Affairs elements as "human terrain scouts" and an argument that Civil Affairs should field specially designated "Civil Reconnaissance Teams," see Andrew J. Bibb, "Civil Reconnaissance Teams: The Expeditionary Arm of Civil Affairs Forces," *Small Wars Journal*, October 3, 2019, https://smallwarsjournal.com/jrnl/art/civil-reconnaissance-teams-expeditionary-arm-civil-affairs-forces. Similarly, for recognition of civil reconnaissance as Civil Affairs's fundamental value proposition to the Joint Force, see Orlando N. Craig, William P. Hurt, Albert W. Oh, and Christopher B. Melendez, "Reconnaissance Found: Redefining Army Special Operations Forces Integration," *Military Intelligence Professional Bulletin*, PB 34-19-2 (April–June 2019), 38.

24. There may be a place for the crosswalk as a presentation tool or a taxonomy for the organization of information. The key point to this discussion is its irredeemable unsuitability as an investigative framework.

25. Current doctrine defines civil reconnaissance as "targeted, coordinated, and planned observation" but offers no useful guidance on how that should be done beyond the ASCOPE/PMESII-PT crosswalk. *Civil Affairs Operations*, 1–3.

26. *Intelligence Preparation of the Battlefield*, section 1.1.

27. For commentary on the "fantasy" of data-driven understanding in conflict, specifically related to the tactical-level flexibility demanded by mission command, see John Q. Bolton, "Modifying Situational Awareness: Perfect Knowledge and Precision are Fantasy," *Small Wars Journal*, June 10, 2018, https://smallwarsjournal.com/jrnl/art/modifying-situational-awareness-perfect-knowledge-and-precision-are-fantasy

28. Chapter 4 notes the limitations of top-down analytical processes and the general absence within US Army doctrine of bottom-up analytical processes or tools. This is a wider issue that transcends discussion of civil reconnaissance: the US military is doctrinally hardwired to take a top-down approach to the challenges it faces, to the great detriment of various facets of the intelligence discipline. It remains to be seen whether the embrace of "mission command" can effect substantive change to this dynamic.

29. The urge to classify networks as "friendly, neutral, or a threat" as per doctrine such as *Network Engagement* is questionable, at best. These terms mislead and confuse far more than they explain. A particular network's posture vis-à-vis American objectives will inevitably be fluid and situational (much like American objectives themselves). Instead of classifying networks according to their position toward the US government, practitioners should understand them on their own terms.

30. An issue discussed in greater detail in Nicholas Krohley, "Moving Beyond the Post-9/11 Manhunt: Translating Tactical Wins into Strategic Success," *Modern War Institute at West Point*, February 6, 2019, https://mwi.usma.edu/moving-beyond-post-9-11-manhunt-translating-tactical-wins-strategic-success/.

31. For discussion of Civil Affairs as an ISR asset in multi-domain operations by Civil Affairs proponent leadership, see Jay Liddick, Thurman "Scott" Dickerson, and Linda K. Chung, "Calibrating Civil Affairs Forces for Lethality in Large Scale Combat Operations," *Small Wars Journal*, March 18, 2019, https://smallwarsjournal.com/jrnl/art/calibrating-civil-affairs-forces-lethality-large-scale-combat-operations.

32. By way of comparison, the author has experience as a civilian advisor to deployed US military forces, a commercial consultant on the Saudi oilfield, an Arabic student at a Syrian public university, an independent conflict researcher in the former Soviet Union, an intelligence advisor to the Iraqi government, and a rural development facilitator in West Africa. The one and only dynamic common to *every single one* of these disparate

situations was the consensus among local national interlocutors that the author was, obviously, an American intelligence officer.

33. Mary Irwin, "A Stranger Among Us: The 83rd Civil Affairs Battalion," *Eunomia Journal*, November 3, 2020, https://www.civilaffairsassoc.org/post/a-stranger-among-us-the-83d-civil-affairs-battalion.

CHAPTER 6

NETWORKS OF INFLUENCE AND ACTION

COLLABORATION IN THE LAKE CHAD BASIN

Dan Collini and Kyle Atwell

The two groups were standing face to face, a mere ten feet apart. On one side were forty-one defectors from the most lethal terrorist group in the world at the time, Boko Haram.[1] On the other side were soldiers from three African Nations, an officer from the French Foreign Legion, a United States Agency for International Development (USAID) representative, and the small group of American Special Forces and Civil Affairs soldiers who brought them all together.

The multinational team had driven hundreds of kilometers across the grasslands of the Sahel, which slowly shifted into sand dunes as they approached Boko Haram territory on the north side of Lake Chad. This was the first international element to encounter Boko Haram defectors, who were famed for their ruthlessness and the kidnapping of hundreds of innocent schoolgirls. What the eclectic team saw that day told a different story, one important for policymakers in Washington, DC, and partnered countries to understand: defectors from Boko Haram were malnourished, disheveled children and teenagers, projecting confusion, anger, sadness, and a lack of hope.

The unprecedented engagement provided critical information to the international community on the actual conditions within Boko Haram. It exposed the network's weakness, which was coercing and deceiving vulnerable youth to join with false promises of wealth and status. Importantly, the engagement happened because a cross-functional team of Civil Affairs and Special Forces professionals worked closely together, mapped the various joint, interagency, and multinational networks—and, ultimately, they convinced various stakeholders who otherwise would not have collaborated to travel together into contested territory in order to engage some of the most vulnerable populations facing Boko Haram. The engagement was such a success that the African military partners involved sought to replicate the mission across the four countries that make up the Lake Chad Basin.

This chapter illustrates key themes discussed in this book. It is a story of adaptive change and a networked approach to security threats and vulnerabilities. It involves the three core competencies of civil network development and engagement: supporting human networks, influencing human networks, and neutralizing human networks.[2] This, in turn, drives civil knowledge integration and widespread interagency success through civil-military integration. This chapter also provides a useful case study for the Civil Affairs practitioner in collaboration with other US Special Operations forces: the concept of the "cross-functional team."

Ultimately, the authors of this chapter argue for the utility of network engagement and demonstrate how practitioners can employ the attendant techniques. Civil Affairs professionals are well postured to design, conduct, and assess network engagement effects. They are not the only ones vested in network engagement efforts—there is typically present a diverse community consisting of development workers, private contractors, NGOs, and other agencies striving to improve local dynamics on the ground. Each brings their own expertise and value to the mission. A key observation is that cross-functional teams derive their influence through force multiplication—they corral dynamic and disparate actors from a multitude of backgrounds to work together in a networked effort to accomplish shared goals. This is absolutely essential, particularly in resource-constrained operating environments, where accomplishing US security objectives relies on achieving objectives through others.

The cross-functional team concept features Special Forces, Civil Affairs, and Psychological Operations professionals working together in a mutually supporting effort to engage in irregular warfare environments. It has been employed worldwide in recent years. Wherever there is a Civil Affairs team, there will inevitably be either a Special Forces or Psychological Operations element close by—most likely both. Although the concept of cross-functional teams is championed within the Army Special Forces community, critical case studies of their effectiveness are few and far between. This inhibits Civil Affairs's ability to learn and gain perspective from its own successes and failures.

THE ESSENCE OF NETWORK ENGAGEMENT

Civil Affairs forces are *the* military asset that bridges the political objectives of the Department of State and the military objectives of the Department of Defense while nesting those objectives neatly within the construct of the host nation government's political appetite for foreign intervention. Civil Affairs thus occupies a critical position in the national security enterprise.

In implementing these objectives, Civil Affairs forces act as a force multiplier, using regional and local networks to implement solutions against enemies and competitors alike. Terror networks like Boko Haram are notorious for operating in decentralized fashion, making them unpredictable and difficult to counter. Greg Wilson highlighted the need for a networked approach in counterinsurgency operations, particularly when these networks transcend international borders:

> A regionally networked approach will optimize US efforts to build indigenous capacity. The enemy is part of a transnational global network and flows across borders in many regions of the world... Terrorists and insurgents use ungoverned areas to their advantage so that efforts by individual states alone will not be effective. The best way to confront a network is to create a counter-network.[3]

Similarly, in the fight against Al-Qaeda in Iraq, General Stanley McChrystal transformed his organization with a mantra written on a white board for everyone in the office to see: "It takes a network to defeat a network."[4] Networked approaches are not proprietary to violent extremist organizations. All aspects of the human domain are inherently made up of networks, as detailed in chapter 4. Thus, the concept of understanding and developing friendly networks to employ against problems is applicable in all environments. This philosophy of achieving results with the help of others is a defining feature of network engagement.

Network engagement increases the capability or capacity of a node, part, or a more extensive network—at least temporarily. The concept organizes and combines attributes from nodes such as will, knowledge, resources, capability, and access, to meet a goal that would be unattainable alone. Networks exist to achieve a purpose, and at least a portion of the network is under some mutual agreement for cooperation. Through this, the entities (nodes) engaged in the process tend to leverage the same or similar pathways to address new challenges or opportunities, sometimes unknowingly, from a more extensive network. If the human domain is the backdrop for the struggle of wills in the twenty-first century, the ability to create information superiority and advantage through networks is crucial.

A New Mission: Three Problems

In 2017, members of a cross-functional team consisting of a small number of Special Forces and Civil Affairs professionals put these concepts into practice in the Lake Chad Basin. The mission's top three tasks were core Civil Affairs objectives: gain access to contested and denied areas, build capacity, and disrupt local support for violent extremist organizations.

The team's partner force was the Special Anti-Terrorism Group - Action Civilo Militaire (hereafter, the Special Anti-Terrorism Group), the sole organization within the Chadian military focused on civil military cooperation, or CIMIC. Time was short for the US team, however, and before the military shifted its focus to the Special Anti-Terrorism Group, there were fractured relationships from previous engagements that required mending with both adjacent US Special Operations entities and the US Embassy.[5] This is reality for any enduring military partnership: relationships over multiple iterations will deviate through personal relationships, participants, and efforts. Therefore, restoring these relationships was a priority, and the cross-functional team's approach paid dividends as they quickly developed rapport and the initial trust needed for both cohesiveness among US Special Operations forces and US Embassy support.

As US soldiers conducted an initial assessment of the operational environment, they found three main problems. First, the threats from Boko Haram and ISIS-West Africa were *regional*, bleeding across the national borders of Cameroon, Chad, Niger, and Nigeria. National boundaries could be ignored by insurgent groups, yet this posed a critical dilemma for counterinsurgency efforts. Boko Haram could freely move across borders, but the US government and the various Lake Chad Basin militaries faced coordination challenges (as it is a significant effort for one country's military to cross into a neighbor's territory). This allowed Boko Haram to leverage border areas for safe haven.

Second, although the Special Anti-Terrorism Group was the most capable Civil-Military Cooperation element in the region, they could not extend their influence across borders, let alone across the region. They were concerned with the threat, impacts, and issues from neighboring countries, but they were primarily focused on their own internal problems.

Third, there was no regional civil-military network to be leveraged for either humanitarian effects or security. For years, a multitude of entities had poured significant resources into the area, to varying effects. A constellation of international military forces, United Nations elements, the African Union, the Lake Chad Basin Commission, and multiple NGOs were all active in the region—but their efforts were not coordinated in any systematic manner across borders.

The essential challenge in the Lake Chad Basin appeared to be how to address a regionally oriented threat group that moved freely across borders. The incoming Civil Affairs and Special Forces elements assessed that the most effective way to counter a regional threat was with a regional response.

BUILDING A LIVING NETWORK

Seemingly, all of the pieces of the puzzle were present, but they had not been assembled. Central to this multipronged effort were the expansion of the Special Anti-Terrorism Group's capacity to coordinate regionally and the simultaneous development of both a *Civil-Military Cooperation operations structure* and a *humanitarian assistance support structure.* The team's goal was to build a network large enough to counter both Boko Haram and ISIS-West Africa. This was to be achieved via a network that could illuminate hidden safe havens, identify drivers of extremism across the region, and provide civil knowledge integration through civil military collaboration. As a drawing on a napkin, it made sense. But the creation of unified Civil-Military Cooperation capabilities across the entire Lake Chad Basin appeared too ambitious, with too many moving parts—at least at first.

Within the first few weeks, the team conducted many engagements that were both ad hoc and planned. As their relationships continued to improve, the team quickly determined the network entities they needed to develop. They identified the partners they would need to increase stability, confirm or deny information, foster legitimacy, and drive unified action. This was accomplished along four overlapping lines of effort. The criteria the team used for prioritizing depended on the will, knowledge, resources, capability, and access of the node. They concurrently focused on these four priorities:

1) Harnessing US Government Resources: Special Operations forces, US Embassy Country-Team

2) Aligning Partner Forces: Special Anti-Terrorism Group, Multinational Joint Task Force, and the Centre for Coordination and Liaison

3) United Nations Coordination: Humanitarian Country Team, United Nations Office for the Coordination of Humanitarian Affairs, United Nations Development Programme, and United Nations High Commissioner for Refugees

4) Addressing Medical Vulnerabilities: Centers for Disease Control, an unnamed medically focused NGO, and the Bill and Melinda Gates Foundation

HARNESSING US GOVERNMENT RESOURCES

The first line of effort was to establish alignment between the US Embassy Country Team and USAID. The Department of State oversaw funding streams that would be essential to the team's efforts. There were challenges along the way, however, as they worked alongside the USAID in securing financing. They used one of the (at least) seven funding streams focused on counterterrorism, the Trans-Sahara Counterterrorism Partnership Program, for several items, but an understaffed US Embassy complicated the process. Later, the team discovered that underlying difficulties resided at a much higher level. A September 2020 report from the State Department's Office of Inspector General audited the Trans-Sahara Counterterrorism Partnership Program. It concluded that "... staffing shortages and continual vacancies at US embassies in the Sahel and Maghreb regions as factors making it difficult to oversee Trans-Sahara Counterterrorism Partnership Program projects...vacancies and lack of resources also affected their ability to carry out the Department's mission."[6] The report also claimed that embassies in all countries in the Lake Chad Basin were categorized as "historically difficult to fill." This issue impacted the efficiency of operations, as well as the goals that the team aimed to achieve.

The US soldiers also looked to bridge a relationship gap between the United Nations Office for the Coordination of Humanitarian Affairs and USAID. However, USAID was partnered with the United Nations Children's Fund and primarily focused on nutrition programs that bled into the efforts of the United Nations Office for the Coordination of Humanitarian Affairs. To collaborate with USAID, the team would need to identify their priorities and appeal to them.

The focus on nutrition programs was a priority for USAID due to the immense number of displaced people in Chad. The country's government provided asylum and allowed organizations to bring humanitarian relief to over 400,000 people. Driving through the landscape and trying to account for all of the tents, camps, and broken shelters draped in humanitarian plastic tarps was time-consuming but necessary to establish ground truth. That said, this was something that USAID could not do without working with other actors who could access contested spaces. Another priority for both USAID and multiple partner forces was establishing information dissemination platforms, such as radio stations, which were used to amplify moderate voices within the population. Multiple prospective partners shared this objective, and it became a vehicle that eventually linked US equities to the partner force and the humanitarian community. It empowered youth programs and the community to conduct something

US soldiers could not accomplish: a campaign by their citizens that elevated the community and countered violent extremism.

ALIGNING PARTNER FORCES

Once the team had oriented itself to the priorities and agencies within the US government, it began to focus on the second line of effort, specifically on the various partner forces and multinational entities within Chad and the broader Lake Chad Basin (to include both government and nongovernmental organizations). As the team engaged with various entities, clear prospective areas of collaboration became apparent.

Special Anti-Terrorism Group

US Civil Affairs had an established relationship with the Special Anti-Terrorism Group. The team was familiar with their capabilities, will, and resources. Similarly, US Civil Affairs also had existing partnerships with two of the other Lake Chad Basin countries: Cameroon's Bataillon d'Intervention Rapide and Niger's Forces Armées Nigériennes. Nigeria did not have a standalone Civil-Military Cooperation-focused unit but traditionally assigned duties to an officer with a military unit as an additional duty.

From the beginning, the US soldiers knew that the Special Anti-Terrorism Group had more experience than other entities throughout the region. The group was small, but it was dedicated, knowledgeable about local civil dynamics, and tactically proficient. This proficiency was a significant positive, but one shortcoming was the group members' inability to develop civil networks. They did not have partnerships with the Multinational Joint Task Force, United Nations entities, or NGOs, despite being in the same city as them. The challenge with the Special Anti-Terrorism Group was not will, capability, or enthusiasm to work with the US—it was identifying and establishing cooperative relationships with other networks. This provided an opportunity for the US to connect

Special Anti-Terrorism Group leadership with other actors who had shared interests.

Multinational Joint Task Force

The Multinational Joint Task Force (MNJTF) was established by the Lake Chad Basin Commission in 1998 to fight highway banditry and other cross-border crimes, but it was later decommissioned. The African Union reactivated it in 2014 and authorized it to conduct missions including combat operations against Boko Haram, intercepting trafficked weapons, freeing hostages, and encouraging defections. It is composed of soldiers from Nigeria, Cameroon, Niger, Chad, and Benin defense forces. In 2015, Boko Haram attacks on MNJTF headquarters in Nigeria prompted the allocation of more troops, expansion of the mandate, and relocation of the headquarters to N'Djamena, Chad. In 2016, an agreement between the European Commission and the African Union Commission further bolstered the Multinational Joint Task Force, referred to as the MNJTF throughout the remainder of this chapter.

The United States, United Kingdom, and France collectively form the P3 Center for Coordination and Liaison, which is headquartered in N'Djamena. It serves as a coordination body to provide technical, financial, and strategic support to the MNJTF. A Special Forces officer serving as the US Liaison was assigned to the Special Operations Command and Control Element – Lake Chad Basin, which was advantageous for partner force relationships and network building. The MNJTF initially operated on a conventional military strategy, which ignored the sociocultural element, until an African-generated initiative at the MNJTF established a J9 Civil-Military Cooperation cell that oversaw regional civil-military support. J9 refers to the staff directorate routinely responsible for civil-military cooperation. This was only a partial solution, however, as this civil-military cell existed only at the strategic level, with limited operational or tactical reach.

The J9's objective was to conduct projects throughout the Lake Chad Basin and build trust between the respective national-level militaries and the local population. Concurrently, the aim was to develop a pro-government message that countered extremist organizations. However, the MNJTF did not have connections with the operational civil-military entities of its various member countries (Cameroon's Bataillon d'Intervention Rapide, Niger's Forces Armées Nigériennes and Special Anti-Terrorism Group - Action Civilo Militaire in Chad, whose headquarters was only two miles up the road from the MNJTF headquarters), the United Nations entities, or any local or international NGOs. As a result, the MNJTF drew from each of its member countries' conventional forces, which had limited civil-military capabilities. These deficiencies meant that the MNJTF could secure international donor funds but lacked the tactical and technical Civil-Military Cooperation capacity to take effective action using these funds, but it also did not have the local or regional network required to execute projects successfully. The MNJTF conducted reconnaissance missions to identify civil-military development projects and, in 2016, had conducted their own regional civil reconnaissance operations. However, they encountered difficulty translating the missions into tangible project proposals and lacked the tactical capacity to follow through.

The US Special Forces liaison to the MNJTF recommended collaboration with the US Civil Affairs Team to improve technical assistance on project proposals. The first key partnership developed was between the US Civil Affairs Team and the Special Forces liaison, facilitated by shared experience as members of the army special operations community. Once a plan had been developed to leverage their respective networks in the country, the cross-functional team developed a strategy to engage both US embassy interagency members and MNJTF partners. The African partners were very receptive to the support. It was a win for the US team. The goal of establishing a *regional Civil-Military Cooperation operations structure* meant linking Cameroonian, Nigerian, and Chadian Action Civilo Militaire forces' tactical actions under the operational umbrella of the J9 Civil-Military Cooperation cell. The US Civil Affairs team in

Nigeria, the Special Operations Command and Control Element – Lake Chad Basin, and Special Operations Command Africa were all supportive, as were Cameroon's defense elements. Further, US Civil Affairs had trained all three nations' civil-military elements, and the MNJTF was aligned with US interests through the P3 Center for Coordination and Liaison, which significantly bolstered this concept.

UNITED NATIONS COORDINATION

The third line of effort was to develop a *humanitarian support structure* centered on reinforcing the coordination, sharing, and deconflicting of projects and activities. The team started with the United Nations Office for the Coordination of Humanitarian Affairs (OCHA—the UN's body for coordinating all relevant humanitarian actors in a country that traditionally handles civil-military interaction). Initial engagements with UN OCHA were promising. Although military personnel were not initially welcome in the joint NGO meetings, US Civil Affairs forces gained access after defining their purely civil-military role.

However, the relationship between security forces and the humanitarian network was immature. To develop it, the team aimed to develop a trustworthy "civil-military working group" through a charter involving the collective NGOs and security elements. This endeavor required the approval of the Humanitarian Country Team (HCT), a strategic and operational forum with representation from the United Nations, International Organization for Migration, NGOs, and International Federation of Red Cross and Red Crescent Societies. The team met with the HCT's Resident Coordinator (also referred to as the Humanitarian Coordinator), a meeting which was successful in part due to the team's knowledge of the region, their understanding of the UN's cluster approach and humanitarian coordination architecture, and their familiarity with the UN-CMCoord (Civil-Military Coordination) Field Handbook.[7] This allowed for a shared understanding among the various doctrinal approaches and contributed to better collaborative efforts.

Due to the shared understanding, the Humanitarian Coordinator increasingly supported efforts to align civil-military activities in the region after the team highlighted and coordinated responses for three areas. The first was to use armed escorts for the UN's humanitarian convoys, given the frequency of attacks against UN assets.[8] As the general rule, and per the UN-CMCoord Field Handbook, humanitarian convoys are not armed, and this requires the approval of the HCT.[9] Second, convoy attacks led to border closures, which negatively impacted socioeconomic variables like goods and livestock trade. The nomads and farmers could neither trade their livestock nor feed them properly, and their herds were a target for plunder as well. This created a security challenge which motivated the Humanitarian Coordinator to cooperate with security personnel and led to the reopening of restrictive border closures that eased some nomadic trade routes and allowed for increased trade.[10] Third, the team developed an information-sharing plan to support the actions of humanitarian groups. US forces concentrated on information sharing at the lowest classification possible. This ensured that there were no issues with potential spillage of classified information and that all relevant information could be shared freely among members of the group. The team prioritized a wide distribution of information to coordinate with civilian agencies, organizations, and NGOs.

The Humanitarian Coordinator established a new meeting schedule to accommodate this concept. The all-civilian coordination meetings continued weekly, as they had previously. In addition, a purely security-focused meeting was scheduled biweekly, and a combined security/civilian meeting was held in the intervening weeks. The Humanitarian Coordinator facilitated the partnership with UN OCHA, which served as a pivotal point in establishing the regional network. These efforts resulted in access to the coordinated efforts of over fifty NGOs in Chad and Cameroon, in addition to the inclusion of more security elements.

ADDRESSING MEDICAL VULNERABILITIES

The final line of effort was slower to materialize, but it eventually emerged in the form of the efforts of the civil-military working group and the non-traditional relationships established by the P3 Center for Coordination and Liaison. This effort focused on medical vulnerabilities (cholera and malaria), and it became the most significant contributor to the team's ability to produce operationally relevant civil reporting. The team developed robust relationships with the Centers for Disease Control (CDC) and an NGO focused on medical treatment, both of which had excellent ground access and abundant information.

Through information sharing, the team received data on over five thousand villages in the region. This was an overwhelming amount of information, which was examined alongside many layers of NGO activity, security force activity, medical supply locations, and other related areas. The relationship with the CDC eventually developed into an approved agreement. The Bill and Melinda Gates Foundation, via the CDC, provided resources and geo-tracking tools containing metadata on locations, timelines, structure types, and populace numbers. The merging of civil information between these organizations and the DoD was pivotal to a synchronized approach in tackling the vulnerabilities that prevented stability throughout the region.[11]

BY-WITH-THROUGH

The relationship between the Civil Affairs team and the US Special Forces Liaison to the P3 Center for Coordination and Liaison was critical to the success of the rotation. This partnership created a nascent special operations cross-functional team, increased access and placement, and rapidly fused multiple interagency capabilities. It was the ideal scenario of the by-with-through approach. Unifying the civil-military capabilities of the entire Lake Chad Basin began to look achievable. Drumming up buy-in and motivation brought together the various entities across the four lines of effort. This aligned capacity, will, resources, access, and ability. The team could now counter regional threats *by* linking and employing both the Special Anti-Terrorism Group and the Multinational Joint Task Force *with* the US Civil Affairs Team and P3 Center for Coordination and Liaison *through* the coordinated and legal framework of the US embassy agreements, European Union, African Union, and the UN's Humanitarian Country Team.

The team's approach enabled a range of important operations. They conducted civil reconnaissance, established a Civil-Military Coordination network, identified viable projects, and assisted the Multinational Joint Task Force J9 in developing project proposals. Operations typically included the strengths of multiple elements of the newly aligned network. Typical missions were purely cross-functional and included the Special Anti-Terrorism Group, the Multinational Joint Task Force, P3 Center for Coordination and Liaison personnel, and the USAID. The team used collaborative engagement plans on long-range civil reconnaissance missions designed to map the human domain. The team also leveraged the legal authorities provided to the Civil Affairs Team that supported minimal risk to mission and afforded the cross-functional team flexibility and the freedom to move throughout the country that many State Department personnel were denied. The team connected MNJTF staff personnel located at the multinational headquarters in N'Djamena, Chad, with Chadian, Cameroonian, and Nigerian civil-military forces with whom they were otherwise not connected. This opened up new opportunities to facilitate a regional civil military effort by building a network that otherwise had not developed prior to the Civil Affairs Team intervention.

Long-range civil reconnaissance missions allowed the team to see beyond the confines of headquarters and the limited perspective available in major cities. These missions brought the team to tribal leaders who described attacks in areas that were unprotected and considered forbidden —the terrorists' network of safe havens. These areas, like the ones along the border between Niger and Chad, were where raids would occur, causing the loss of livestock, resources, and freedom of movement for local farmers, herdsmen, and nomads trying to make it to market. Local soldiers would also find themselves subject to attacks and raided, which further inhibited security in the areas given the inadequate resources. To counter this, Civil Affairs forces, working through the cross-functional concept, engaged with the local populace, the host nation military, and NGOs. The result from this concept was better information gained, enhanced relationships between NGOs and military units, and better navigation of friendly tribal networks that improved the exposure of existing vulnerabilities.

These reconnaissance missions culminated in the face-to-face encounter with forty-one Boko Haram defectors, which is referenced at the start of the chapter. This breakthrough validated the efficacy of the network and prompted further efforts to expand it. The team refined their understanding of the operational environment, and, three weeks after the first encounter, they met forty-seven more defectors, proving that the efforts of the Chadian, Cameroonian, and Nigerian civil-military units, synchronized by the MNJTF (with the assistance of the US team), were achieving the desired effects. The cross-functional team soon became the go-to resource for information about extremists and defectors.

The resulting insights provided a deeper understanding of the situation in the Lake Chad Basin. The team delivered weekly reports to the State Department's counter–Boko Haram working group. There, the team served as the subject matter experts on the complex reasons for recruitment *and* defection. Their interactions with the NGOs and the civil-military working group (which they had helped to establish at UN OCHA) led them to realize that no one had a clear view of the wider dynamics of defection from Boko Haram. How many defectors were there? What was the rate of defection? What were the drivers of defection? How were defectors related to the movement of displaced people?

New policies were needed for evaluating the next steps involving the defectors. One key step included establishing a disarmament, demobilization, and reintegration program for the defectors in Chad. The program was modeled on Nigeria's Operation Safe Corridor, which the team had previously observed and advised on.[12] The overall work to establish a program fell to, among others, the individual countries, the African Union, the Lake Chad Basin Commission, the United Nations, and NGOs.

Operationally, the cross-functional team gathered support not only from Chad but from neighboring countries as well. The next step in putting this new network to use was to plan cross-border civil reconnaissance with the small coalition's collective partner forces. The concept garnered initial support because it was a low-risk mission tied to Civil-Military Cooperation efforts (and more importantly, it was not a kinetic operation). Support for the mission in Cameroon was received from the US Embassy Country Team, adjacent US Special Operations forces in the region, and their civil-military forces. The MNJTF was supportive and approved internal resourcing as well as security support. This included the support of the Cameroonian MNJTF sector commander, who agreed to provide a security element and civil-military representation. Moreover, he agreed to work with the operational component, raising the level of collaboration.

Despite the buy-in, the team never executed the cross-border operation due to the last-minute approval revocation by the US Embassy Country Team in Chad. The mission had not been approved prior to the outgoing ambassador's departure, and the successor was not willing to support the mission. As happens all too frequently, the rotation of personnel within the US government undermined months of promising work. The cancellation was particularly frustrating to partner forces, who had embraced the concept and shown powerful initiative.

Frustrations aside, the network the team helped establish was proving its value and dynamism. This network rapidly evolved to operate without US support. Its autonomy enabled US Civil Affairs forces to be relocated so that they could support other areas in need of assistance. The team continued the weekly engagements with the counter–Boko Haram working group. Ultimately, the strategic effects, and other activities, prompted visits by an under secretary of state and a deputy assistant secretary of defense. This visit shined a political light on the work the team had accomplished. The team explained the methods they had used, how the friendly network had been established, and how the network had been employed to meet key objectives related to the mass displacement of civilians and the reintegration of Boko Haram defectors.

Valuable Insights

Networks are inherently unstable. Like social movements (and civil society itself), cooperation is driven by innumerable factors that are subject to change. This is especially true when a network gathers increased attention, resources, or stress. Continued participation in these networks may appear to be costly or unnecessary. However, practitioners and planners must understand and embrace the nature of networks. Like a car, the maintenance of networks must be conducted deliberately and periodically to prevent breakdowns. The cross-functional team did just that with the network in the Lake Chad Basin. The network evolved over time, continually adding, replacing, and removing entities at specific intervals.

Network engagement can be a powerful tool; if planners and practitioners intend to attempt to influence systems, they must also consider where and when action may create an undesired reaction. For those entrenched in a battle of narratives and counternarratives, network engagement will be scrutinized, manipulated, and mischaracterized by competitors. Stagnation is a risk as well. Activity creates expectations. Inaction can lead to frustration and grievance. The team faced the dangers of stagnation when the US Embassy Country Team halted these operations for an extended period, following the cancellation of the cross-border operation described.

In the end, the regional civil network's effectiveness proved enduring. In Chad, for the first time, the MNJTF, along with the Special Anti-Terrorism Group, partnered with NGOs during the multinational military exercise Flintlock. Eventually, cross-border missions were authorized. The special operations element that replaced the team was able to conduct cross-border civil reconnaissance and civil engagement in Cameroon. Similar operations were then mounted in Niger, and cross-functional forces conducted long-range reconnaissance missions into Cameroon. Ultimately, a light footprint package of US Civil Affairs and Army Special Forces Soldiers was able to facilitate an extended network of multinational military personnel, US interagency actors, and non-governmental organizations toward the common objective of engaging the population and countering Boko Haram influence in the Lake Chad Basin. This case study highlights the valuable contribution US Civil Affairs assets can make toward facilitating networks of access and influence that serve to advance US national security interests.

NOTES

1. Katie Pisa and Time Hume, "Boko Haram Overtakes ISIS as World's Deadliest Terror Group, Report Says," *CNN*, November 19, 2015, https://www.cnn.com/2015/11/17/world/global-terror-report.

2. Department of the Army, *Network Engagement*, ATP 5-0.6 (Washington, DC: Department of the Army, 2017), section 1.1, https://armypubs.army.mil/epubs/DR_pubs/DR_a/pdf/web/ARN3696_ATP%205-0x6%20FINAL%20WEB.pdf.

3. Gregory Wilson, "Anatomy of a Successful COIN Operation: JTF-510 OEF Philippines." *Military Review: The Professional Journal of the US Army* 86, no. 6 (2006): 13–14, https://doi.org/100-06-11/12.

4. Stanley McChrystal, *Team of Teams: New Rules of Engagement for a Complex World* (New York: Portfolio/Penguin, 2015), 84.

5. Civil Military Support Elements are Civil Affairs Teams deployed under the United States Special Operations Command's Civil-Military Engagement program of record. This enables special operations Civil Affairs forces to maintain a persistent presence in Title-22 environments.

6. US Department of State Office of Inspector General, *Audit of the Department of State Bureau of African Affairs Monitoring and Coordination of the Trans-Sahara Counterterrorism Partnership* (Washington, DC: US Department of State, 2020).

7. United Nations Office for the Coordination of Humanitarian Affairs, *UN-CMCoord Field Handbook 1.0* (Geneva: United Nations, 2018).

8. Andrew Esiebo, "After Attack on Convoy, UN Suspends Aid Delivery in Areas of Restive North-Eastern Nigeria," *UN News*, last modified July 29, 2016, https://news.un.org/en/story/2016/07/535772-after-attack-convoy-un-suspends-aid-delivery-areas-restive-north-eastern; and Andrew Esiebo, "UNICEF Working at 'Full Strength' in North-East Nigeria, despite Attack on Aid Convoy," *UN News*, last modified August 1, 2016, https://news.un.org/en/story/2016/08/535862-unicef-working-full-strength-north-east-nigeria-despite-attack-aid-convoy.

9. United Nations Office for the Coordination of Humanitarian Affairs, *UN-CMCoord Field Handbook 1.0* (Geneva: United Nations, 2018).

10. Notably, it took all four priorities being concurrently actioned to ultimately identify the safe havens and identify ways to counter this regional issue.

11. Unfortunately, some of these tools and resources are no longer available due to policy changes in the DoD. For explanation, see Jim Garamone, "New Policy Prohibits GPS Tracking in Deployed Settings." *DOD News*, August 6, 2018, https://www.defense.gov/Explore/News/Article/Article/1594486/new-policy-prohibits-gps-tracking-in-deployed-settings/.
12. International Crisis Group, "An Exit from Boko Haram? Assessing Nigeria's Operation Safe Corridor." International Crisis Group, last modified March 19, 2021, https://www.crisisgroup.org/africa/west-africa/nigeria/b170-exit-boko-haram-assessing-nigerias-operation-safe-corridor.

CHAPTER 7

THREE TRIBES TO ONE

INTEGRATING CIVIL AFFAIRS

Assad Raza and Susan Gannon

The US Army Civil Affairs Corps is at an inflection point. A critical capability in competition and conflict, US Army Civil Affairs must position itself to meet future requirements as a *total force*. This can be achieved via full integration of both the active component (AC) and reserve component (RC). The purpose of this chapter is to examine the challenges to integration and propose solutions to optimize the capabilities presented by active- and reserve-component US Army Civil Affairs.

This chapter reviews past initiatives and policies across the different services pertaining to active and reserve component organizational structure and integration. Understanding these cross-component initiatives can provide the army with options to achieve total integration of its Civil Affairs capability. Integration of the army's Civil Affairs capability would draw on the strengths that lie within each component, mitigating shortfalls while increasing readiness and interoperability, as well as providing service members options to serve across components.[1] Additionally, this improved integration of the army's Civil Affairs capability aligns with the drive toward an inclusive "3-D" (Diplomacy, Development, and Defense) approach to long-term stability, as outlined in the State Department's 2018 Stabilization Assistance Review.[2]

BACKGROUND

In 1987, the Nunn-Cohen Amendment to the 1986 Goldwater-Nichols Department of Defense Reorganization Act created the position of Assistant Secretary of Defense for Special Operations and Low-Intensity Conflict, the United States Special Operations Command (USSOCOM), and the attendant line of special operations funding.[3] However, Secretary of Defense Caspar Weinberger initially excluded active and reserve components of Civil Affairs and Psychological Operations as force structures under USSOCOM. It was not until 1993 that the US Army Civil Affairs were designated as special operations forces.[4] This included Civil Affairs's one active-duty battalion, the 96th Civil Affairs Battalion, as well as the reserve component's two-star command, the US Army Civil Affairs and Psychological Operations Command (USACAPOC). Until 2006, USACAPOC was responsible for all US Army Civil Affairs, both active and reserve, under the US Army Special Operations Command (USASOC).

At present, US Army's Civil Affairs comprises approximately ten thousand service member positions across the active and reserve components. The 95th Civil Affairs Brigade is aligned to special operations units, and the only conventional forces active-duty Civil Affairs unit, the 83rd Civil Affairs Battalion, will be deactivated by 2024, as depicted in figure 5.

Figure 5. Active component formations.

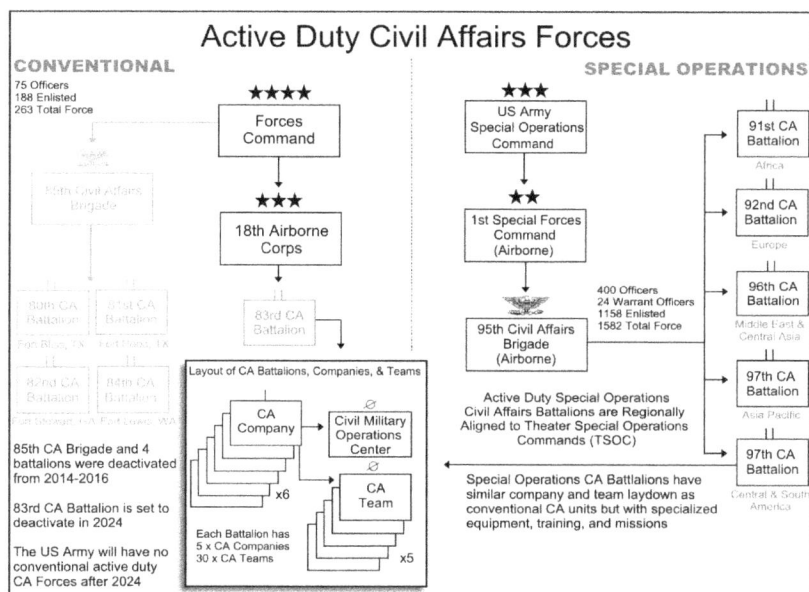

Source. Adapted from the US Army John F. Kennedy Special Warfare Center and School (SWCS), Civil Affairs proponent office PowerPoint slides, Fort Bragg NC (October 29, 2021).

The remaining 82% of Civil Affairs resides in the Army Reserve, as seen in figure 6. These forces are primarily organized within four separate one-star level Civil Affairs Commands (CACOM), each with two subordinate brigades and their subordinate battalions. Additionally, the reserve component has two separate regionally aligned brigades at United States European Command and United States Indo-Pacific Command, as well as one battalion-aligned United States Northern Command. To give readers a better understanding of Civil Affairs within the Department of Defense, figure 7 shows US Marine Civil Affairs (the evolution of Marine Civil Affairs is in chapter 8).

Figure 6. Reserve component formations.

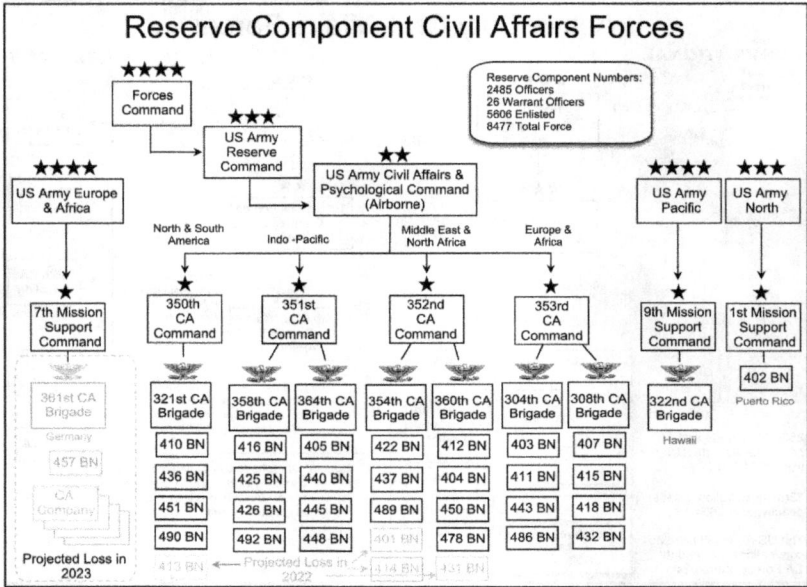

Source. Adapted from the US Army John F. Kennedy Special Warfare Center and School (SWCS), Civil Affairs proponent office PowerPoint slides, Fort Bragg, NC (October 29, 2021).

Figure 7. US Marine Corps Civil Affairs.

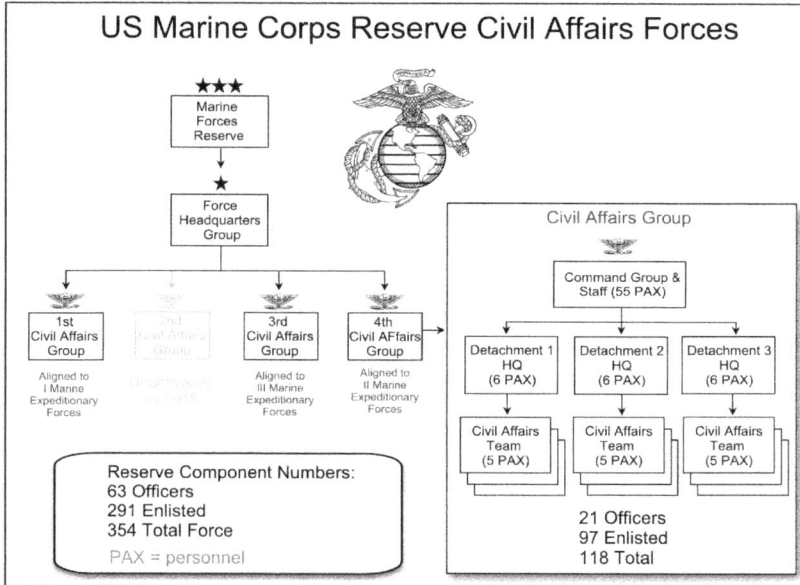

Source. Adapted from USMC Civil Affairs Forces Overview by USMC Deputy Commandant for Information: Civil Affairs presentation to the Office of the Secretary of Defense.

Table 1. Structural comparison of Civil Affairs and traditional sized units.

Service and Component	Type of Unit	Number of Type of Units in 2022	Total Personnel per Unit
US Army (Active Duty)	Infantry Brigade	13	4,560
US Army (Active Duty)	Civil Affairs Brigade	1	1,582
US Army (Reserves)	Civil Affairs Brigade	8	924
US Marines (Reserves)	Civil Affairs Group	3	118

Source. Adapted from Congressional Budget Office, *The U.S. Military's Force Structure: A Primer,* (2021 Update) and information provided by service components.

Current force structure dates back to 2006 when the US Army, at the direction of the Office of the Secretary of Defense, separated the active and reserve components of Civil Affairs between USASOC and US Army Reserve Command (USARC). According to Dr. Alfred Paddock's 2012 article in the *Small Wars Journal*, "the process that led to Deputy Secretary of Defense Gordon England's 2006 decision began with a series of notes to senior DoD officials from Secretary of Defense Donald Rumsfeld during the period January 2004 to March 2005. These notes principally questioned whether or not Civil Affairs should be in special operations."[5]

In the context of the times, fighting two insurgencies in Iraq and Afghanistan, the majority of reserve component Civil Affairs forces were supporting conventional forces in counterinsurgency operations, whereas the majority of active component Civil Affairs forces supported special operations forces conducting counterterrorism operations. The correspondence between Secretary Rumsfeld and senior military leaders ultimately led to the split among active and reserve Civil Affairs, with active duty integrated within special operations and the reserve supporting conventional forces. This decision was made despite the advice from senior military leaders who advocated keeping the entirety of US Army Civil Affairs within special operations.[6]

In 2008, the House Armed Services Committee released its findings on the Provincial Reconstruction Teams used in Iraq and Afghanistan. The findings included several concerns with the employment of the DoD's Civil Affairs capability.[7] As a result, the National Defense Authorization Act of 2009 directed the Office of the Secretary of Defense to prepare a report on Civil Affairs. Although there were several issues, one specific area of focus was "whether the programmed Civil Affairs force structure between active and reserve components is balanced and appropriate."[8] This report highlighted that, following the 2006 split, there continued to be issues with the current Civil Affairs force structure. The report also questioned whether imbalances between the reserve and active components were aligned with future demands. The 2006 division of Civil Affairs had placed over 82% of the force into the reserve component, despite heavy demand to support the wars in Iraq and Afghanistan. This split led to a drastic difference in the resources supporting readiness available to each component to include specialized equipment, operations, and training.[9]

In 2008, Secretary of Defense Robert Gates issued DoD Directive 1200.17, *Managing the Reserve Components as an Operational Force*, establishing policies to integrate all active and reserve component forces "as a total force based on the attributes of the particular component and individual competencies."[10] These policies included cross-component assignments. In 2012, Secretary of the Army John McHugh issued Army Directive 2012-08 (Army Total Force Policy or ATFP) with additional policies for integrating the army's active and reserve components.[11] By 2016, the army implemented the Associated Units Pilot Program, a pilot program pairing units from active duty, the reserves, and the national guard.[12] The program consisted of mostly brigade combat teams from the Army National Guard, which were paired with active-duty divisions (or vice versa). A few reserve sustainment units also participated in this program. However, no Civil Affairs units were selected to participate in this pilot program, which was a missed opportunity to deliver better integration across the Civil Affairs *total force.*

WHAT CAN THE ARMY DO?

The army can establish a Civil Affairs Total Force Policy (CATFP) that leverages the momentum of the DoD *total force* concept and the Army Total Force Policy. A CATFP would include organizational concepts to assist with integrating active and reserve Civil Affairs units to provide the army with a unified and interoperable capability. This policy would consist of different organizational structures that include a mix of multicomponent units, associate units, and fully integrated Civil Affairs units across special operations and conventional forces.

This effort would integrate the three "tribes" of US Army Civil Affairs: active component special operations forces, active component conventional forces, and reserve component conventional forces. The result would be a multifaceted Civil Affairs force postured to respond to both irregular warfare and global competition. In turn, this would also help strengthen Civil Affairs's brand, narrative, and value to the Joint Force.

Understanding the "total force" concept across DoD helps the US Army Civil Affairs—warrior diplomats—develop organizational structures to increase interoperability across components. Moreover, integration provides the Joint Force a seamless Civil Affairs capability across the range of military operations to support the 2018 *National Defense Strategy* in global competition. For this reason, the remainder of the chapter will examine the challenges to cross-component integration across the services and propose solutions for Civil Affairs.

To facilitate the understanding of the different organizational structures across the services, this chapter will use the following definitions:

> Multi-component units – units made up of personnel from more than one component (active duty, National Guard or Reserves), whose intent is to integrate, to the maximum extent possible within regulatory and legal constraints, resources (manpower, equipment, and funding) from more than one component into a cohesive, fully capable unit.[13]

> Associate units – separate units of different components that share the equipment of one unit (usually the active component unit) to accomplish particular missions. These units are located in proximity of one another; they divide aircraft/weapon system maintenance and flying responsibilities and tasks but maintain a separate chain of command (Normally used in the Air Force between active duty and Air National Guard).[14]

> Integrated units – units where full-time reservists and civilians work alongside full-time active personnel—all of them doing permanent work. Reserve statutes set the minimum limits on days to be served, and it is common for reserve unit personnel to be employed up to full- time via flexible workdays/hours.[15]

This chapter uses a literature review of relevant articles, doctrine, policies, and reports on military services' organizational concepts for active and reserve integration. References include lessons learned by other services on organizational integration, with the chapter elaborating as to how to best implement them for Civil Affairs. Recommendations include changes across doctrine, organization, training, material, leadership and education, personnel, facilities, and policy (DOTMLP-PF). Overall, this chapter contends that the integration of Civil Affairs forces would improve readiness and resources to meet future operational requirements.

Integration Across the DoD

All the military services within the DoD, including the US Coast Guard, have found innovative ways to integrate active and reserve components.

Each service combined active and reserve units differently to meet their unique challenges. For example, the US Air Force established multicomponent units to retain human capital and minimize overhead costs by having components share aircrafts. The United States Coast Guard fully integrated its reservists under one active-duty commander to provide active units an appropriate mix of personnel to meet real-world missions. The US Marines assigned active-duty personnel to reserve units as Inspectors-Instructors (I&I) to assist with training.

The army has associated or paired reserve and guard units with active-duty forces. When done successfully, the integration of active and reserve forces can increase readiness, reduce costs, and retain human capital across components.[16]

In 2004, Deputy Chief of Staff for Air Force Plans and Programs Lieutenant General Duncan McNabb presented three compelling reasons for active and reserve integration before the Armed Services Committee:

1. Integration allows balancing personnel tempo, or days deployed, appropriately among the components.

2. Integration plays to the strengths of each component.

3. Integration provides a continuum of service, an expansion of institutional knowledge, and the preservation of human capital.[17]

At that time, the air force had successfully integrated several active, reserve, and Air National Guard units. For example, in 2002, the air force stood up its first integrated unit, the 116th Air Control Wing, which merged all three components.[18] Within three months, it deployed eleven aircraft and 750 personnel across Iraq and Afghanistan.[19] The commander, Brigadier General George T. Lynn, said, "we integrated successfully and went to war successfully at the same time."[20] The 116th Air Control Wing demonstrated that these organizational concepts can be successful with cross-component integration to meet operational requirements. But the air force was not the first success story; the Coast Guard had introduced a similar plan back in the mid 1990s.

In 1994, the Coast Guard established its active- and reserve-integration plan, known as "Team Coast Guard."[21] This plan prompted the Coast Guard's long-term initiative to restructure both components entirely under one active command. Although the integration did have challenges, such as a reduction in command positions for reserve officers, most Coast Guard reservists are now assigned to active units as individual augmentees. This plan consisted of:

> 1. Restructuring the Coast Guard Reserve at the field level by placing reservists under the direct operational control of the augmented active command.

> 2. Integrating active and reserve administrative control structures.

> 3. Eliminating reserve unit commanding officers, except in units needing special training, such as port security units.

> 4. Developing a reserve personnel allowance list that assigns each selected reserve billet a unique identifying number.

> 5. Integrating district readiness and reserve division functions into other staffs.[22]

Although successful, the implementation of this change caused several organizational challenges, such as a lack of reserve leadership in active units to advocate for the unique needs of reservists. For this reason, in 2014, the Coast Guard published a policy called Reserve Force Readiness System (RFRS) Staff Elements Roles and Responsibilities.[23] This policy provided a service-wide structure to better align reserve personnel requirements and readiness and to maintain unit strengths to facilitate surge requirements for operational needs. It also established a Senior Enlisted Reserve Advisor program to advise active-duty commanders on all aspects of their reserve personnel.[24]

The Marine Corps did something similar by assigning individual active-duty marines to reserve units. To assist reserve units in maintaining readiness, the Marine Corps assigns active-duty personnel, known as Inspectors and Instructors (I&I), to reserve units.[25] A reserve unit's I&I integrates within the different staff sections to assist with organizing, training, and administering for future operational requirements.[26] According to a study conducted by the Institute for Defense Analysis, reserve units within the Marine Corps experienced fewer training and administrative challenges than US Army reserve units because of the marines' integration.[27] (There will be more on Marine Civil Affairs in chapter 8).

In 2007, the RAND Corporation published a study on organizational designs for active and reserve integration. This study aimed to identify organizational concepts to improve readiness, reduce costs, and facilitate mission accomplishment for the total force.[28] For this study, the authors identified the following goals and subgoals that merit consideration in developing a strategy to integrate active and reserve Civil Affairs:

1. Improve readiness.

- Improve accomplishment of missions and goals.

- Improve readiness to accomplish missions and goals.

- Facilitate active ownership of appropriate training and readiness standards for all components and appropriate resourcing to accomplish assigned missions.[29]

2. Improve efficiency.

- Achieve better availability of human capital.

- Foster seamless movement among active and reserve units.

- Share professional experience and coaching.

- Balance personnel tempo or days deployed.

- Optimize the unique capabilities and strengths of each component.

- Lower cost.

- Lessen active duty deployment numbers.

- Increase capital asset utilization. Use the least costly mix of personnel to accomplish the mission.[30]

Department of Defense Directive 1200.17 advises all the service secretaries to "integrate AC and RC organizations to the greatest extent practicable, including the use of cross-component assignments, both AC to RC and RC to AC. Such assignments should be considered as career-enhancing and not detrimental to a service member's career progression."[31] This directive is another reason the US Army should consider, at a minimum, implementing cross-component assignments for its Civil Affairs forces. These assignments would provide officers and enlisted soldiers from both components the opportunity to be exposed to cross-level experiences throughout the Civil Affairs total force.

In 2015, Congress established the National Commission on the Future of the Army in the National Defense Authorization Act for Fiscal Year 2015.[32] This commission examined the entire US Army force structure to include their implementation of the ATFP. In January 2016, the commission published its final report, which provided sixty-three recommendations on how the army can restructure the active and the reserve components to meet its total force policy.[33] Although both documents focus more on combat units—for example, Brigade Combat Teams and Combat Aviation Brigades—the recommended findings below could support the army's development of a CATFP:

> Recommendation 27: The Secretary of the Army should review and assess officer and NCO positions from all components for potential designation as integrated positions that would allow individuals from all components to fill positions to foster an Army Total Force culture and expand knowledge about other components.[34]

> Recommendation 28: The Secretary of the Army should develop selection and promotion policies to incentivize Regular Army,

Army National Guard, and Army Reserve assignments across components and within multi-component units.[35]

Recommendation 32: The Army should continue using multicomponent units and training partnerships to improve Total Force integration and overall Army effectiveness.[36]

Recommendation 36: The Army should develop and implement a pilot program to assign Regular Army officers and enlisted soldiers to Army Reserve full-time support positions within one year of publication of this report and evaluated in two years to determine the effectiveness of such a program.[37]

Recommendation 38: Congress should authorize and direct the Secretary of the Army to establish a substantial multi-year pilot program in which recruiters from all three components are authorized to recruit individuals into any of the components and receive credit for an enlistee regardless of the component.[38]

INTEGRATION IN ARMY CIVIL AFFAIRS

Drawing from the lessons learned by sister services, as well as the recommendations of the previously mentioned studies, the Army Civil Affairs proponent should carve a path forward for the integration of active and reserve Civil Affairs forces under a multicomponent command. This would allow commanders to balance forces to meet operational requirements and resolve the disparities and tensions that resulted from the 2006 split. Currently, the parochialism of the three "tribes" of Civil Affairs impedes the ability to present as one unified capability to the army. Integration would improve readiness and training and share the burden of deployments among component members. Moreover, integration would facilitate a continuum of service for Civil Affairs forces and the development of a shared identity and culture among active and reserve components. An example of this model is the 1st Special Forces Command organizational architecture, which includes five active-duty Special Forces groups and two Army National Guard Special Forces groups.

Although the commission's recommendations were published in 2016, they still provide the army with a framework to develop a Civil Affairs pilot program. However, the greatest challenge with implementing a pilot program will be cultural differences and mistrust among the tribes of Civil Affairs. The only way for this program to be successful is to convince all stakeholders of the advantages to improve readiness and provide the army with a more capable Civil Affairs force that maximizes the benefit and uniqueness of each component.

Like any change, the integration of active and reserve Civil Affairs forces will bring disruption, creating challenges across the traditional capability framework, which includes doctrine, organizations, training, material, leadership, and education. Consequently, the integration should be monitored carefully to ensure these challenges are turned into opportunities and do not hurt those units participating.

The challenges to integration outlined below have been modified from the 2007 RAND study on active and reserve component integration.[39]The chapter authors gathered information from various sources, including interviews with senior military leaders. For this section, we identified the most significant challenges believed to impact Civil Affairs *total force* integration:

- Command relationship between components

- Operational availability of reserve forces

- Component specific funding

- Training availability of reserve forces

- Training standards

- Promotion and command opportunities

- Organizational culture and identity

-Drill and training periods

-Actual facilities

-Geographical disbursement of active and reserve forces

Funding constraints and geographical disbursement will be significant contributors to the challenges for integrating active and reserve Civil Affairs forces. Civil Affairs can learn from some of the difficulties associated with the initial implementation of the Associated Units Pilot Program. For example, the commander of the 173rd Brigade Combat Team in Vicenza, Italy, was dependent on the Texas National Guard to fund the 1-143rd Infantry battalion to participate in an integrated training exercise for which sufficient funds were not allocated. This shortfall negatively impacted training and the commander's responsibility to validate the unit.[40]

Another example was the division level multicomponent pilot unit program which partnered the 25th Infantry Division (ID) with the Hawaii National Guard. However, the Hawaii National Guard could not support the Main Command Post Operational Detachment associated with the 25th ID headquarters.[41] Subsequently, the responsibility was passed to the reserve component, which US Army Indo-Pacific was hesitant to support due to its ability to fill billets on account of geographic limitations. Distance between units is a critical factor with the integration of RC units with AC units. Moreover, location will impact everything from funding for travel to increased training days for RC to meet mission requirements.

Additionally, readiness differences can impact the implementation of CATFP. Generally, the reserves are constrained by funding and training days compared to their active-duty counterparts. In 2018, during a hearing to the Senate Appropriation Committee, Army Reserve Chief Lieutenant General Charles D. Luckey stated, "if sequestration budget caps return in FY 2020, the Army Reserve will incur significant risk in training, facility restoration and modernization, and equipping and modernization programs vital to winning the Nation's wars."[42] Hence, personnel and equipment may not be fully prepared or compatible when integrating with AC units.

The army's shift toward lethality and great power competition may also negatively impact Civil Affairs readiness. According to a RAND study, current processes for resourcing and training tend to focus on brigades and lethality. This puts the entire Army Reserve at a disadvantage, as it is mostly made up of sustainment units.[43] However, the integration of active-duty and reserve Civil Affairs could give the force access to modernized equipment and contribute to the long-term, sustainable readiness of the total Civil Affairs force.

Another major challenge is the enduring identity- and culture-based differences between active and reserve Civil Affairs. Shafi Saiduddin and Robert Schafer suggested the difference in capabilities and training under one career field is central to Civil Affairs's identity issue.[44] This identity issue is compounded by the real-life differences between active and reserve forces. Additionally, they stated that identity within Civil Affairs is based on component and command relationship; for example, "active versus reserve" and "special operations versus conventional."[45] Although these identity issues are not unique to Civil Affairs, they will be a formidable barrier to integration. Moreover, these identity challenges are exacerbated by the fact that active-duty forces because they are full time, have significantly more access to training and are thereby often technically and tactically more proficient and aligned with assigned missions. Army Reserve training is, by design, less frequent and requires a longer lead time to amass the same level of technical capability, often not fully realized until units reach the mobilization platform.

All organizations have a unique culture in which they operate. Over time, these cultural norms become embedded in every aspect of an organization, from systems to people. For example, AC personnel are more accustomed to the special operations culture than RC, who have usually supported conventional forces since the 2006 split. Thus, any attempt to integrate active and reserve Civil Affairs under one organization must consider the potential resistance from the cultural differences.

One key aspect of successfully integrating active and reserve component Civil Affairs forces is to mitigate resistance during the transition. Alexandria Patricia Braica claims that involving organizational members early in the planning process can replace insecurities and reduce members' resistance to change.[46] Sibel Caliskan and Idil Isik also noted that members' understanding of the reasons and perceived ability to successfully change can reduce any resistance.[47] Additionally, Mark Mueller-Eberstein, in his TEDx presentation, claims leaders must communicate the positive impacts that address both members' concerns and the adverse effects if the organization does not change.[48] Thus, communicating and engaging with both AC and RC Civil Affairs personnel and other stakeholders early on can help prevent resistance throughout the integration process.

For example, knowing the cultural differences between active and reserve forces, Secretary of Defense William Cohen issued a memorandum in 1997 that reinforced the need for component integration to address cultural barriers to the *total force*:

> I ask each of you to create an environment that eliminates all residual barriers—structural and cultural—for effective integration within our Total Force. By integration, I mean the conditions of readiness and trust needed for the leadership at all levels to have well-justified confidence that Reserve Component units are trained and equipped to serve as an effective part of the joint and combined force within whatever timelines are ser [sic] for the unit—in peace and war...Our goal, as we move into the 21st century, must be a seamless Total Force that provides the National Command Authorities the flexibility and interoperability necessary for the full range of military operations. We cannot achieve this as separate components.[49]

However, two decades later, the army continues to face cultural divisions between components.[50] These cultural differences drastically impact the effectiveness of the *total force* to meet emerging requirements. Therefore, the CATFP should focus on how to optimize Civil Affairs while putting cultural biases into consideration for future integration efforts.

APPLICATION TO CIVIL AFFAIRS INTEGRATION

Now is the time to change the organizational structure for Civil Affairs, uniting the tribes to increase effectiveness, efficiency, and strengthen the warrior diplomat community. The 2018 *National Defense Strategy* states, "department leaders will adapt their organizational structures to best support the Joint force. If current structures hinder substantial increases in lethality or performance, it is expected that Service Secretaries and Agency heads will consolidate, eliminate, or restructure as needed."[51] Thus, the *National Defense Strategy*, the commission, and the ATFP provide leaders the organizational frameworks to put a CATFP into action. The integration of active and reserve forces will not only support the *National Defense Strategy* and ATFP but also increase performance and illuminate many of the unique capabilities found only within Civil Affairs.

The CATFP could start by implementing a pilot program to integrate AC and RC Civil Affairs forces. The Civil Affairs proponent should continue to monitor updates as the army continues to change doctrine and policies to meet ATFP requirements. For example, the ATFP recommended changes with Army Regulation (AR) 500-5, *Army Mobilization*, to streamline the mobilization process for RC forces to meet mission requirements.[52] The recommended ATFP changes for army regulations are intended to move the army toward a total force that would support the implementation of a CATFP. Additionally, the Civil Affairs proponent should conduct an independent assessment of army regulations and policies to determine recommended changes and request exceptions to expedite the integration of AC and RC Civil Affairs forces.

To better capitalize on Civil Affairs's capabilities across both commands and components, the Civil Affairs proponent should implement a combination of associated units, multicomponent units, and fully integrated unit approaches. For example, associate (or pair) a reserve Civil Affairs battalion with the 95th Civil Affairs Brigade. This partnership would allow the 95th Civil Affairs Brigade to approve training and assess the readiness of a reserve battalion while enabling the reserve battalion to train alongside its active-duty special operations counterparts. Over time, this integration would enhance the readiness of reserve battalions and cross-level deployments, easing the high demand for active-duty forces.

Another approach would be the development of a multicomponent Civil Affairs Command, alternately commanded by a reserve and an active-duty Civil Affairs brigadier general. This structure would include a staff mixture of active and reserve personnel at all echelons, to include moving administrative control of the 83rd Civil Affairs Battalion from United States Army Forces Command (FORSCOM) to this multicomponent command. This structure would be one step forward to fully integrating active and reserve units under a single command, with the goal of cross-leveling experiences and validating compatibility.

For all the other reserve Civil Affairs units, Civil Affairs should follow the marines' I&I duty model and assign active-duty soldiers to reserve units as mentors to assist with training.[53] Active-duty staff would be a mixture of officers and enlisted personnel, working alongside unit leadership with a focus on training and readiness and deploying alongside them.

Civil Affairs forces, dependent on components, have different levels of training and experience. Most glaringly apparent is the disparity between the qualification of RC and AC officers. In the RC, units recruit both qualified and unqualified Civil Affairs officers because there is no assessment program as in the AC. The unqualified officers complete a hybrid three-phase qualification course consisting of two 30-day periods of in-resident training and several months of structured online training. This approach varies greatly from the nearly year-long training pipeline consisting of language training, regional studies, and Civil Affairs common core that AC officers experience. The differences are largely due to logistics—RC soldiers typically cannot support the AC's lengthy training pipeline when balancing civilian job requirements. One way to address the gaps in training and readiness between components is to assign AC instructors to USACAPOC's 1st Training Brigade. The assignment of AC instructors could assist RC with developing and implementing a continuous training program to level the training between components. Over time, this could increase progress toward qualification and closing the gap of qualified personnel between AC and RC. This program focuses only on core Civil Affairs qualification training and does not include elements specific to special operations Civil Affairs forces.

Regarding collective training, the cross-pollination of AC and RC across multicomponent units can increase unit readiness. Either associated or a fully integrated multicomponent command, the partnership will force AC and RC to identify areas to train together. Just like the units participating in the Associated Units Pilot Program, the controlling headquarters (either AC or RC) would be responsible for:

- approving the training program of the associated unit

- reviewing readiness reports

- assessing resource requirements

- validating compatibility; this is the authority that moves farthest from the established concept of AC commanders simply assessing readiness and resourcing, as it specifies that compatibility will be assessed using "integrated training exercises" (Acting Secretary of the Army Patrick Murphy's 2016 memorandum)[54]

Therefore, the higher Civil Affairs unit, either AC or RC, would be ultimately responsible for the training and readiness for the other component's units.

One of the benefits of the integration of AC and RC Civil Affairs forces is the access to modernized equipment. Historically, there has always been a modernization gap between AC and RC forces. The FY

2017 National Guard and Reserve Equipment Report (NGRER) states: "Due to the impacts of the Budget Control Act of 2011, the Department is witnessing a decline in RC equipment procurement funding, in some cases falling back to pre-9-11 levels or even lower."[55] Therefore, the sharing of equipment between components can close the interoperability and training gap between AC and RC units.

For example, the Joint Light Tactical Vehicle will be fielded across the army for over twenty years.[56] Throughout the fielding period, the sharing of equipment for training between components would provide not-yet-fielded units access to modernized equipment. Units participating in the Associated Units Pilot Program have done it before. For example, "the 1st Cavalry Division loaned M1 tanks and Bradley fighting vehicles to the Mississippi National Guard for its Multi-Echelon Integrated Brigade Training exercise on Fort Hood."[57] Although the sharing of equipment will not expedite the fielding process, it will provide Civil Affairs forces access to modernized equipment and ensure standardization in training across Civil Affairs. Additionally, as much of Civil Affairs forces' core work is done on digital systems, it is imperative that Civil Affairs forces in both components have access to the same software and associated support infrastructure.

More integration of AC and RC Civil Affairs units would increase opportunities for leaders to fill critical positions across components and potential promotions. The cross-pollination of leaders, both officers and noncommissioned officers, will increase understanding and close the cultural gap between components. For example, the marines place their AC I&I in key positions: "I&I personnel normally occupy key staff leadership positions, such as the training chief of a battalion or as the S-3/S-4. I&I staff provide leadership continuity when selected reservist (SELRES) leadership is not drilling, and they assist in planning training and unit development."[58]

Additionally, AC can fill an agreed-upon percentage of RC command and senior enlisted slots within the Civil Affairs Commands. This offers

AC soldiers the opportunity to command that isn't available in the AC. The placement of leaders across the Civil Affairs force will not only contribute to unit readiness but also close the cultural gap and provide Civil Affairs a more unified voice with the army. This cross-pollination would especially benefit units at the battalion level. The RC regularly struggles to build a sufficient pool of command candidates and the AC Civil Affairs force lacks sufficient command bullets, thereby stymying career growth.

Facilities and locations can be a challenge for implementing a CATFP. The RC units are spread across the United States while the AC units are all located at Fort Bragg, North Carolina. Therefore, more analysis of facilities and geographic locations must be researched to determine unit associations that minimize challenges with AC and RC integration. Collocating active-duty Civil Affairs formations at some of these RC locations could present opportunities for education or other career-enhancing activities. For instance, the 351st Civil Affairs Command in Mountain View, California, is near large tech companies like Facebook and LinkedIn and universities like Stanford. Key locations like this can provide the Civil Affairs Corps an excellent opportunity to increase community pairing and push toward more military-civilian integration with high-tech firms.

Lastly, the Civil Affairs proponent should establish a corps charter similar to the *Abrams Charter* developed for the US Army Rangers in 1974.[59] Then Chief of Staff of the Army General Creighton Abrams wanted leaders from ranger battalions to rotate back to conventional infantry units to expose those units to ranger standards. With multicomponent units and other cross-component initiatives, Civil Affairs can develop a similar program to cross-pollinate conventional and special operations Civil Affairs experiences across the total force. This final initiative would contribute to the balance of capability and expertise across AC and RC from the unit to the individual level.

Conclusion

The army published its Army Total Force Policy in 2012 to define steps and guidance to integrate all components to meet the DoD's goal for a total force. US Army Civil Affairs should take the commission's recommendations and the lessons learned by other services and those army units participating in pilot programs to develop a Civil Affairs-specific multicomponent program. Due to the ratio of AC to RC Civil Affairs units, a CATFP should include different types of organizational structures to integrate components. Examples include multicomponent units led by either component and embedding AC Civil Affairs mentors and leaders into RC units that are not partnered with AC units in an associated unit program.

The integration of AC and RC will create several opportunities for Civil Affairs's total force. One example is to train and develop Civil Affairs forces across both components, to include synchronizing RC units' annual training with AC collective training events. Another is for AC Civil Affairs soldiers to fill critical billets that may be difficult to fill in the reserves, like operations and command positions. These opportunities can increase lines of communication between components, lessen the cultural differences, improve readiness, and retain human capital to meet future operational requirements.

However, more collaborative discussion among senior army leaders is required to help identify AC and RC Civil Affairs force integration goals. This should include identifying individual positions and units that would participate across the three different integration structures: multicomponent, associate units, and integrated units. These efforts require buy-in from Civil Affairs leadership to facilitate integration efforts and overcome the cultural differences and mistrust between components. Without a Civil Affairs Total Force Policy and leadership support at all levels, any integration effort will be virtually impossible to implement. The next chapter dives deeper into Marine Corps Civil Affairs and how they are evolving to improve the efficacy of information operations.

NOTES

1. Assad Raza, "True Civil Affairs Integration: From Three Tribes to One," *Small Wars Journal*, October 7, 2019, https://smallwarsjournal.com/jrnl/art/true-civil-affairs-integration-three- tribes-one.
2. US Department of State, "Stabilization Assistance Review: A Framework for Maximizing the Effectiveness of U.S. Government Efforts to Stabilize Conflict-Affected Areas - United States Department of State" (US Department of State, 2018), https://www.state.gov/reports/stabilization-assistance-review-a-framework-for-maximizing-the-effectiveness-of-u-s-government-efforts-to-stabilize-conflict-affected-areas-2018/.
3. Christopher Paul, Isaac R. Porche, and Elliot Axelband, "The Transition to and Evolution of U.S. Special Operations Command." In *The Other Quiet Professionals: Lessons for Future Cyber Forces from the Evolution of Special Forces*, 15–22. RAND Corporation, 2014, https://www.jstor.org/stable/10.7249/j.ctt1287m89.10?seq=1#metadata_info_tab_contents.
4. Kathleen H. Hicks and Christine E. Wormuth, *The Future of U.S. Civil Affairs Forces* (Washington, DC: Center for Strategic & International Studies, February 2009), https://csis- prod.s3.amazonaws.com/s3fs-public/legacy_files/files/publication/130409_Hicks_FutureCivilAffairs_Web.pdf.
5. Alfred H. Paddock, "The 2006 'Divorce' of US Army Reserve and Active Component Psychological Operations Units," *Small Wars Journal*, March 3, 2012, https://smallwarsjournal.com/jrnl/art/the-2006-"divorce"-of-us-army-reserve-and-active-component- psychological-operations-units.
6. Hugh Van Roosen, "Implications of the 2006 Reassignment of U.S. Army Civil Affairs" (master's thesis, U.S. Army War College, 2009), https://apps.dtic.mil/dtic/tr/fulltext/u2/a494806.pdf.
7. Kathleen H. Hicks and Christine E. Wormuth, *The Future of U.S. Civil Affairs Forces*.
8. Ibid., viii.
9. Ibid., 37.
10. Ellen M. Pint, Christopher M. Schnaubelt, Stephen Dalzell, Jaime L. Hastings, Penelope Speed, and Michael G. Shanley, *Review of Army Total Force Policy Implementation* (Santa Monica, CA: RAND, 2017), https://apps.dtic.mil/dtic/tr/fulltext/u2/1057218.pdf.
11. Ibid., 11.
12. Ibid., 33.

13. Harry J. Thie, Roland J. Yardley, Peter Schrimer, Rudolph H. Ehrenberg, and Penelope Speed, *Factors to Consider in Blending Active and Reserve Manpower Within Military Units* (RAND Corporation 2007), 6, https://www.rand.org/content/dam/rand/pubs/monographs/2007/RAND_MG5 27.pdf.

14. Ibid., 14.

15. Ibid., 6–7.

16. Ibid., 37.

17. US House of Representatives, Testimony of Lieutenant General Duncan J. McNabb Deputy Chief of Staff for Air Force Plans and Programs Before the United States House of Representatives Committee on Armed Services Subcommittee on Total Force Regarding Adequacy of The Total Force, March 10, 2001, https://www.globalsecurity.org/military/library/congress/2004_hr/040310-mcnabb.html. Beverly Isik and Paul Ross, "First Future Total Force Wing Proves Successful," *U.S. Air Force News*, July 27, 2005, https://www.af.mil/News/Article-Display/Article/133860/first-future-total-force-wing-proves-successful/.

18. Beverly Isik and Paul Ross, "First Future Total Force Wing Proves Successful," *U.S. Air Force News*, July 27, 2005, https://www.af.mil/News/Article-Display/Article/133860/first-future-total-force-wing-proves-successful/.

19. Ibid.

20. Ibid.

21. Thie et al., *Factors to Consider in Blending*, 56.

22. Ibid.

23. Commandant, United States Coast Guard, "Reserve Force Readiness System (RFRS) Staff Element Responsibilities," Instruction 5320.4A, November 6, 2014, https://www.reserve.uscg.mil/Portals/2/Documents/Directives/CI_5320_4A.pdf?ver=2017-01-25-160025-570.

24. Ibid.

25. Thie et al., *Factors to Consider in Blending*, 66.

26. John Morrison, John Metzko, and Charles Hawkins, *Planning and Preparing for Training in Reserve Component Units* (Alexandria, VA: Institute for Defense Analysis, 2002), https://apps.dtic.mil/sti/pdfs/ADA4 09161.pdf.

27. Ibid.

28. Thie et al., *Factors to Consider in Blending*, 8.

29. Ibid.

30. Ibid.

31. Department of Defense, DoD Directive 1200.17, *Managing the Reserve Components as an Operational Force* (Washington, DC: Department of Defense, October 29, 2008), 6, https://www.esd.whs.mil/Portals/54/Documents/DD/issuances/dodd/120017p.pdf.

32. National Commission on the Future of the Army, *Report to the President and the Congress of the United States* (Arlington, VA: United States. National Commission on the Future of the Army, 2016), https://www.hsdl.org/?abstract&did=789780.

33. Ibid.

34. Ibid., 65.

35. Ibid.

36. Ibid., 68.

37. Ibid., 69.

38. Ibid., 73.

39. Thie et al., *Factors to Consider in Blending*, 34.

40. Pint et al., *Review Army Total Force*, 36.

41. Ibid.

42. US Senate Appropriation Committee, Defense Hearing of Lieutenant General Charles D. Luckey, 33rd Chief of Army Reserve and 8th Commanding General, US Army Reserve Command, April 17, 2018, https://www.appropriations.senate.gov/imo/media/doc/041718%20-%20FY19%20CAR%20Luckey%20Testimony.pdf.

43. Pint et al., *Review Army Total Force*, 53.

44. Shafi Salduddin and Robert Schafer, *Optimizing Civil Affairs through Branding and Narrative Strategies*, Civil Affairs Issue Papers (The Civil Affairs Association/ Association of the United States Army), vol. 5 (2018–2019): 27.

45. Ibid., 29.

46. Alexandra Patricia Bracia, "Fundamentals of Change Management," *Studia Universitatis "Vasile Goldis" Arad.Seria Stiinte Economice* 23, no. 4 (2013): 138–149, https://www.proquest.com/scholarly-journals/fundamentals-change-management/docview/1664920678/se-2.

47. Sibel Caliskan and Idil Isik, "Are You Ready for the Global Change? Multicultural Personality and Readiness for Organizational Change," *Journal of Organizational Change Management* 29, no. 3 (2016): 404–423, https://doi.org/10.1108/jocm-07-2015-0119.

48. Mark Mueller-Eberstein, "Lead and Be the Change," YouTube, TEDxRainer, December 11, 2012, https://www.youtube.com/watch?v=yv-QiSvuLLM.

49. Pint et al., *Review Army Total Force*, 8.

50. See National Commission on the Future of the Army, *Report to the President and the Congress of the United States*, 59–60, for a discussion of the cultural challenges in the US Army.

51. Summary of the 2018 *National Defense Strategy* of The United States of America: Sharpening the American Military's Competitive Edge, 10, https://www.hsdl.org/?abstract&did=789780

52. Pint et al., *Review Army Total Force*, 26.

53. Melissa Martens, *Working Together to Accomplish the Mission: Inspector-Instructor Duty*, Marines official website, August 20, 2019, https://www.marforres.marines.mil/Marine-Reserve-News-Photos/Marine-Reserve-News/Article/910927/working-together-to-accomplish-the-mission-inspector- instructor-duty/.

54. Ibid., 33.

55. Pint et al., *Review Army Total Force*, 63.

56. Arthur J. Villasanta, "New JLTV Combat Trucks to Enter U.S. Army Service in Jan. 2019," *Wall Street News*, January 3, 2019, http://wallst-news.com/new-jltv-combat-trucks-to-enter-u-s-army-service-in-jan-2019/.

57. Pint et al., *Review Army Total Force*, 66.

58. Thie et al., *Factors to Consider in Blending*, 68.

59. Asymmetric Warfare Group, "Abrams Charter in Effect at the AWG," US Army, January 18, 2017, https://www.army.mil/article/180709/abrams_charter_in_effect_at_the_awg.

CHAPTER 8

JOINT INFORMATION FUSION AND SYNERGY

OPPORTUNITIES FOR COLLABORATION WITH UNITED STATES MARINE CORPS CIVIL AFFAIRS

Diana X. Moga and Robert Boudreau

The US Army, United States Navy, United States Marine Corps, and the US Air Force each possess unique capabilities to serve the Department of Defense. Though some capabilities overlap, such as aviation and infantry, their missions remain distinct by design. Today, only the marines and army have Civil Affairs personnel. The navy disbanded its last Civil Affairs unit in 2014, and the air force never had Civil Affairs forces. Like their army counterparts, Civil Affairs marines serve to align host-nation civilians' interests with the commander's objectives. Civil Affairs marines accomplish this by using soft skills to create partners and establish buy-in with civilian leaders. But the army, marines, and other US government agencies can improve collaboration. Internal silos persist, forming barriers among the services that undermine joint effectiveness.[1]

Because today's multi-domain operating environment is complex and dynamic, it is not enough for Civil Affairs to integrate outside of the military. Civil Affairs must also integrate laterally, with sister services and other US government agencies. Whether the marines serve the Office of Security Cooperation at a US embassy or with a field commander, integrating Civil Affairs across agencies is critical. As expressed in the Marine Corps Doctrinal Publication 1-4, *Competing*, the Marine Corps must operate across a spectrum of competition, where a range of violent and nonviolent activities support strategic competition efforts.[2] Improved collaboration, increased opportunities for information sharing, and a culture of open cooperation between Marine Corps and Army Civil Affairs personnel improves joint capabilities along this competition continuum. This chapter calls attention to the increased complexity of the world and the need to identify and break down silos within the DoD.

THE STRUCTURE OF MARINE CORPS CIVIL AFFAIRS

Marine Corps Civil Affairs saw substantial growth in the years immediately following 9/11 due to a spike in demand for specialists in civil-military operations. Recent experiences in Operation Iraqi Freedom and Operation Enduring Freedom marked a turning point for the Marine Corps, when commanders on the ground confronted a situation fundamentally impacted by the civil environment. As a result, the Marine Corps saw the need for dedicated Civil Affairs personnel, and it created standing Civil Affairs units and trained full-time Civil Affairs specialists.[3]

When deployed, Marine Corps Civil Affairs forces augment the Marine Air-Ground Task Force (MAGTF) staff with insight and influence capabilities pertaining to the civil environment.[4] The MAGTF is a foundational, integrated combined-arms concept with aviation, ground combat, logistics, and command headquarters elements. In simple terms, the MAGTF organizes, dissolves, and reassembles to accomplish specific missions. All Marine Corps units are task-organized into a standing Marine Expeditionary Force (MEF) and are further task-organized into smaller expeditionary MAGTFs for specific missions. Civil Affairs billets typically fit within the MAGTF structure as part of the operations, information operations, or fires and effects coordination cells. Civil Affairs marines focus attention externally by assessing the host nation and internally by integrating within the MAGTF structure.

Close working relationships and collaboration with Army Civil Affairs and other DoD components is not a cultural norm at present. There exists a very limited (to nonexistent) working knowledge within Marine Civil Affairs groups of Army Civil Affairs missions and tasks, even when the two entities are operating concurrently within a shared Area of Responsibility. For example, when a Marine Civil Affairs team deployed to Guatemala as part of the Special Purpose MAGTF in 2019, army Civil Affairs had an established presence with an enduring mission in the same area, but collaboration between the units occurred only a few days prior to the marines arriving in the country. This caused friction between overlapping Civil Affairs activities and highlighted some missed opportunities for mutually supporting one another's missions.

With the end of the Global War on Terrorism, Marine Corps Civil Affairs has pivoted from a focus on post-conflict rebuilding operations to one on pre-conflict stabilization and geopolitical competition activities. Consequently, civil-military operations have evolved to meet different strategic goals. Key purposes of Civil Affairs activities include influencing the civil environment by conveying a positive message to the host nation and transmitting civil information within the DoD. The need to improve cross-agency collaboration has heightened importance today because the variety of missions the Marine Corps faces means more stakeholders have a role in military operations. Whether Civil Affairs marines provide support to DoD medical readiness exercises or support host-nation government activities, they must leverage relationships with the DoD and Department of State (DoS) for maximum effectiveness.

As the US military enters a down-cycle of deployed activity following the wars in Iraq and Afghanistan, the health and strength of Marine Corps

Civil Affairs is tenuous. The section that follows shows a historical trend in which the Marine Corps invests in Civil Affairs capabilities during a conflict, and when the conflict is over and demand subsides, Civil Affairs forces are cut back and resources are redirected to other areas. When the next conflict arises, the Marine Corps is behind in reinvigorating its civil environment capabilities. This is the prospect the US faces today. The Marine Corps needs a standing capability in good health *ahead* of the next conflict. Because it is vitally important to maintain a Civil Affairs capability, Marine Corps Civil Affairs must offer a strong return on investment across the competition continuum.

THE EVOLUTION OF CIVIL-MILITARY OPERATIONS

The Marine Corps has prepared infantry leaders to conduct civil-military operations for over a century. The Marine Corps' early-twentieth-century involvement in a series of Central American and Caribbean conflicts (the so-called "Banana Wars"), and subsequently in the Vietnam War, framed the way in which marines approach civil-military operations today.[5] In Panama, the Dominican Republic, Haiti, and Nicaragua, counterinsurgency operations helped shape the Marine Corps' understanding of stabilization activities.[6] The Marine Corps' philosophy to root out malign actors by military force served as a means of achieving stability in the region.[7] This led to long-term occupation, however, and seizure of government institutions. During the United States' 1915 occupation of Haiti, for example, the marines assumed control of customs, law enforcement, tax collection, and other civil administrative functions within the Haitian government. These were some of the Marine Corps' earliest experiences wherein the military took responsibility when operations interfered with the basic functioning of the host nation's society.

For civil-military operations, the lessons from this period were memorialized in the Marine Corps' *Small Wars Manual* of 1940, last reviewed for republication in 1990.[8] At the time of the manual's first publication, the Marine Corps' focus centered on maintaining civil government while functioning as an occupying force. Until the mid-twentieth century, civil-military operations existed simply as a subset of tasks for that occupying force. Nevertheless, the marines, in principle, recognized restoration of civil order as the overall goal of military intervention:

> In assisting any country to restore peace and order, it is not the policy of the United States Government to accept permanent responsibility for the preservation of governmental stability by stationing its armed forces indefinitely in the foreign country for that purpose. The United States forces seek to restore domestic tranquility as soon as possible and to return the normal functions of government to the country concerned.[9]

How to restore "domestic tranquility," and determining when the host nation has reached that state, lies at the heart of a well-defined purpose for civil-military operations. But the ramifications of having only a murky definition would play out again for the Marine Corps in future conflicts.

By the 1960s, the US government shifted its focus toward countering Russia's increasing influence throughout the world. The Cold War offered a clear, bipolar international system with the obvious geostrategic objectives to crush the communist threat. Yet, this macro-level objective did not translate easily to national or local policies. The US military found itself embroiled again in a range of small wars—most notably a counterinsurgency campaign in Vietnam.[10] This prompted the Marine Corps to revisit civil military operations in the context of "pacification," with the Combined Action Program in 1965.

Vietnam

In Vietnam, the Marine Corps' military strategy went beyond its approach during the Banana Wars, with the additional objective of winning over the civilian population in a bid to undermine the Viet Cong insurgency. Civic action figured prominently during the Vietnam War, particularly so in the I Corps region in the northern part of South Vietnam. In concert with the "clear, hold, and build" counterinsurgency strategy, then

Lieutenant General Lewis William Walt, the commander of III Marine Amphibious Force (MAF), recognized that it was not enough to rid rural villages of the enemy.[11] He also saw that a successful stabilization campaign had to include legitimate local governance that connected the people to the central South Vietnamese government.[12] In the midst of counterinsurgency operations, Marines with III MAF engaged in the "Civic Action Program." The program sought to win over the populace and restore stable government, thereby reducing insurgent activity. Over time, the outline for the Combined Action Platoons (CAPs)—first devised in 1965 by 3rd Battalion, 4th Marine Division in the Phu Bai Province—emerged in the form of a marine squad and a navy corpsman embedded with a Vietnamese platoon.[13]

Despite localized successes with many parts of the Combined Action Program, the employment of civic action did little to impact the complex political situation in Vietnam. It is important to note that these civic action organizations within the CAP had a different purpose than that of the regular Civil Affairs forces. The mission of the Combined Action Program was to achieve security by training, advising, and integrating the South Vietnamese Popular Force soldiers with US marine platoons.[14] The goal of the Civil Action Program was to enhance the lives of Vietnamese people and offer them a reason to support their government, and the mission of army Civil Affairs was to serve as the primary interface between the military and the civilians.[15] Both Army Civil Affairs and Marine Corps CAP performed civic action in rural villages.

By mid-1970, demand for the Combined Action Program declined as the Republic of Vietnam's confidence in administering the rural areas grew.[16] The Marine Corps eventually dissolved the program, and US forces withdrew from Vietnam. Though the activities of the CAPs overlap with those of Civil Affairs, the Marine Corps never employed trained Civil Affairs personnel in Vietnam.

Desert Shield and Desert Storm

In 1990, the Marine Corps staged units in Saudi Arabia prior to the Iraq invasion, deployed the 3rd Civil Affairs Group (CAG) to the Middle East, and went to work building partner relationships in Jubail.[17] Immersing troops in a strict Islamic culture created friction for them; many Saudis found it anathema that Americans had even set foot on soil so close to Mecca and Medina.[18] Nevertheless, the Civil Affairs marines seized the opportunity to coordinate support with the US Army Reserve's 403rd Civil Affairs Group and developed ties with government, business, and law enforcement officials.[19]

As combat operations began, the Civil Affairs footprint in Saudi Arabia increased as the 4th CAG sent reinforcements. Civil Affairs marines increased their liaison activities with business and local leaders and assisted the Saudis in establishing an emergency operations center for civil defense.[20] The Civil Affairs marines also led a program to integrate Kuwaiti volunteers as linguists, marking a notable "shift into the divisions and brigades afloat as well as into psychological operations teams as [the invasion] approached."[21]

With the conflict intensifying, the 3rd CAG focused on managing food and resources to prevent civilian interference in combat missions.[22] After a month of fighting, coalition forces expelled the Iraqis from Kuwait, and the 3rd CAG shifted to assist the Kuwaitis in restoring civil control, aiding displaced civilians and refugees, and providing humanitarian relief.[23]

Operations Desert Shield and Desert Storm marked the first large-scale Marine Corps Civil affairs deployment. Many of the Civil Affairs activities resembled the tactical missions defined in doctrine today, but certain critical elements were missing. First, although the CAGs coordinated with the host-nation and other partners, they did not establish a formal civil-military operations center (CMOC) to centralize coordination efforts. Today, CMOCs are routinely set up for military and civilian stakeholders to coordinate Civil Affairs activities. Second, there was no formal planning staff position for Civil Affairs. Hindsight shows the ad hoc employment of Civil Affairs resulted in measurable success during Operation Desert Shield and Operation Desert Storm, but present-day practitioners recognize the value added in conducting civil analysis as part of the collective staff planning phase prior to arrival in theater.

The Global War on Terrorism

In the early 2000s, the 9/11 attacks prompted the US government to embark on ambitious campaigns in Iraq and Afghanistan. The US military again found itself engaged in a counterinsurgency fight, where achieving trust from the populace could make or break the success of the entire campaign. Both campaigns saw the robust incorporation of civil-military operations into the Marine Corps' extensive combat engagements.

At this point in Marine Corps history, the best practice for Civil Affairs employment was limited to employment on a reactive, "as needed" basis. Civil considerations typically existed near the end of a long list of other strategic and tactical considerations, and early planning did not involve specialists focused on the civil environment. As a result, the early days of the Iraq and Afghanistan campaigns saw artillery and infantry units functioning as provisional Civil Affairs units.[24] Over time, commanders increasingly saw the value of employing Civil Affairs to facilitate combat maneuver.

Further along in the campaign, the Marine Corps embraced the return to counterinsurgency warfare, recognizing the need to understand cultural aspects of the operating environment.[25] This focus on irregular warfare led to the 2005 creation of the Center for Advanced Operational Cultural Learning (since renamed the Center for Regional and Security Studies), directed by then Lieutenant General James Mattis.[26] The center issued publications such as *Operational Culture for the Warfighter*, which emphasized the importance for training all deploying marines on host nation culture.[27] It is evident throughout contemporary irregular warfare and counterinsurgency literature that the Marine Corps came to recognize civilians as the key to success.[28] Unfortunately, this focus came several years into the Global War on Terrorism, after many missteps and missed opportunities with the civilian population.

Much has been written about policy and tactical failures surrounding the wars in Iraq and Afghanistan.[29] Then Secretary of State Colin Powell warned that by toppling an existing regime, the United States would become responsible for governance in the face of inevitable insurgencies.[30] But contemporary Marine Corps commanders did not seem to understand what then Lieutenant General Victor Krulak had recognized during the Vietnam War: protecting the civilian population is the most important ingredient for the success of any counterinsurgency campaign.[31] Instead, commanders used Civil Affairs marines to manage the Commander's Emergency Response Program (CERP), through which US government funding was used to build schools, repair infrastructure, and other similar projects.[32] Rather than using Civil Affairs as a means to understand and influence civilians in Iraq and Afghanistan, the Marine Corps sought to use "money as a weapons system"—injecting massive economic stimuli into local economies in a questionable effort to foster political stability.

Employing Civil Affairs as a capability primarily to administer human-itarian projects was a disaster for two reasons. First, the campaigns in Iraq and Afghanistan suffered from a fundamental misunderstanding of the civil environment. Information-gathering activities often became a secondary emphasis, at the expense of funded projects. Second, CERP spending on projects failed to provide value because many projects lacked essential levels of understanding and communal buy-in. Put simply, Civil Affairs forces were repurposed as project managers to achieve commanders' goals. Ironically, many projects failed because the US military lacked precisely the sort of local insight that Civil Affairs forces should have been providing.[33]

Over time, as combat units deployed to Afghanistan and Iraq, the mantra of "winning hearts and minds" resounded so strongly that, for some commanders, Civil Affairs missions became part of routine operations. Lieutenant Colonel Chris O'Donnell, a retired Civil Affairs reserve officer who was deployed in 2010 with a Civil Affairs team supporting the 3rd Battalion, 5th Marine Regiment, recalled his experiences when he arrived in Sangin, Afghanistan. When he tried to integrate civil considerations into the battalion's planning, he found it difficult to overcome the staff attitude that "we already do that stuff."[34] In reality, however, the commander's Civil Affairs reach did not extend much beyond identifying reconstruction projects within the area.[35] To provide value to the commander and the staff, Lieutenant Colonel O'Donnell's team focused on civil reconnaissance and social network analysis, which involved preparing analysis of the key leaders and other stakeholders. As reconstruction efforts progressed, follow-on units could build upon the information gathered by Lieutenant Colonel O'Donnell's team. However, transferring this knowledge to follow-on units proved difficult and did not easily scale into a larger or repeatable model across Afghanistan.

The Marine Corps' approach in Iraq and Afghanistan gradually shifted to security cooperation missions in the transitional/reconstruction phase of operations.[36] Civil Affairs employment became more nuanced. For example, the Marine Corps created and employed Female Engagement Teams (FETs) in Afghanistan, primarily to focus on the female demographic of the population.[37] Then Brigadier General Lawrence Nicholson, recalling his experiences as the II Marine Expeditionary Brigade commander from May 2009 to April 2010, "found that the FET team was exceptionally good at working with Afghan men. Afghan men were much less reticent about coming up and telling our women any number of things."[38] These comments are reflective of the overriding attitude about the efficacy of the FET program. However, an applied knowledge services think tank assessed in a 2015 report that "very little independent analysis has been carried out [regarding FETs], and unclear functions and a desire to be useful meant there was great pressure to report FETs as successful without really understanding cultural dynamics."[39] The FET concept highlighted the unsettling trend that, once again, well-intentioned and innovative programs for addressing civil considerations came too late and amid so much pressure that results and improvements became virtually impossible to assess.

Similarly, Lieutenant Colonel Aniela Szymanski, then a major who was deployed in 2010 as a Civil Affairs team leader with the 3rd Battalion, 2nd Marine Division to the Now Zad district of Helmand Province, Afghanistan, noted that Civil Affairs could have provided an even greater impact if commanders had focused more on interagency coordination and incorporated civil considerations at earlier planning stages.[40] In one example, she observed how the US Drug Enforcement Agency made sophisticated plans to disrupt poppy farming (which fuels illegal opium trafficking) in a failed attempt to promote stability in the area. But everyone overlooked the Afghan women; no agency made plans to engage half the population in the battle to win hearts and minds.[41]

History painfully repeated itself in the failures to obtain enduring success in Iraq and Afghanistan. Despite the developments in Civil Affairs capabilities, the purpose behind the activities became lost in a sea of ill-defined objectives and misapplication of resources, all of which came too late in the campaign. The core purpose of Civil Affairs is to understand and influence the civil environment, but the application of Civil Affairs stopped at the basic execution of civic action-type projects.

New Applications for Civil Affairs

In the wake of the Global War on Terrorism, there is renewed focus on redefining Civil Affairs activities. To break away from the reconstruction-focused model, doctrinal updates and senior-level discussions within the Civil Affairs community are refocusing Civil Affairs as an information-related capability. Information-related activities, such as messaging and information collection, are especially critical during the entirety of the competition continuum. Employed in this context, Civil Affairs marines focus heavily on civil information via civil reconnaissance and civil network analysis.[42]

Marine Corps Civil Affairs personnel have engaged with myriad exercises and operations, both joint and within the MAGTF construct, to execute information-operations tasks in a pre-conflict environment. For example, in the summer of 2019, US Marine Sergeants Daniel Echeverri and Adonis Duarte detached from the 4th Civil Affairs Group to augment the Army Civil Affairs team attached to the *USNS Comfort* (as part of Operation Enduring Promise, led by US Southern Command's Joint Task Force Bravo). The joint Civil Affairs team augmented the *USNS Comfort*'s mission to provide medical services to civilians in twelve Caribbean and South American countries by managing resources, coordinating with host nation government officials, and assisting the host-nation population in gaining access to the medical and dental services offered by the ship.

By expanding on new ways to apply Civil Affairs, the Marine Corps has uncovered new opportunities. As an information dissemination tool on the *USNS Comfort*, for example, Civil Affairs could convey important information to community leaders about the arrival and departure of the *USNS Comfort*, its humanitarian mission, and the specific medical and dental services available to local civilians. As it was, a poor understanding of the medical offerings aboard the *USNS Comfort* and the country teams on the ground at the US embassies meant that much of this information never made it to the host-nation civilians. This led to unused port capacity, misinformation, and missed opportunities to treat more people. The Marine Corps has an appetite for seeking joint Civil Affairs opportunities and at the very least is always looking for new ways to passively gather information on the civil domain. This team in particular served as the eyes and ears of the Marine Forces South commander, offering new situational awareness on the *USNS Comfort* mission for the Marine Forces South staff.

In fall 2019, Civil Affairs marines Major Chris Bridger and Staff Sergeant Abdiel Solisromero attached to the 2nd Battalion, 6th Marine Division, as part of Marine Rotational Force-Europe (MRF-E). MRF-E fell directly under the US Marine Corps Forces component command and established a rotational presence in Norway that facilitated military exercises in the

Nordic regions, increasing interoperability with allies and improving Marine Corps cold weather and mountain warfare proficiency.[43] As part of the rotational force, Major Bridger and Staff Sergeant Solisromero assumed their Civil Affairs roles within the information-related capability cell in the battalion operations section. They engaged in messaging to convey the enduring support from the United States via community relations events. The team also connected with the Norwegian Home Guard, which is the rapid mobilization force in the Norwegian military. The MRF-E mission to facilitate military exercises in the Nordic region leveraged Civil Affairs capabilities to strengthen country-to-country relations. However, Major Bridger and Staff Sergeant Solisromero participated in the second-to-last MRF-E rotation, as the Marine Corps discontinued the mission in 2020.

These vignettes connect to several trends within Civil Affairs. First, the effectiveness of deployed Civil Affairs units is largely a byproduct of the talents of specific individuals. This is an organizational weakness within the Civil Affairs community. The limitations of Civil Affairs training, resources, and methodologies are such that individuals must find their own way to operationalize the mixture of soft and technical skills that are imparted during the Marine Corps' four-week training program. For example, Civil Affairs training emphasizes culture and civil-environment-orientation skills from more of an intelligence perspective, but contemporary missions demand information-related skills. Civil Affairs should not solely be a personality-driven endeavor. Second, many formerly recurring missions with Civil Affairs participation are being discontinued, modified, or have come and gone as one-off opportunities. There is no plan for a repeat of the *USNS Comfort*'s mission, and the MRF-E rotation is no more. These anecdotes serve as indicators of the Marine Corps' longstanding struggle with maintaining a consistent and continuously improving Civil Affairs capability in peacetime and finding meaningful training and development opportunities.

JOINT EMPLOYMENT, RESTRUCTURING, AND
CIVIL-INFORMATION CHALLENGES

In 2014, the navy's Maritime Civil Affairs and Security Training Command (MCAST) folded its colors, and in so doing ended the navy's primary means of supporting the US Embassy Country Teams' strategic and security assistance plans.[44] Now, the Marine Corps must fill the navy's capability gap. Writing in 2019, the commandant noted that the Marine Corps is poised to "maximize our inherent relationship with the navy, along with our expertise coordinating elements of the MAGTF, to effectively coordinate across all warfighting domains to support the Joint force."[45] The Marine Corps supports the Joint Force, and not just the navy, in civil-military operations throughout the world. In addition to improving training to include data-related skills, Civil Affairs marines must adopt a 180-degree approach to improve upon relationships, information flow, and collaboration and communication with adjacent units and agencies.

Across the spectrum of joint operations, consensus and unified effort are achieved through coordination with partners both inside and outside of the military.[46] Nonetheless, the ways in which Civil Affairs personnel across organizations collect, analyze, and share civil information remains a severely limiting factor for meaningful collaboration both within the MAGTF and with external partners. Every engagement with host-nation civilians presents opportunities for passive information collection and messaging. Following an engagement, Civil Affairs marines will typically produce a situation report or a civil information management report for the MAGTF staff. But beyond this, there exists no consistent format or platform for sharing information across units, let alone across services or agencies. For example, each Civil Affairs group applies its own preferred version of civil information management, which exacerbates the problems of segregating information in "stovepipes" and "silos," as will be discussed further next. The resolution of these concerns is all the more urgent due to Civil Affairs's reframing as an information-related capability. If

Marine Corps Civil Affairs is in the "information business," Marine Corps Civil Affairs needs the training and tools to fulfill this critical mission.

To support the reframing of Civil Affairs as an information-related capability, the Marine Corps has established three MEF Information Groups (MIGs), each aligned with a MEF command.[47] The MIGs exist to support operations in the information environment.[48] Within the MIGs, Civil Affairs should be heavily used as a tool for collecting, analyzing, and disseminating civil information. In addition, Civil Affairs can assist with developing battlespace awareness, informing target audiences, fostering relationships with key leaders in the civil network, and influencing operations in coordination with military-information support operations and other special technical capabilities.

A further challenge for Civil Affairs will be to find creative ways to support operations in the information environment, where there is no boots-on-the-ground presence. In a 2020 interview, Lieutenant General Lori Reynolds, Deputy Commandant for Information, noted that, to achieve effects in the information environment, marines need not always be on the ground to inform or influence the population.[49] At present, however, this capability is aspirational. Formal training does not equip Civil Affairs marines with the tools to engage effectively in a remote or distanced environment. That said, this limitation will not prevent innovators, for example, from finding ways to conduct civil reconnaissance in a virtual environment. Echoing chapter 5 on civil knowledge integration, Civil Affairs marines will draw upon their operational art. But a fundamental aspect of effective integration is consistency, and that will be impossible to achieve without improved training and updated doctrine.

Civil Affairs remains a key factor in conducting civil-network analysis and identifying the critical nodes within the civil environment. In a recent interview, Lieutenant Colonel Korvin Kraics and Lieutenant Colonel Jahn Olson, Civil Affairs planners who led teams assigned to III MEF, described their role as providing the "glue" between the military and civilians—understanding the region, recognizing cultural intricacies, and connecting with organizations on the ground.[50] In the context of great power competition, persistent civil engagement will demonstrate the US military's commitment as the "partner of choice, fully capable, ready to respond...and [one that is] not going to leave. [It is] the trusted organization...the organization of good faith."[51] At the joint level and within the MAGTF, Civil Affairs must improve upon its ability to take in large volumes of data, analyze that data, and share useful information. Technology is one part of the solution to this challenge. Enhanced investigative and analytical methods are another. Finally, improved training and education are required to enable Civil Affairs marines to leverage these tools and resources toward the production of consistent, actionable reporting for commanders, their staff, and external agencies.

Within the Marine Corps, an organizational tendency to "stovepipe" or "silo" civil information has been a recurring problem. Case in point: the Marine Corps Civil Information Management System (MARCIMS), the official platform for civil information, does not allow Civil Affairs personnel to share data and integrate data across the Joint Force.[52] Current practitioners have sought alternative platforms, such as the Protected Internet Exchange (PiX) which is accessible beyond the US military to federal agencies with a need for access.[53] The use of PiX has opened up new opportunities to collaborate and to share geospatial, humanitarian, infrastructure-related, demographic, and other kinds of data across agencies. However, PiX has its own limitations. PiX does not "talk" to the Joint Force's other data management systems and requires extra steps and work-arounds to migrate complex civil data into other classified or unclassified systems. Standing alone, it cannot solve all of the information management needs of US agencies.

As the multi-domain operating environment becomes more complex, civil information management will become a more critical Civil Affairs activity. The MIG construct holds promise as a path to better management and integration of civil information across the MAGTF and opens the door to better interagency coordination. As the name itself would suggest, the CAGs should align their information-related capabilities with the MIGs and support planning and mission execution in the information environment. Trends also suggest that Marine Corps Civil Affairs may be integrated with other information operations specialties (psychological operations and strategic communications) to create a single occupational field. If this happens, the need to manage and integrate both classified and unclassified information should create an incentive for the rapid development of improved platforms for storing, using, and disseminating information.

BREAK DOWN THE SILOS

Civil Affairs exists to inform a commander on the human domain and to influence and support civil-military operations. This chapter has highlighted examples of tactical-level excellence in that regard. Yet, the execution of Civil Affairs tasks is largely meaningless in and of itself. Civil Affairs activities must be integrated into operational and strategic frameworks and aligned with interagency efforts. Coordination and information sharing are paramount.

Even so, the 2019 Marine Corps Civil Affairs Concept rightly under-scored the importance of keeping Civil Affairs personnel forward deployed, which would "provide a proactive posture, and enhance American access and influence abroad."[54] Operations "must be coordinated, integrated, and deconflicted with the activities of interorganizational partners, including various [host nation] agencies within and en route to and from the operational area."[55] One strong argument for the early employment of Civil Affairs marines in planning relates to the 38th Commandant's Planning Guidance, which states that "rather than heavily investing in expensive or exquisite capabilities...naval forces will persist with much smaller, low signature, affordable platforms that can econom-ically host a dense array of lethal and nonlethal payloads."[56] Fundamen-tally, Civil Affairs focuses on one thing: crossing the military divide into the civilian environment. No technology produced to date can replicate or replace the face-to-face observation, communication, and learning that takes place through tactical employment of Civil Affairs teams on the ground.

Civil Affairs offers the ultimate low-signature, low-cost, and high-impact capability to understand the civil environment. Many nations desire reassurance that the United States is committed to supporting their mutual strategic interests but do not want an overt visible mani-festation of power in their territory.[57] By keeping a persistent forward presence, Marine Corps Civil Affairs would reinforce the notion that the United States is committed to strong, enduring partnerships, without overemphasizing lethality. Civil Affairs teams, operating with minimal equipment while maintaining a mindset for broad engagement, hold immense potential as a resource-light means to increase a commander's operational reach. By maintaining a persistent forward presence and consistently engaging civilian stakeholders, Marine Corps Civil Affairs can sustain relationships and ensure access for the United States in the future joint operating environment. By breaking down silos and working together with allies, sister services, and across agencies, Civil Affairs can reach a new level of impact across the Joint Force.

NOTES

1. Stephen Goto, "Civil Information: CA is Missing the Moment," *Small Wars Journal*, September 22, 2016, https://smallwarsjournal.com/jrnl/art/civil-information-ca-is-missing-the-moment.
2. USMC MCDP, 1-4 *Competing* (Washington, DC: Dept of the Navy, 2020), 1–6.
3. Vera Zakem and Emily Mushen, *Charting The Course for Civil Affairs in the New Normal* (Arlington, VA: CNA Analysis & Solutions, July 2015), https://apps.dtic.mil/sti/pdfs/AD1014508.pdf.
4. Colonel Valerie Jackson, interview by USMCR, *One CA Podcast* (Civil Affairs Association), April 8, 2018.
5. Although Civil Affairs was not a doctrinally distinct concept prior to the Vietnam era, in practice, the Marine Corps was providing support to civil administration, conducting civil network analysis, and managing other aspects of civil-military operations in small wars and other engagements.
6. Lester D. Langly, *The Banana Wars: United States Intervention in the Carribean, 1898–1934* (Rowman & Littlefield Publishers, 2001), 2.
7. Ibid., 158.
8. US Marine Corps, *Small Wars Manual*, FMFRP 12-15. Revered and relied upon by Marines for more than half a century to carry out small-scale operations, the *Manual* was last reviewed for republication in 1990 after review, it was simply reissued, and includes the original chapters on coordination with the Department of State; host-nation civil-military relationships; managing government functions, including law enforcement, public utilities, business trade and taxation; and holding elections. 13-7, 13-23.
9. Ibid., 457.
10. Ronald E. Hayes II, "Combined Action: U.S. Marines Fighting a Different War August 1965 to May 1971," *Marines in the Vietnam War Commemorative Series* (US Marine Corps History Division, 2019), 2.
11. Ibid., 8.
12. Ibid.
13. Ibid., 5; and Nicholas J. Schlosser, *U.S. Marines and Irregular Warfare - Training and Education, 2000–2010* (US Marine Corps History Division, 2015), 17. At this time in Vietnam, Marine Corps Civil Affairs did not exist, and so the Marines found support from the US Army, which landed

the 29th Civil Affairs Company to support III MAF activities in the I Corps region. The Marine Corps established an organic Civil Affairs capability in February 1966 with the Marine Corp Reserve's 4th Civil Affairs Group, activated at the Navy Yard in Washington, DC. This unit never mobilized during Vietnam. It is difficult to account for the transferable lessons from the Combined Action Program and to tell whether those lessons were passed on to the 4th Civil Affairs Group following the war.

14. Ibid., 13.
15. Ibid., 10, 25.
16. Ibid., 49.
17. Charles J. Quilter II, USMCR, *U.S. Marines in the Persian Gulf 1990–1991: With the I Marine Expeditionary Force in Desert Shield and Desert Storm* (Washington, DC: US Marine Corps History and Museums Division, 1993), 65–66.
18. Ibid.
19. Ibid., 27.
20. Ibid., 65–66.
21. Ibid., 66.
22. Kathleen H. Hicks and Christine E. Wormuth, *The Future of U.S. Civil Affairs Forces* (Center for Strategic & International Studies Report, February 2009), 7, https://csis-website-prod.s3.amazonaws.com/s3fs-public/legacy_files/files/publication/130409_Hicks_FutureCivilAffairs_Web.pdf .
23. Ibid.
24. Schlosser, *U.S. Marines and Irregular Warfare*, 45–46.
25. For example, *see* Colonel Stephen S. Evans (compilation), *U.S. Marines and Irregular Warfare, 1898–2007: Anthology and Selected Bibliography* (Marine Corps University Press, 2008), pt. 7.
26. Barak A. Salmoni, "Advances in Predeployment Culture Training: The U.S. Marine Corps Approach," *Military Review* (US Army University Press; November–December 2006): 80.
27. Barak A. Salmoni and Paula Holmes-Eber, *Operational Culture for the Warfighter: Principles and Applications* (Quantico, Marine Corps University Press, 2008), 3.
28. For example, see ibid., 3. Candidly, the authors of that volume noted that "[i]n recent years, 'Irregular Warfare' (IW) has been the framework through which the US and allied militaries have thought about military

operations," tacitly acknowledging that the Marine Corps had shifted from its historical naval approach to operations to a land-based mindset.

29. For example, see R. Jeffrey Smith, "US Military Admits Major Mistakes in Iraq and Afghanistan," *The Atlantic*, June 11, 2012, https://www.theatlantic.com/international/archive/2012/06/us-military-admits-major-mistakes-in-iraq-and-afghanistan/258339/; Jason Dempsey, "Coming to Terms with America's Undeniable Failure in Afghanistan," *War on the Rocks*, February 11, 2019, https://warontherocks.com/2019/02/coming-to-terms-with-americas-undeniable-failure-in-afghanistan/; and Anthony H. Cordesman, "America's Failed Strategy in the Middle East: Losing Iraq and the Gulf," *CSIS*, January 2, 2020, https://www.csis.org/analysis/americas-failed-strategy-middle-east-losing-iraq-and-gulf.

30. Tom Friedman, interview by Robert Siegel, "Powell's Cautions on Iraq," *All Things Considered*, April 20, 2004, https://www.npr.org/templates/story/story.php?storyId=1844476.

31. Ronald E. Hayes II, "Combined Action: U.S. Marines Fighting a Different War August 1965 to May 1971," *Marines in the Vietnam War Commemorative Series* (US Marine Corps History Division, 2019), 2.

32. James Jabinal and Valerie Jackson, "Forward and Enduring - Rethinking Civil Affairs," *Marine Corps Gazette*, September 2019, WE45, https://mca-marines.org/wp-content/uploads/Jabinal-Jackson.pdf.

33. Special Inspector General for Afghanistan Reconstruction, *What We Need to Learn: Lessons from Twenty Years of Afghanistan Reconstruction* (August 2021), 60.

34. Lieutenant Colonel Christopher O'Donnell, USMCR (ret.), interview by Diana X. Moga and Robert Boudreau, January 22, 2021.

35. Others have noted the tendency to equate success with dollars spent. See, for example, Matthew F. Cancian, "Counterinsurgency as Cargo Cult," *Marine Corps Gazette* (January 2013).

36. J. P. Hesford and Paul Haskins, "U.S. Marine Corps Security Cooperation," *The DISAM Journal* (September 2008).

37. Julia L. Watson, "Female Engagement Teams: The Case for More Female Civil Affairs Marines," *Marine Corps Gazette*, July 2011.

38. Lawrence D. Nicholson, interview conducted by Michael I. Moffett on June 9, 2010, in David W. Kummer, *U.S. Marines in Afghanistan, 2001-2009 - Anthology and Annotated Bibliography*, Marine Corps History Division (Quantico: US Marine Corps History Division, 2014).

39. Brigitte Rohwerder, "Lessons from Female Engagement Teams," GSDRC Applied Knowledge Services, 2015, https://gsdrc.org/publications/lessons-from-female-engagement-teams/.
40. Aniela Szymanski, "A Woman in Charge: A Civil Affairs Marine Team Leader Experience in Afghanistan," *Marines at War - Stories from Afghanistan and Iraq* (Marine Corps University Press, 2016), 145–147.
41. Ibid., 144, 149.
42. Jabinal and Jackson, "Forward and Enduring - Rethinking Civil Affairs," WE46.
43. US Marine Corps, "Marine Rotational Force- Europe Transfer of Authority Ceremony," Marines official website, https://www.marforeur.marines.mil/News/News-Article-Display/Article/2206102/marine-rotational-force-europe-transfer-of-authority/.
44. Matthew Daniels, "Navy Disestablishes MCAST," Defense Visual Information Distribution Service, May 16, 2014, https://www.dvidshub.net/news/130141/navy-disestablishes-mcast.
45. Department of the Navy, *Commandant's Planning Guidance.* https://www.marines.mil/Portals/1/Publications/Commandant's%20Planning%20Guidance_2019.pdf?ver=2019-07-17-090732-937.
46. US Joint Chiefs of Staff, *Joint Publication 1 – Doctrine for the Armed Forces of the United States* (2017), II–8.
47. US Marine Corps, *Marine Air Ground Task Force Information Environment Operations Concept of Employment* (July 6, 2017), 2, https://www.trngcmd.marines.mil/Portals/207/Docs/wtbn/MCCMOS/FINAL%20MAGTF%20IE%20OPS%20CoE%202017-07-06.pdf?ver=2017-11-16-090225-057.
48. Ibid.
49. Lieutenant General Lori Reynolds, USMC, interview by Beverly Kirk, "Marines on the Information Battlefield," *Smart Women, Smart Power Podcast* (Center for Strategic & International Studies, 2020), https://www.csis.org/node/55495.
50. Jahn Olson and Korvin Kraics, USMC, interview by Rob Boudreau, *One CA Podcast* (Civil Affairs Association, 2021).
51. Ibid.
52. Diana X. Moga and Abraham Blocker, "Technology Innovations in Information Operations," *Eunomia Journal* (2020), https://www.civilaffairsassoc.org/post/technology-innovations-in-information-operations.

53. Paul J. Hendrick, Edward B. Lescher, and Matthew T. Peterson, "Digital Civil Reconnaissance," *Eunomia Journal* (2020) https://www.civilaffairsassoc.org/post/digital-civ-recon.

54. Robert Bodreau, Don Newberry, and Richard Phillips, "The 2019 Marine Corps Civil Affairs Concept: An Ambitious Step Toward Improved Integration," *Small Wars Journal*, October 14, 2019, https://smallwarsjournal.com/jrnl/art/2019-marine-corps-civil-affairs-concept-ambitious-step-toward-improved-integration.

55. US Joint Chiefs of Staff, *Joint Publication 1 – Doctrine for the Armed Forces of the United States*, II–13.

56. Department of the Navy, *Commandant's Planning Guidance.*

57. Anthony P. Terlizzi, "The Civil Affairs Force: A Reimagining," *Marine Corps Gazette* (March 2020), 20.

CHAPTER 9

BUILDING A GLOBAL
CIVIL-MILITARY NETWORK

Christopher Holshek

"When you go alone, you go fast; when you go together, you go far."

–Cyrus H. McCormick [1]

Civil Affairs is the US military's primary capability for civil-military engagement and likewise for the maintenance of civil-military relationships. Across the rest of the NATO alliance, these tasks fall principally to Civil-Military Cooperation forces. CIMIC forces are also military forces which are subtly different yet broadly comparable and interoperable with Civil Affairs forces. This chapter argues for enhanced collaboration between Civil Affairs and CIMIC, which would be a powerful means through which the West could pursue its strategic objectives without resorting to armed conflict. [2] The following discussion examines how such collaboration can raise Civil Affairs's profile within the US military as a competitive asset, and also surveys the NATO and UN versions of CIMIC, as well as those of the United Kingdom, Canada, and Australia.

The impetus for collaborative civil-military action goes back to the Cold War, when the collective moral and material power of the transatlantic alliance bested the Soviet Union. What has made NATO more than just a political or military alliance—the resiliency and strength of which has endured well beyond its expected shelf life—has been a transcontinental community sharing the values of freedom, liberal democracy, and free markets. Taken for granted since the Cold War, a global network as such is even more vital in an era in which strategic competition has taken precedence over operational conflict. The cross-cultural bonds of networked civil-military enterprises constitute one of the West's greatest competitive advantages, and these bonds can be cultivated and sustained through enhanced partnership between US Civil Affairs forces and their CIMIC counterparts.

Strategic competition is a clash of civilizations: a moral, societal, and political struggle among (and within) states, pitting authoritarianism against democracy. The goal of strategic competition is "winning without fighting by leveraging all elements of national power," as Army Chief of Staff General James McConville has stated.[3] The military—as much an instrument of diplomacy as it is of war—has a critical enabling role.

Influence capabilities such as Civil Affairs, Psychological Operations (PSYOP), Information Operations (IO), and Foreign Area Officers (FAOs) should take center stage in this effort. Civil Affairs constitutes an ideal capability in military support to competition. Within this framework, one of Civil Affairs's most important roles is to develop and leverage civil networks. As highlighted in chapter 6, Civil Affairs does this by, with, and through a vast array of military and civilian partners.

A key objective of the latest *National Security Strategy* and *National Defense Strategy* is to "strengthen alliances and attract new partners." At the 2020 Civil Affairs Association Symposium, retired US Army lieutenant general and former Defense Security Cooperation Agency director Charles Hooper stressed how mutually beneficial global alliances provide decisive advantages over geopolitical competitors. "The challenge is not attracting new partners, it is about retaining partners," he warned. "Our engagement with our partners must be persistent, not episodic, to build the long-term relationships that provide our partners with the value they desire and [to] build human capital" that, in turn, can be leveraged to prevail in competition and crisis management as well as conflict. "We're not building nations anymore," he concluded. "We're building networks."[4]

In a hyperconnected, information-intensive global security ecosystem, a persistent global civil-military network would be a geostrategic game-changer. To build it, it must be institutionalized within a structured international collaborative framework among civil-military professionals. This requires a far more deliberate collaborative effort between US Civil Affairs and their CIMIC counterparts around the world.

NETWORKING IN A COMPETITION CONTINUUM

"Military competition encompasses the range of activities and operations employed to achieve political objectives, and to deny adversaries the ability to achieve objectives prejudicial to the United States," states the latest *Civil Affairs Operations* doctrine (*FM 3-57*). The document calls competition "the condition when two or more actors in the international system have competing and potentially incompatible interests but neither seeks to escalate to open conflict in pursuit of those interests."[5]

Access, influence, and legitimacy are vital positional advantages in competition. This is especially true when US forces act as the "visiting team," lacking firsthand cultural knowledge. According to the US Army War College's online publication forum *War Room*, the aim of strategic competition is to gain and retain access and influence to preserve a rules-based international order favorable to Western values.[6] These positional advantages come largely through the security cooperation activities and persistent forward presence of influence capabilities like Civil Affairs, whose reconnaissance, engagement, and networking enable strategic depth, situational understanding, and early warning.

Access, influence, and legitimacy begin with *knowledge*. Among the persistent shortcomings of US Civil Affairs, during and since the Cold War, has been its broad unfamiliarity with its CIMIC partners in NATO and the UN, even though the US is a founding member of both organizations. There is little-to-no discussion of CIMIC in US civil-military doctrine, nor is there any CIMIC orientation for most Civil Affairs personnel. Nor, to date, has there been any exchange of permanent liaisons or representatives at respective Civil Affairs and CIMIC proponent offices or major commands. Closer institutional ties would enable Civil Affairs to leverage more steadily their CIMIC counterparts' unique local access, insight, legitimacy, and influence, helping US forces overcome their characteristic insularity and self-referencing and make it more of the learning organization it needs to be to win in strategic competition.

By building an enterprise of civil-military enterprises, Civil Affairs could harness thousands of interpersonal bonds and scores of interorganizational connections, to the great benefit of the commanders and statesmen they support. Such an effort will require structure and foresight. Forces like Civil Affairs and CIMIC should collaborate institutionally to establish the human, strategic, and operational capital necessary to succeed in the human domain.

The Benefits of Going Global

The reasons for greater Civil Affairs–CIMIC networking and interoperability run along institutional as well as strategic and operational lines. Robust and overlapping networks of civil-military professionals will generate access and influence in support of strategic assessment and warning, strategic and operational vision, more coherent operational preparation of the environment, regional and cultural understanding and civil knowledge, political-military and command decision-making and coalition decision cycles, civil-military integration, risk management and mitigation; information operations, stabilization and civil or societal resilience, anti-access/area denial; force protection, measures of effectiveness and performance, and many other desired outcomes.

In strategic competition, knowledge is power—at times, more in relation to *whom* one knows than what. Whether for combat operations, irregular warfare, gray-zone encounters, or continuous competition with state and nonstate actors, advantage falls to the force that acculturates a superior learning network. A trademark attribute of civil-military professionals is their ability to find answers (more so than knowing them offhand)—Civil Affairs's most competent professionals are consummate networkers, which is a diplomatic skill. Besides, the exchange of intellectual capital, doctrinal insights, tactics, techniques, procedures, and other "best practices" advances the overall state of the art. It also sharpens the acumen of forces that struggle to maintain relevance in military cultures that favor the physical over the psychological, and the tactical over the strategic.

Civil Affairs and CIMIC face a constant struggle to be seen as something other than "force multipliers," "enablers," or "combat support," rather than as maneuver forces in the human domain and the moral spaces or war and peace. By rebranding themselves as such—with unique access and influence in a global civil-military engagement enterprise with a vastly expanded mission template—they can more coherently expand and advocate their strategic and operational value. They can also integrate their competencies to much greater effect, something that equally benefits the people they support and themselves.

At the same time, Civil Affairs and CIMIC are gravitating toward greater integration with other information-related capabilities such as PSYOP, FAOs, cyber, and public affairs. As a force for influence, Civil Affairs gains advantage through knowledge of regional and local dynamics. International, interorganizational relationships are an unmatched channel through which that knowledge can be gained. As an expeditionary force, these warrior diplomats must help overcome the inherent American handicap of being a "visiting team" in having to win access, influence, and legitimacy. Ties to NATO CIMIC, for example, are helping Civil Affairs relearn coordination norms in more politically mature countries (rather than the failed or fragile states they were in for the last two decades).[7]

NATO's Contribution

Among civil-military enterprises, Civil Affairs is the elder statesman, dating back to the late nineteenth-century, whereas NATO and UN versions entered the scene in the late twentieth and early twenty-first centuries. But "civil affairs" denotes a military capability for what the rest of the world brands as "CIMIC," which is both a capability (in the form of specially trained and designated CIMIC forces) and an activity (insofar as any member of the military can partake in civil-military cooperation in the course of their duties, and thus perform "CIMIC"). NATO CIMIC is the most commonly referenced among civil-military enterprises. It is also the template for most national civil-military concepts, in and outside of NATO. The majority of NATO (and many non-NATO) nations either cite NATO civil-military policy and doctrine directly or leverage it heavily in their own national concepts. There is one major exception to this: the United States, whose civil-military doctrines overlook it.

The European answer to Civil Affairs, NATO CIMIC has its origins in early 1980s Germany. The CIMIC operational concept centered around liaison and civil-military coordination in support of two major tasks: minimizing civilian interference in military operations and facilitating wartime logistical support to NATO formations. While the latter function has lessened in importance, the former task remains a major feature of NATO CIMIC. As the Cold War ended, NATO fielded a CIMIC doctrine and organized into two groups, above and below the Alps. CIMIC Group North became the CIMIC Centre of Excellence in The Hague in 2001. Much like the US Army John F. Kennedy Special Warfare Center & School, the CIMIC Centre of Excellence oversees doctrinal and force integration as well as training and education of NATO CIMIC forces.

CIMIC Group South gained a more operational role with increasing "out-of-area" missions in Iraq and Afghanistan, becoming the NATO Multinational CIMIC Group in 2009. Based in Motta di Livenza, Italy, the Multinational CIMIC Group is under the direction of the J9 in the Partnership Directorate at Supreme Headquarters Allied Powers Europe. Essentially a multinational CIMIC battalion, it deploys on the orders of the Supreme Allied Commander Europe orders to integrate civil considerations into NATO operational planning, support stabilization and reconstruction, or conduct CIMIC advisory missions in Africa.

As a capability, NATO CIMIC enjoys clear executive authority in NATO's Military Committee. As an activity, it differs from Civil Affairs operations in that CIMIC receives strategic direction and politico-military guidance, first from the North Atlantic Council's strategic concept of "comprehensive engagement" (i.e., civil-military and multiagency engagement) and then from the policy of civil-military interaction, which is "founded on communication, planning and coordination that all NATO military bodies share and conduct with international and local non-military actors."[8] CIMIC, then, is the military capability that NATO possess to coordinate civil-military interaction on the ground. Given the essentiality of clear strategic and political-military direction in competition, this is a distinct comparative advantage.

Compared to US civil-military policy and doctrine, NATO civil-military interaction policy (*MC 411/2*) and CIMIC doctrine (*AJP 3.19*) assume a less direct role for the military in population engagement. Being a multinational framework, it pays particular heed to civilian direction of military activities. Civil-military transition management in NATO CIMIC is also more elucidated. Seen as "negotiated processes with the host nation and other actors," they are "non-linear and dependent on host nation political processes and interests, which may change over time." *AJP 3.19* also prioritizes earliest transition planning, pointing out how "interaction with multinational and interagency actors, as well as those within the host nation, provides an effective means for building shared ownership and understanding of transition activities." [9]

NATO CIMIC aims less to be a sensor of civil threats (in contrast to Civil Affairs's civil reconnaissance) or to directly influence populations. Instead, it emphasizes civil analysis in cooperation with civilian entities to help commanders have common understanding of the civil environment. For political reasons, NATO CIMIC activities cannot target their own or allied country populations, much like Civil Affairs cannot operate domestically under the Posse Comitatus Act. This precedence of analysis over engagement is also limited by the small size and limited professional specialization of most NATO CIMIC forces. (Keep in mind the total number of all CIMIC forces of all kinds in the world would still be a fraction of the twelve thousand plus designated Civil Affairs personnel in the US Army and Marine Corps.)

Within the NATO comprehensive approach and civil-military interaction concepts that frame CIMIC, military support to "non-military actors and the civil environment" is limited to creating conditions that support the accomplishment of the military mission. NATO CIMIC doctrine acknowledges cross-cutting topics (protection of civilians; children and armed conflict; women, peace, and security; and cultural property protection) that require constant consideration. Although they "fall outside of the military responsibilities," these issues are nonetheless central to contemporary military operations. [10]

In some ways, NATO CIMIC concepts are comparatively progressive. The 2018 version of CIMIC doctrine, for example, already discusses the role of gender advisors and staff processes to integrate gender perspective into planning, execution, and evaluation of military operations. (The 2021 US Civil Affairs doctrine mentions neither gender nor the DoD's *Women, Peace and Security Strategic Framework and Implementation Plan* approved the year prior.)[11] That version of *AJP 3.19* notes how a mixed gender force enhances information-sharing and is "instrumental in garnering trust and credibility."[12] It also notes how CIMIC information gathering should not be conflated with intelligence and how the military should use the lowest classification possible to promote civil-military information sharing.[13] This emphasis, as well as the importance of civil-military transition management in multinational civil-military enterprises as in NATO or the UN, are particularly important baseline considerations for a global civil-military network. At the same time, interallied civil-military integration for cognitive warfare and societal resilience to counter hybrid warfare has gained importance.[14] Civil Affairs–CIMIC collaboration along these lines would be especially synergistic and highly productive.

In recognition of the need for a transatlantic civil-military network, the CIMIC Centre of Excellence initiated a CIMIC-CA Synchronization Project in 2020, along three lines of operation. First were the simultaneous education and training of Civil Affairs and CIMIC personnel on respective policy mandates, authorities, capabilities, and limitations, especially in support of vulnerable member states. Second was harmonization of NATO and US civil-military doctrines. The third was formalized relations between the CIMIC Centre of Excellence and US Army John F. Kennedy Special Warfare Center and School, along with professional organizations like the Civil Affairs Association. The project has created institutional impetus to stimulate the synchronization of comparative advantages, facilitate a professional interorganizational learning network, and share operational insights in civil-military competition for influence.

The United Nations as a Global Civil-Military Enterprise

Gaining and maintaining access and influence in a global civil-military network necessitates understanding UN as well as NATO concepts that inform the civil-military enterprises of most partner nations. With over ninety-thousand military personnel deployed to twelve field missions, the UN oversees the operations of the largest collective civil-military stabilization force in the world. Most are in Africa, a pivotal region of strategic competition. African-troop and police-contributing countries, in turn, provide about 50 percent of the UN's uniformed personnel. The African

Union draws from UN civil-military coordination templates informing the civil-military doctrines of many troop contributing countries.

UN field missions pose risks and opportunities for US geostrategic interests because the involvement of competitors like Russia and China has grown—which enables them not only to provide greater access and influence in the pursuit of regional interests but also to shape institutional, policy, and operational changes to UN peace operations. At the same time, greater US military staff involvement at UN headquarters and field missions offer opportunities to counter such ambitions. Concurrently, US personnel gain positional advantage through having their own access, influence, and legitimacy, developing experience in multinational coalitions, improving peacekeeping capacity-building programs, and building goodwill.[15]

With the exception of Civil Affairs teams supporting counterterrorism in Africa (exemplified in chapter 6), many of them have conducted building-partner capacity missions with little knowledge of the doctrinal frameworks to which their partners most refer. Instead, they often defer to US civil-military doctrines (e.g., Civil Affairs doctrine Field Manual 3-57) to teach international partners that work more within multinational frameworks than their American mentors. Civil Affairs doctrine contains valuable tactics and techniques (e.g., civil reconnaissance and civil engagement, which, in fact, have gained greater traction in UN civil-military guidelines). However, US civil-military capacity building would be even more effective if presented in the context of peace and stability operations under integrated, civilian leadership and a multilateral mandate under which most of these forces tend to operate. The implied task is that Civil Affairs needs to learn more about its audience.

Looking beyond Africa, one can see that many UN troop and police contributing countries in Latin America and Asia also reference the two parallel but complementary UN frameworks for civil-military coordination: UN-CMCoord and UN-CIMIC. UN-CMCoord is the humanitarian concept for "the essential dialogue and interaction between civilian and military actors in humanitarian emergencies that is necessary to protect and promote humanitarian principles, avoid competition, minimize inconsistency and, when appropriate, pursue common goals."[16] US forces have experienced this framework, having provided humanitarian aid in response to the 2010 Haiti earthquake and numerous natural disasters in the INDOPACOM region.

UN-CIMIC is a military staff function (rather than a type of operation) that facilitates the interface among the military, police, and civilian components of an integrated UN field mission—as well as among military forces and various humanitarian and development actors, local authorities, donor agencies, NGOs, host governments, and civil-society organizations. "Civil engagement," now an operational term in the revised *UN Infantry Battalion Manual*, includes a new requirement for each battalion to field an engagement platoon of four teams of four personnel (much like Civil Affairs's deployed team structure) to promote civil stability and interact with local authorities and populations—all to improve UN mission situational understanding of the *human terrain*.[17]

The UN has contributed greatly to the global civil-military enterprise. One example is the integrated field mission model of operationalized civil-military interagency cooperation. Another is the *human security* concept from the 1994 *Human Development Report* that prioritizes the protection of civilians in stabilization.[18] Peacebuilding and conflict prevention, as operational concepts, also grew from this. More recently, deployed UN engagement platoons and CIMIC staff must comprise at least 50 percent women, per the Secretary General's gender mainstreaming strategy under UN Security Council Resolution 1325—a far bolder move than in the 2019 *United States Strategy on Women, Peace and Security* or the aforementioned 2020 DoD framework.[19]

Partner Nation Mindsets
The British and Canadian armies do not have formal civil-military doctrines for what they often refer to as "CIMIC." Instead, they cite

NATO civil-military policy and doctrine. At the same time, however, they have consistently taken a more operationally integrative approach to CIMIC than most military forces, including the US. Although allied armies are similarly preoccupied with major combat operations, given their much smaller size, they are more open to a "small-war" or irregular warfare methods—a comparative advantage over US land forces, whose more conventional "big-war" and "warfighting" mentality views Civil Affairs as working mainly for reconstruction and stabilization. For the British and Canadians, therefore, CIMIC is more a mindset of many than it is a skill set of a specialized few. The idea that every officer must know CIMIC and that every soldier has a CIMIC mission has won easier application to gray-zone competition for them than for Americans.

In the British Army, the gravitation to small-war approaches has led to the Integrated Operating Framework, which distinguishes "operating" from "warfighting."[20] In an era of persistent competition, unconventional and conventional deterrent postures must be more dynamically managed. Of interest to Civil Affairs, the Integrated Operating Framework also calls for the forward deployment of "civil-military relations" personnel— with a near-term focus on engagement and a long-term focus on standoff capabilities in a layered approach to British military strategy. Training and exercising with partners are paths to build capacities and relationships in target countries. Civil-military capabilities have a key role in these efforts, understanding context and aligning partners with shared values and aspirations. For this reason, the Integrated Operating Framework places a premium on building alliances and improving interoperability, especially with US forces.

Canadian CIMIC comes under the direction of the Canadian Peace Support Centre and the Canadian Army's Influence Activities Task Force. The Canadians use "CIMIC," "PSYOP," and "IO" more integrally in their operational language, with CIMIC-PSYOP teaming in deployed units at operational and tactical levels. This is remarkable, given how much Civil

Affairs-PSYOP operational integration remains a struggle in conventional US Army formations.

The Canadian Army's Influence Activities Task Force also has considerable experience in CIMIC-PSYOP integration, including Provincial Reconstruction Teams in Afghanistan and support to the international delivery of humanitarian aid and disaster response. To obtain non-military viewpoints, the Influence Activities Task Force shares information with international organizations, NGOs, local and foreign governments and militaries, the media, and affected populations to assess effects delivery as much for mission preparation as execution. Social media analyses are also leveraged. The emphasis on civil analysis from steady-state cooperation with civilian entities comprises the main institutional effort in Canadian CIMIC-PSYOP operational readiness, much as NATO CIMIC does in its support of civil-military interaction. These have important learning implications for Civil Affairs in military support to strategic competition.

In addition to more traditional techniques, Canadian CIMIC-PSYOP activities, especially in humanitarian assistance and disaster response, feature *communicating with communities.* Key leader engagement is also driven by influence mapping and civil needs assessments drawn from steady-state open-source data collection. The resulting civil knowledge helps support a more holistic intelligence picture as well as media and message analysis, monitoring related portals and apps, and "horizon scanning"—first, to improve common civil operational picture; second, to influence target populations more comprehensively; and third, to better anticipate threats from the civil environment.

Australian CIMIC offers additional resources and insight as well as breadth of coverage to the global network. Much of its formative experience comes from its own civil-military affairs operations in Vietnam. During and after the Cold War, Australian Defense Force civil-military capability developed along the lines of emerging NATO CIMIC doctrine as well as from the US Civil Affairs in deployments to the Balkans, Iraq, and Afghanistan. Then came its involvement in UN peace operations and regional actions in the Western Pacific, such as the Australian-led International Force East Timor and humanitarian operations after the 2004 tsunami in Indonesia and typhoons in the Philippines. Throughout these years, the eclectic Australian civil-military learning experience has drawn from military-heavy combat, counterinsurgency, and stabilization operations to civilian-led complex emergency responses.

As a result, close cooperation with a wide array of governmental and nongovernmental organizations at national and multinational levels has shaped a whole-of-government approach to civil-military integration that echoes growing recognition in the US of the need for more intense civil-military, interagency, and interorganizational interoperability for strategic competition. From an operational as well as interagency perspective, civil-military-police coordination leverages the unique capabilities of individual agencies and the diversity of different expertise, roles, responsibilities, and approaches to planning through a collaborative culture among three major components (much as UN-integrated field missions do). These three components—the civilian, military, and police components—make up the unified Australian Government Civil-Military Centre. Although each agency has well-developed processes to meet internal requirements, they also "leverage the value that comes from bringing together diverse approaches, skills and ways of thinking."[21] This has important implications considering the growing threat of dark networks and illicit (e.g., multinational criminal) organizations linked to malevolent actors, from adversarial states to violent extremist syndicates, in a strategic competition environment.

What most of the NATO, British, Canadian, and US civil-military approaches have in common is that they see civil-military capabilities as an operational tool for military command and control, conducted in the service of the commander in the execution of military tasks. In the Australian and UN versions—and in NATO civil-military interaction—civil-military enterprises fall under civilian interagency coordination frameworks. This has enabled system-wide policies and mechanisms adaptable to a wide range of missions and circumstances. In many respects, this more confederated approach could be a conceptual model for a global civil-military network for influence.

Nevertheless, there are more complementarities (if not compatibilities) among all these civil-military approaches than at first glance. Most major international players are realizing, in different ways, how the complex strategic and operational landscape impacts civil-military approaches. They also increasingly understand the need for comprehensive, collaborative, and coordinated approaches focused more on community-based civil society solutions to national and international security challenges—again, reflecting more inherently democratic approaches to societal issues and the values that come with these approaches. The key for any civil-military practitioner is to learn enough about these varying but overlapping approaches to facilitate greater networking and interoperability while protecting the integrity of equities among disparate multilateral, regional, and national organizations working for a common purpose, the synergy of which is far greater than the sum of its parts. This, in essence, is the civil-military operational art.

An Opportunity for American Leadership

There is a clear case for greater Civil Affairs networking and interoperability, particularly among NATO and partner states that contribute to UN peace operations. Operationalizing this network's collective power, however, first requires institutionalizing it. A global network of civil-military enterprises will generate its own momentum once sufficient organizational impetus is reached. The NATO CIMIC Centre of Excellence's focus on doctrine and education is a starting point. Initiative from Europe is both timely and needed, yet there is also a clear opportunity for American leadership in this process because the United States owns the world's largest, most established and experienced, and best-developed civil-military enterprise. The following courses of action could help bring this network to a desired tipping point:

- Ensure discussion in FM 3-57 *Civil Affairs Operation Joint Publication* and JP 3-57 *Civil-Military Operations* of NATO and UN CIMIC/CMCoord doctrines, their major differences with US doctrine, and their significance to Civil Affairs. This would improve American interoperability with military partners more used to operating under UN mandate, in NATO operations, or in support of international humanitarian assistance.

- Familiarize Civil Affairs personnel on NATO and UN CIMIC doctrines, organizations, and operations in the Civil Affairs Qualification Course and at unit levels. The US Army John F. Kennedy Special Warfare Center and School and major US Army and Marine Corps Civil Affairs commands need not develop any curriculum for this. Instead, they can leverage, for example, the short online course the NATO CIMIC Centre of Excellence has prepared for this very purpose as well as information from the US Army Peacekeeping and Stability Operations Institute.

- For Civil Affairs units preparing to deploy on overseas missions associated with the UN, the special warfare center and school could also make available the US-based Peace Operations Training Institute online course Civil-Military Operations in Peace Operations for an appropriate introduction to American officers on UN-CIMIC, UNCMCoord, and how civil-military integration works in a UN field mission. For even deeper dives, there is a UN Integrated Training Service special training module on UN-CIMIC, United Nations Institute for Training and Research training modules on civil-military coordination, as well as the Office for the Coordination of Humanitarian Affairs' Civil-Military Coordination eCourse on UNCMCoord. All these should be recognized as Civil Affairs training resources.

- Conversely, as part of mission preparation, Civil Affairs personnel should be prepared to provide Civil Affairs/Civil Military Operations familiarization and interoperability briefings to their CIMIC partners, as well as brief US regional and task force command contacts on interoperability with CIMIC.

- In order to build relationships, Army and Marine Corps Civil Affairs commands can also invite personnel from these organizations and/or their CIMIC partners to their commands, to participate in planning conferences, exercises, and provide allied and partner CIMIC insights and perspectives. Web-based meeting technologies enable this in lieu of travel resources.

- As the largest stakeholder in the Civil Affairs community, the US Army Civil Affairs and Psychological Operations Command should deploy a reserve component Civil Affairs field-grade officer with CIMIC experience working as a military representative of the Civil Affairs Corps at the CIMIC Centre of Excellence to improve interoperability and for Civil Affairs–CIMIC coordination. This evokes the forward deployment engagement of the British Integrated Operating Framework.

- With respect to Chinese and Russian military penetration of UN field missions, US Army Civil Affairs and Psychological Operations Command in particular should have in its annual Program Objective Memorandum (POM) deployments of twenty to thirty personnel (including a significant number of women) as part of the US Military Observer Group - Washington, a multiservice national strategic contingent managed by the US Army G-3/4/7 staff in the Pentagon. These "strategic scouts" and "strategic enablers" would form a cadre of Civil Affairs personnel with priceless global networks and inside knowledge of UN operations (and the access and influence that comes with it).[22] Civil Affairs personnel would epitomize the idea of global warrior diplomats, bringing even greater value to the commands they support. US Army Civil Affairs and Psychological Operations Command should also include in its POM the assignment of one or two senior Civil Affairs officers to serve continuously at the UN Office of Military Affairs for access and influence on UN strategic military planning and doctrinal development at the UN headquarters in New York, as retired Major General Hugh Van Roosen has done.

- Along all these lines, military civil-military institutions should not overlook the value of related professional associations such as the Civil Affairs Association, as well as private-sector partners in human, behavioral, and cyber sciences and technologies. They are positioned to provide practical and informal incentives

to global civil-military networking, as well as contribute to
intellectual capitalization and operational enrichment in ways that
organizations under stringent government regulations cannot.

Going Farther Together

Interaction between soldiers and civilians is as old as peace and war.
Civilians have always been present in war zones, often at the center of
gravity in determining winners and losers. The civil-military enterprise
is an inherently *strategic* endeavor, regardless of naming, doctrinal
approach, mission, and operational setting. At its most basic level, it
involves managing the interaction between military and civilian actors
with respect to political, security, humanitarian, developmental, and other
social challenges to attain larger strategic goals. Across that continuum,
it is the management of the transition from conflict to peace and from
military to civilian dominance of that process. It is at the nexus of
winning without fighting by bringing in all elements of national power and
generating positional advantage through greater influence and access.

Especially at tactical levels, civil-military professionals must *think
globally and act locally* (or think strategically and act tactically), artfully
leveraging and integrating comparative advantages while mitigating
risks and limitations. Far too often misconstrued as an exercise in public
affairs or community outreach, the civil-military enterprise is gaining
appreciation as an instrument of strategic narrative because of its ability
to reach populations directly or by, with, and through critical partners
who either serve as influencers or influence them.

Given the gravity and complexity of their mission, civil-military
personnel must possess first-rate cognitive capacities, knowledge, and
networks. They must be multitalented; highly anticipatory as well as
adaptive; have superior assessment, planning, and project management
capabilities; and also be skilled in negotiation and mediation across
cultural and interorganizational lines. More than being able to think
outside the box," they must be able to understand and explain the "box"
they and those they work for, by, with, and through are already in, from

multiple perspectives. They must contend with a plethora of policy and operational frameworks, working effectively in and between military and civilian worlds—as such, they must be multicultural and multilingual. They must also be effective speakers and writers. All this requires, as the British, Canadians, and Australians emphasize, is a mindset more than a skill set. As warrior diplomats, they should be among the first, rather than later, draft picks for the military-support-to-competition roster.

In this context, the idea of diversity as a source of organizational strength takes on even greater importance. In a collaborative, global civil-military network, a more conscientious leveraging of the comparative advantages of partnership generates outcomes that no one partner alone can produce. This is the inherent advantage of alliances whose forces come from open, pluralistic, and democratic societies—networks and networking themselves being inherently collaborative and democratic. It also presupposes maintaining an interorganizational learning culture that values the contribution of even the smallest of partners. As for the largest of them, it presumes the greatest among leadership traits: humility.

What binds protagonists in this metaculture—whether civilian, police, or military—is a sense of public service to three constituencies: the interests of the countries they come from, the host nation and local communities they assist, and the international community whose collective power they represent and have stake in. Among the most effective ways they influence others is through their own behavior. In this century, *Military Strategy in the 21st Century* notes that "strategic advantage will emerge from how we engage with and understand people and access political, economic, and social networks to achieve a position of relative advantage that complements American military strength. The state that best understands local context and builds a network around relationships harnessing local capacity is more likely to win the twenty-first-century 'struggle for the flanks.' In this connected world, even more than before, the decisive battle will occur before the first shot is fired as actors compete to amplify internal divisions and develop key partnerships."[23]

That sounds a lot like a global network of twenty-first century warrior diplomats, working together to go farther and not just faster.

NOTES

1. Cyrus H. McCormick, "Men and Teamwork," *The Harvester World* (Chicago: International Harvester Company, 1917).
2. Nicholas Krohley and Stefan Muelhich, "NATO CIMIC & US Civil Affairs: Doctrinal Review & Comparative Assessment," *NATO CIMIC Centre of Excellence*, June 15, 2022, https://www.cimic-coe.org/resources/ ccoe-publications/nato-cimic-us-ca-doctrinal-review-and-comparative- assessment.pdf. Notably, the term "CIMIC" refers to both a capability (trained and designated CIMIC forces), as well as a joint function that can be performed by all NATO personnel (the act of engaging/cooperating with civil actors). These issues are addressed throughout this chapter.
3. James, C. McConville, *Army Multi-Domain Transformation Ready to Win in Competition and Conflict*, Chief of Staff Paper #1 (Unclassified Version) (Washington, DC: Headquarters, Department of the Army, 2021), i.
4. Christopher Holshek, ed., *Civil Affairs: A Force for Influence in Competition; Civil Affairs Issue Papers, Vol. 7, 2020–2021* (Arlington: Association of the United States Army, April 2021), 6.
5. FM 3-57, *Civil Affairs Operations* (Washington, DC: Headquarters, Department of the Army, 2021), 3–19.
6. Tom Harper and James Armstrong, *The Era of Constant Competition – Purposes and Principles* (Carlisle: Army College War Room, July 29, 2021).
7. Csaba Szabó and Robert Nicholson, "Civil Affairs and Civil-Military Cooperation: A Hybrid Solution to Defeat Hybrid Threats," in *Civil Affairs Issue Papers, Vol. 7, 2020–2021* (Arlington, VA: Association of the United States Army, April 2021), 49.
8. North Atlantic Council Military Committee (MC) 0411/2, *NATO Military Policy on Civil-Military Cooperation (CIMIC) and Civil-Military Interaction (CMI)* (Mons, Belgium, SHAPE, May 12, 2014), 4.
9. Transition management is discussed in AJP 3.19, *NATO CIMIC*, 5-5/6.
10. AJP 3.19, *NATO CIMIC*, 1–10.
11. Jim Garamone, "DoD Unveils Women, Peace, Security Strategy," *DoD News* (Washington, DC: Department of Defense), June 11, 2020.
12. AJP 3.19, *NATO CIMIC*, 1–12
13. Ibid., 2–3 and 4–5/6.
14. This is discussed more deeply in chapter 3. "Cognitive warfare" is a concept that is quickly gaining recognition in both US and NATO

operations narrative. To learn more, go to the Allied Command for Transformation "Innovation Hub" page on cognitive warfare: www.innovationhub-act.org/content/cognitive-warfare. See the CCoE website https:///www.cimic-coe.org.

15. See Bryce Loidolt, *Doing Well by Doing Good? Strategic Competition and United Nations Peacekeeping* (Washington, DC: Center for Strategic Research Institute for National Strategic Studies National Defense University, 2021); as well as Christopher Holshek, "American Needs Peacekeeping Missions More than Ever," *Foreign Policy*, November 10, 2015.

16. Office for the Coordination of Humanitarian Affairs (OCHA) Civil-Military Coordination Section (CMCS), *UN-CMCoord Field Handbook*, version 1.0 (Geneva: UN OCHA, October 2015), 7.

17. Office of Military Affairs, *United Nations Infantry Battalion Manual (UNIBAM)*, 2nd ed. (New York: Department of Peace Operations, January 2020); see especially 17–18 and 67–68.

18. United Nations Development Programme, *UN Development Report 1994* (New York: Oxford University Press, 1994).

19. US Department of State, *United States Strategy on Women, Peace and Security* (Washington, DC: US Department of State, 2019).

20. UK Ministry of Defense, *Introducing the Integrated Operating Concept* (MoD Abbeywood South, Assets Publishing Services, 2020).

21. Australian Government Civil-Military Center website, http://www.acmc.gov.au/.

22. For a greater explanation of the terms "strategic scouts" and "strategic enablers," see Christopher Holshek, "American Needs Peacekeeping Missions More than Ever." See also his "U.S. Military Observers and Comprehensive Engagement," *Small Wars Journal*, February 10, 2011.

23. Charles Cleveland, Benjamin Jensen, Susan Bryant, and Arnel David, *Military Strategy in the 21st Century: People, Connectivity, and Competition* (Amherst, NY: Cambria Press, 2018), 4.

Conclusion

Arnel P. David, Sean A. Acosta, and Nicholas Krohley

A new great game is underway. The United States and its core allies are engaged in a global competition for power and influence. This competition is taking place in a fragmenting international order, where the structures and norms of the recent past are increasingly obsolete. The US remains at war among people, all over the world. Whereas "some will argue that technology will simplify future military operations, the evidence overwhelmingly indicates that warfare remains a fundamentally human endeavor."[1] This book is a clarion call to build and improve capabilities for the human domain. These are capabilities that, despite their small size and limited footprint, deliver disproportionate results and return on investment.

MASTERING THE PLAYING FIELD

To compete and win in the new great game, the US military requires a detailed, up-to-the-minute understanding of the playing field (which is constantly shifting), the rules (which are being continuously rewritten and frequently ignored anyhow), opponents (who may or may not declare themselves as such), and the global community of spectators (who have a habit of jumping in and out the game when it suits them). There is no referee.

Such an environment calls for a network of sensors that can deliver a granular, nuanced understanding of the state of play—and who can, in turn, be leveraged to shape the game in America's favor. Conventional wisdom in Western defense circles is that technological innovation—specifically in the fields of artificial intelligence, machine learning, and edge computing—will transform the military's ability to understand operational environments.[2] The evangelists of technology offer an alluring narrative, which features understanding at the push of a button and data-driven predictive forecasting. We, the editors, are deeply skeptical of this view. Human beings are required to make sense of the human domain, and humans still possess the best "processor" ever created.

There is a clear risk in the future that the trend-chasing embrace of technology as an analytical panacea will bring an explosion of quant-backed departments and programs. Technology firms and defense contractors will reap fortunes—but to what end, if they are unable to explain the world around us?

This is not an argument against technology. Rather, it is a recognition of what technology and data-driven analysis can and cannot do. To make sense of the world, patterns and correlation are not good enough. The US government needs causal understanding achieved via human insight. As the US military grows increasingly dependent on technology, an investment in human capability is essential to counterbalance and provide deep context. Civil Affairs forces, operating on the ground among people, are a cost-effective choice to complement technological developments.

The Case for Warrior Diplomats

This book opened with a survey of America's geopolitical landscape. Chapter 1 explored how, as the international system disaggregates, local fault lines take on strategic significance. The erosion of international structures and norms demands an agile approach to alliance-building and the management of international relations, which must grow from the mastery of local detail. Chapter 2 examined how the rise of competition in the space between peace and all-out war requires creative thinking, the anticipation of second- and third-order effects, and recognition of the *opportunities* inherent in such ambiguity. Chapter 3 highlighted the need to rethink and reframe America's approach to the human domain, highlighting the shortcomings of the status quo.

This book has also argued for the importance of warrior diplomats, particularly from the US military's Civil Affairs community. At present, the US military is the dominant instrument of American influence abroad. Putting aside the desirability of this state of affairs and the intentionality through which this came to be, it is a matter of fact. And—barring seismic shifts in the State Department's operational posture, risk appetite, and staffing levels—this fact will not change for the foreseeable future. In the new great game, the US military thus has to play a range of vital roles, which transcend the application of violence.

The gray zone, where the US engages in competition without escalating to large-scale conflict, is filled with ambiguity. Chapter 2 argued that this ambiguity should be viewed opportunistically. However, this requires the US government to be comfortable being uncomfortable. The military must understand (and invest in) the few capabilities—most notably, Civil Affairs—that are able to maneuver in this environment.

This book has offered ideas as to how Civil Affairs can become a more effective geopolitical weapon. Civil Affairs has not reached its full potential. Part of the blame lies within Civil Affairs, which needs to become sharper and more consistent and put forward a clearer value proposition to the Joint Force. This is not simply a marketing challenge. If Civil Affairs were as formidable as it needs to be, the Civil Affairs "brand" would have established itself already. Concurrently, Civil Affairs's customers across the Joint Force can make better use of this capability—a shift that requires the US military to make clear what, precisely, it wants from Civil Affairs. Civil Affairs should be the US military's premier network of human sensors across the spectrum of conflict, monitoring the civil dynamics that comprise the vast majority of any operational environment.

This book has laid out several paths through which these objectives might be realized. Chapter 4 explained how civil reconnaissance delivers essential knowledge. These contextual insights must become a core feature of intelligence analysis. Until this occurs, and until the US military adopts an intelligence architecture that examines opposing forces as an integral feature of the human context in which competition and conflict occur, the US will remain unable to make sense of its strategic environment.[3] Chapter 5 argued that the methods through which civil considerations are assessed and operationalized require urgent and radical change and further explained how civil reconnaissance could be integrated into the military's central nervous system—thereby addressing architectural faults in America's intelligence apparatus. Chapter 6 offered a vignette of civil engagement and network development, showcasing Civil Affairs's unique capability to harness civil and military networks and then employ them against destabilizing vulnerabilities.

The final three chapters of this book offered suggestions on how the civil-oriented capabilities of the US military and its allies could be enhanced. Chapter 7 laid out the benefits of further integrating the US Army components of Civil Affairs forces. The greatest disservice done to Civil Affairs and its ability to support the Joint Force was the 2006 decision to remove the reserve component of US Army Civil Affairs from US Special Operations Command. "The Divorce," as this event has become known within Civil Affairs, has badly undermined training, manning, and equipping units of action. US Army Civil Affairs and Psychological Operations Command has yet to recover and struggles to recruit, educate, train, and deploy, competent Civil Affairs forces. Meanwhile, their active-duty special operations Civil Affairs counterparts in the 95th Civil Affairs brigade are narrowing their skillsets and rebranding to specialize and differentiate from the reserves.

Chapter 8 argued for enhanced cooperation between US Army and Marine Corps Civil Affairs and the need to break down silos within the Department of Defense and fuse Civil Affairs activities with other information-related capabilities. Chapter 9 explained how Civil Affairs forces can leverage the access and insights of its CIMIC counterparts around the world, creating a global influence network. Across each of these chapters, recurring themes included the need for integration and unity of effort and the key role of Civil Affairs as a low-cost, high-impact catalyst of action.

RETHINKING STRATEGIC COMPETITION

Although the strategic competition paradigm is endorsed in the introduction of this book, insofar as it describes an international system in entropy, wherein aspiring powers compete for influence, a critical caveat is necessary with respect to how strategic competition is understood and operationalized.

The prevailing narrative features the United States in competition with a select few opponents.[4] In this framing, the vast majority of the world serves as the backdrop for elite rivalry. Africa is a place in which the US competes for influence with China. Eastern Europe is a place where the US competes with Russia. The Middle East is a place where the US battles to maintain a (marginally) favorable status quo, in the face of an openly hostile Iran and opportunistic encroachment by Russia and China alike. Southeast Asia (and, remarkably, Latin America) are places where the US checks Chinese encroachment. Jihadist terrorism sporadically registers on America's strategic radar, but it no longer holds the spotlight.

At a strategic level, this may seem a coherent approach. The United States' national security interests are being contested by these select few opponents. Surely, the US should frame the new great game accordingly?

This framing is illusory, however, and dangerous. There is a reason why, for all the effort devoted to grand strategy, that the United States consistently fails to translate theory into action. It is easy to sit in Washington or London and speak of the new great game as a head-to-head contest among aspiring great powers (just as it was easy, for the past two decades, to pontificate about a global war on terrorism). Within these paradigms, the US is overwhelmingly concerned with its foes, who are easily identified. The US focuses on their words, their objectives, their capabilities, and their actions. *They* are the competitors. The US will defeat *them*. The US may pay lip service to winning a war of ideas and the mantra that "the human terrain is the decisive terrain," but the US is overwhelmingly focused on the application of power against specific targets.

If the US adopts this mindset in the new great game, it will continue its twenty-first-century losing streak. The United States has not lost the war in Afghanistan due to a lack of insight into the Taliban or an inability to sufficiently disrupt and degrade its operational networks. The opposite is the case: the US has lost the war in Afghanistan because its military failed to understand the majority of Afghans, who are *not* the Taliban, and the ways in which civil dynamics have enabled the Taliban to adapt and regenerate, while Afghan governance and security provision remained woefully inadequate.

Similarly, the failures in Iraq were not a byproduct of the US military's inability to find, fix, and finish members of Al-Qaeda, the Islamic State, or the constellation of Shi'a militias that have fought against the US in that theater. Instead, the US military proved unable to navigate the fault lines of Iraqi society at the tactical level, while being repeatedly outmaneuvered by Iran at the strategic level (due, in large measure, to Iran's vastly superior knowledge of the operational environment).

Looking more broadly at the post-9/11 campaign against jihadist terrorism, one can see that the potency of this threat is, inarguably, more formidable in 2023 than it was on September 10, 2001. This is despite a steady drumbeat of tactical successes over two decades of intensive targeting. Time and again, America's enemies have adapted and regenerated, sustained via robust root structures that sink deep into localized features of the human terrain—root structures that are not captured within the analytical processes that drive military action.

It is a truism that "all politics is local." In a domestic context, Americans grasp this intuitively. For reasons unknown, the US has failed to appreciate that this holds for geopolitics as well.[5] Strategic competition is not simply a global contest among aspiring hegemons in which the features of the playing field are secondary to the actions of the main competitors. The reality of the current geopolitical environment is that local concerns have global resonance.[6] From the Black Sea region to the Sahel and to the Mekong River Basin, fundamentally *local* dynamics set the stage for the new great game. Victory will go to whoever masters the details of the operational environment.

This is where the warrior diplomat has a vital role to play. Although the US is engaged in competition with China, Russia, and Iran while facing threats of jihadist terrorism, the US would be doing itself a devastating disservice if it were to approach the rest of the world on the basis of its utility in these contests.

It is transparent (in a bad way) that US foreign policy engagement in much of sub-Saharan Africa is downstream of concerns about China. The same is true for US engagement in Iraq vis-à-vis Iran. There is tremendous risk inherent in a worldview wherein the US government instrumentalizes its bilateral relationships with smaller powers in pursuit of strategic advantage. This instrumentalization is readily apparent to those on the receiving end and provokes cynicism and frustration. Ultimately, it is exploitative and self-defeating. The West must do better.

TAKING THE OFFENSIVE

George Washington opined "...that offensive operations, oftentimes, is the *surest*, if not the *only* (in some cases) means of defense."[7] The words of America's first president are just as relevant today as they were then. Strategists and pundits proclaim the inevitability of a rising China. To date, China spreads its global reach via economic and political deals with despots, as seen in Cambodia, Zimbabwe, and Venezuela.[8] These "deals," which come under China's One Belt, One Road initiative, offer a brutally honest view of what it means to align with China's vision of the future: crippling debt servitude to China, the corrupt enrichment of the ruling elite, and the stifling of democratic reforms.

Russia, for its part, seeks to spread discord and disruption within its near abroad—yet shows little aptitude beyond creating geopolitical messes. Russia's performance in Ukraine since February 2022 has been the most extreme example. Previously, the Kremlin's "hybrid warfare" prowess had received breathless praise from pundits, despite a shocking failure in Donbas in 2014 (where the Russians proved unable to mobilize coherent local support, despite overwhelmingly favorable demographics and a populace that had been steeped in Russian propaganda for generations).

Finally, Iran exerts influence, and kinetic power, through its regional web of proxy militias, prompting talk of a "*Shi'a* crescent" from Tehran to the Mediterranean. Upon closer examination, however, Iran's proxy forces find themselves on increasingly shaky ground—most clearly in Iraq, where they are principally employed in the crushing of democratic street politics and have categorically failed to mobilize substantive popular support at the ballot box. In every case, ordinary civilians are suffering, while the United States and its allies are on the defensive.

Why are the US and its allies on their collective back foot? Retired US Army general Charles Cleveland made this salient point at a conference with UK special operations forces: "The Achilles heel of every authoritarian government is its people."[9] There is a clear opportunity to appeal to the people who inhabit contested terrain. The world is increasingly wary of economic and political predation at the hands of China. This is particularly true in South and Central America. Ecuador, for example, has found itself indebted to China, following the construction of a $19 billion dam that was touted as the answer to poverty and high energy costs.[10] This dam is now inoperable due to shoddy construction. Domestic energy costs remain unchanged, while the government strains under a staggering debt burden (and China has acquired 80–90 percent of the country's oil exports at a premium rate).[11]

In an effort to put the United States and others on notice, Russia's state-run media released a list of "unfriendly countries."[12] Embarrassingly for Russia, however, the list was dominated by former members of the Soviet Union and Warsaw Pact, showing how Russian aggression has poisoned popular perceptions among populations that Russia considers to be well within its sphere of influence. Fallout from the 2022 invasion of Ukraine has guaranteed the toxicity of Russia's reputation for generations, while pushing more and more European states to seek protection from within the NATO alliance.

It is time for the United States and its allies to take the offensive in the human domain. The new great game will not be won with tentative defensive actions. It is time to deal with Chinese economic aggression while developing and expanding existing partnerships offering viable alternatives.[13] It is time to address Russia's toxic behavior and discard the United States' baseless respect for the Kremlin's soft power. It is time for the United States to align with the ordinary people of the Middle East, who suffer at the hands of Iran's proxy militias.

This approach requires granular knowledge of local dynamics and the ways in which these dynamics resonate upwards to the strategic level. American foreign policy must be designed and executed with grounding in local specificity. The undoing of American grand strategy for generations has been caused by plans and polices being crafted by individuals who are dangerously insulated from ground truth—not simply because of their physical distance from contested terrain but because local detail is not adequately captured and integrated within the intelligence architecture that drives strategic decision-making.

Which organization within the Department of Defense, or any other US government agency for that matter, is postured to investigate, analyze, and offer insight into the human domain? Civil Affairs sits at the top of the list. The only way to make informed strategic decisions is to first understand the context in which challenges and opportunities emerge. This can be achieved via civil reconnaissance, as conducted by Civil Affairs forces—but, as argued in chapter 5, only if such investigation is properly situated within America's intelligence architecture. Furthermore, the critical undertaking of civil network engagement creates bilateral relationships, if properly and *genuinely* developed, that will confer the competitive advantage that the United States seeks. Indeed, "the decisive battle will occur before the first shot is fired as actors compete to amplify internal divisions and develop key partnerships."[14]

PREPARING FOR THE NEXT FIGHT

This book advocates for a range of new ideas that would help reframe the US government's perception of the current geopolitical environment and enable the US and its allies to recalibrate their sensors and refine the tools with which policy is developed and implemented. There is a clear gap between the soldier and the diplomat that must be bridged. Absent clear policy aims informed by a granular understanding of ground truth, violence by military force begets more violence. The military winds up "fighting without winning."[15] Meanwhile, diplomats are unable to gain the necessary access and develop the needed relationships in order to seize the initiative on contested terrain.[16]

Both civilian and military leaders have a natural tendency to focus on macro-level dynamics rather than on the local drivers of violence and instability.[17] The US military is notably and dangerously reluctant to empower its frontline personnel to draw strategic inferences from tactical realities. The siloed nature of the civil-military divide inhibits the resolution of protracted conflict, despite the evident complementarity of these capabilities. This lack of coordination costs lives and loses wars. Given the need to compete in contested, dangerous places and there being no substitute for ground context, the nation needs a cadre of professionals capable of operating in such complex settings. These are the warrior diplomats.

The US needs to invest in human capabilities that will magnify power, suffuse legitimacy, and increase influence in the new great game. Presently, the US military does not know how to *look* at civil dynamics and has no viable framework to prioritize, investigate, and operationalize them.[18] As such, the United States is utterly adrift in the human domain. Military commanders are often unsure as to how Civil Affairs forces should be utilized, and Civil Affairs itself struggles to articulate a clear value proposition. To address this are the following three interconnected recommendations to policymakers within the US national security enterprise:

First, the US military must adopt a new investigative framework for the human domain, which integrates contextual understanding into enemy-centric intelligence. This is a call to reexamine the military's intelligence architecture—the structures and systems through which the United States makes sense of the world and the place of adversaries therein. The current siloed approach, in which intelligence professionals examine opposing forces while capabilities like Civil Affairs examine the ground upon which the military confronts them, is fatally flawed. These parallel lines of inquiry cannot be fused together retroactively. It is not possible to establish causal relationships between the actions of foes and the human context in which they occur if the two are not investigated within a single, coherent process.

The root-map construct has been offered as a key element of a revised intelligence architecture. Such an approach would broaden the view of enemy-centric intelligence, breaking down silos to capture an opponent's connectivity to the wider human domain. The root map would thereafter provide Civil Affairs with clear investigative tasking, establishing an analytical bridge between enemy-centric intelligence and civil reconnaissance. At the same time, additional innovation is needed in relation to current American approaches to cognition and influence. The US military needs to solidify concepts like cognitive warfare and the human domain itself. The US arsenal needs humans who can understand and influence other humans. A small sliver of the military can provide this capability at scale, but policy direction is needed to achieve results.

The second recommendation is a fundamental reorganization of the Civil Affairs enterprise to include a close examination of authorities and ownership. At the moment, the Civil Affairs community lacks coherence, vision, and a sense of urgency to effect change. What does the US military want and need from Civil Affairs? How is that demand signal translated into staffing, training, and deployment posture? Resolving these questions requires external input from stakeholders outside of Civil Affairs. It also requires Civil Affairs's leadership to articulate its own vision for the capability—as much of the US military's senior leadership simply does not know what it wants from Civil Affairs.

To date, no such vision has been offered from within Civil Affairs. Senior leader advocacy is absent, with minimal representation at the Pentagon. The divide between the active-duty and reserve components continues to grow. Without vocal, visionary leadership and senior-level policy implementation, the nation's warrior diplomats will never reach their full potential.

The Civil Affairs community requires restructuring with an emphasis on multicomponent integration. More urgently, however, it needs an honest evaluation of what Civil Affairs forces can actually achieve. Civil Affairs forces are spread far too thinly and have consistently underwhelmed their customers. The reserve component's longstanding posture as an under-resourced and under-trained "jack-of-all-trades" cannot continue.[19] Nor can active-duty forces continue to repeatedly shift direction in their push toward professionalization. Civil Affairs as a whole needs a narrowed, refocused mission set, from which shortfalls in structure, training, education, and readiness can be remedied.

Our third and final recommendation is to focus the entire Civil Affairs enterprise on the provision of insight into the playing field of conflict and competition. To be taken seriously, Civil Affairs forces need an identity based on valued contributions and known outputs: Civil Affairs forces must master a limited number of critical tasks. This book has advanced the importance of understanding and contextual insight—a vision of Civil Affair as warrior diplomats, the essential global scouts in the new great game.

Absent an urgent course correction, Civil Affairs will continue on a trajectory of accelerating decline and disinvestment. This course correction can be done via the professionalization of how civil reconnaissance is conducted and the standardization of deliverables that drive civil knowledge integration. Civil reconnaissance and civil knowledge integration should therefore be added to the universal joint task list. This is necessary to provide military institutions with the direction, focus, and resources to train on what is *essential*. Doing so will mean that Civil Affairs can optimize its role within the Joint Force so that the US military as a whole might remedy a weakness that has subverted its effectiveness for decades.

NOTES

1. US Department of the Army, *Army Doctrine Publication 1, The Army* (Washington, DC: Government Printing Office, 2012).
2. This sentiment is strong within defense. There are countless efforts to integrate AI/ML into military operations. See Adam Frisk, "What is Project Maven? The Pentagon AI project Google employees want out of," *Global News*, April 5, 2018, https://globalnews.ca/news/4125382/google-pentagon-ai-project-maven/.
3. Nicholas Krohley and Stefan Muehlich, "Who Cares About Context: The Case for Getting Serious in the Civil Environment," *Modern War Institute*, July 20, 2022, https://mwi.usma.edu/who-cares-about-context-the-case-for-getting-serious-in-the-civil-environment/.
4. Marcus Hicks, Kyle Atwell, and Dan Collini, "Great-Power Competition is Coming to Africa: The United States Needs to Think Regionally to Win," *Foreign Affairs*, March 4, 2021, https://www.foreignaffairs.com/articles/africa/2021-03-04/great-power-competition-coming-africa.
5. This is a major finding in peace research. See Severine Autesserre, *The Frontlines of Peace: An Insider's Guide to Changing the World* (New York: Oxford University Press, 2021).
6. Dominic Tierney, "The Future of Sino-U.S. Proxy War," *Texas National Security Review* 4, no. 2 (Spring 2021), https://tnsr.org/2021/03/the-future-of-sino-u-s-proxy-war/.
7. George Washington, "From George Washington to John Trumbull, 25 June 1799," in *The Papers of George Washington*, Retirement Series, vol. 4, *20 April 1799–13 December 1799*, ed. W. W. Abbot (Charlottesville: University Press of Virginia, 1999), 156–159.
8. Ryan Dube and Gabrielle Steinhauser, "China's Global Mega-Projects Are Falling Apart," *The Wall Street Journal*, January 20, 2023, https://www.wsj.com/articles/china-global-mega-projects-infrastructure-falling-apart-11674166180
9. Charles T. Cleveland, "On a Theory of Special Warfare," Land Special Operations Conference, United Kingdom, April 21, 2021.
10. Frederico Rios Escobar, "It Doesn't Matter if Ecuador Can Afford This Dam. China Still Gets Paid," *New York Times*, December 24, 2018, https://www.nytimes.com/2018/12/24/world/americas/ecuador-china-dam.html.
11. Ibid.

12. Peter Dickinson, "Putin's Imperialism Turns Neighbors into Enemies," *Atlantic Council*, April 27, 2021, https://www.atlanticcouncil.org/blogs/ukrainealert/putins-imperialism-turns-neighbors-into-enemies/.

13. Economic aggression is a term coined by H. R. McMaster to describe China's debt entrapment tactics. For more information read H. R. McMaster, *Battlegrounds* (New York: HarperCollins Publishers, 2020).

14. Charles T. Cleveland, Benjamin Jensen, Susan Bryant, and Arnel P. David, *Military Strategy in the 21st Century: People, Connectivity, and Competition* (Amherst, NY: Cambria Press, 2018) 4.

15. See Emma Sky, interview by Peter Roberts, *Western Way of War*, https://rusi.org/sites/default/files/wowow50-transcript.pdf.

16. Nadia Schadlow, *War and the Art of Governance: Consolidating Combat Success into Political Victory* (Washington, DC: Georgetown University Press, 2017).

17. Celestino Perez, Jr., "Strategic Discontent, Political Literacy, and Professional Military Education," *Strategy Bridge*, January 14, 2016, https://thestrategybridge.org/the-bridge/2016/1/7/strategic-discontent-political-literacy-and-professional-military-education.

18. Nicholas Krohley and Stefan Muelhich, "NATO CIMIC & US Civil Affairs: Doctrinal Review & Comparative Assessment," *NATO CIMIC Centre of Excellence*, June 15, 2022, https://www.cimic-coe.org/resources/ccoe-publications/nato-cimic-us-ca-doctrinal-review-and-comparative-assessment.pdf.

19. Stefan Muehlich and Nicholas Krohley, NATO CIMIC and US Civil Affairs Doctrinal Review & Comparative Assessment, published by NATO CIMIC Centre of Excellence, The Hague, June 2022, https://www.cimic-coe.org/resources/ccoe-publications/nato-cimic-us-ca-doctrinal-review-and-comparative-assessment.pdf.

INDEX

About the Editors

Sean A. Acosta is a senior noncommissioned officer in the US Army. He has deployed multiple times to Southwest Asia, the Caribbean, and Africa in support of special operations missions. He holds a bachelor's degree from Norwich University. He was a founding member and Co-Editor-in-Chief of the *Eunomia Journal*, a publication focused on the human domain and the military forces operating within it.

Arnel P. David is a colonel in the US Army and a PhD student at King's College London. He has a mix of conventional and special operations assignments with six combat tours of duty in the Middle East, Central Asia, and the Pacific. He holds masters' degrees from the University of Oklahoma and the US Army Command and General Staff College Local Dynamics of War Scholar Program. His last publication was *Military Strategy in the 21st Century*.

Nicholas Krohley is the Principal of FrontLine Advisory and a specialist in civil reconnaissance. He is an advisor on the human domain of conflict and competition, working with the US government and its allies worldwide. Dr. Krohley, who earned his PhD at King's College London, publishes widely in military journals and is the author of *The Death of the Mehdi Army: The Rise, Fall, and Revival of Iraq's Most Powerful Militia*.

About the Contributors

David Allen (OBE) is a lieutenant colonel in the British Army. He is currently a unit commander and is a PhD Candidate at Cranfield University with masters' degrees from Cranfield and Kings College London.

Kyle Atwell is an Army Officer, cofounder of the Irregular Warfare Initiative, instructor in the Social Sciences Department at West Point, and nonresident senior fellow at the Atlantic Council. He has operational experience in West Africa, South Korea, Germany, and Afghanistan.

Guy A. Berry, Jr. is a Civil Affairs non-commissioned officer still serving on active duty. He has deployed twice to the Middle East and three times to East Africa. He holds a bachelor of science in Management from Excelsior College.

Rob Boudreau is a major in the United States Marine Corps Reserve and has served as a Civil Affairs Officer and a Judge Advocate. Rob holds a juris doctor from Boston University and bachelor's and master's degrees from SUNY Albany.

Kevin Chapla is a US Army major serving as a Middle East and North Africa Foreign Area Officer with experience in Africa and the Indo-Pacific. Kevin holds a master's degree in Security Studies from Georgetown University.

Dan Collini is a retired Civil Affairs officer with operational experience in Afghanistan and Africa. He served as a Joint Chiefs of Staff Fellow and contributed to cybersecurity policy at the National Security Council. Dan received a master's degree from Georgetown University and holds Executive Certificates from both Harvard University and Cornell University.

Susan Gannon is a US Army colonel and the commander of the 36oth Civil Affairs Brigade. She holds a bachelor's degree from the University of Pittsburgh, a master's degree from Webster University, and was an Army War College Fellow at Tufts University.

Christopher Holshek is a US Army Civil Affairs retired colonel, CA Association Vice President for programs and events, edits the Civil Affairs Issue Papers and is Distinguished Member of the CA Corps. His insights reflect four decades of US, NATO, and UN civil-military engagement.

James P. Micciche is a US Army strategist with operational and deployment experience in the Middle East, Africa, Afghanistan, Europe, and Indo-Pacific. He holds degrees from the Fletcher School at Tufts University and Troy University.

Diana X. Moga is a major in the US Marine Corps Reserves. She is an associate at J. P. Morgan and holds a bachelor of science from the United States Naval Academy.

Aleksandra Nesic is Senior Social Scientist at Valka-Mir Human Security and a visiting professor at the Joint Special Operations University. Her research focus is cognitive warfare and violent extremism. She holds a PhD in Political Psychology and Conflict Analysis.

Albert Oh is an active duty Foreign Area Officer. He has served at the JFK Special Warfare Center & School and 98th Civil Affairs Battalion. He holds a master of international public policy from Johns Hopkins University and a bachelor of science from West Point.

Assad Raza is a retired US Army Civil Affairs Officer. He holds a bachelor's degree from the University of Tampa, a master's degree from Norwich University, and a master in military art and science from the US Army Command & General Staff College.

Kyle Staron is a Presidential Management Fellow at the Department of State, overseeing security cooperation in east Africa. He is also a Civil Affairs officer with deployments to Afghanistan, Bahrain, and Niger. He holds a bachelor of science from the United States Military Academy and a master of arts from Columbia University.

Lucas Vaughan is a staff sergeant in the US Army. He is the enlisted lead of the Civil Knowledge Integration Section at the 96th Civil Affairs Battalion and holds a bachelor's degree from Lubbock Christian University.

CAMBRIA RAPID COMMUNICATIONS IN CONFLICT AND SECURITY (RCCS) SERIES

General Editor: Geoffrey R. H. Burn

The aim of the RCCS series is to provide policy makers, practitioners, analysts, and academics with in-depth analysis of fast-moving topics that require urgent yet informed debate. Since its launch in October 2015, the RCCS series has the following book publications:

- *A New Strategy for Complex Warfare: Combined Effects in East Asia* by Thomas A. Drohan
- *US National Security: New Threats, Old Realities* by Paul R. Viotti
- *Security Forces in African States: Cases and Assessment* edited by Paul Shemella and Nicholas Tomb
- *Trust and Distrust in Sino-American Relations: Challenge and Opportunity* by Steve Chan
- *The Gathering Pacific Storm: Emerging US-China Strategic Competition in Defense Technological and Industrial Development* edited by Tai Ming Cheung and Thomas G. Mahnken
- *Military Strategy for the 21st Century: People, Connectivity, and Competition* by Charles Cleveland, Benjamin Jensen, Susan Bryant, and Arnel David
- *Ensuring National Government Stability After US Counterinsurgency Operations: The Critical Measure of Success* by Dallas E. Shaw Jr.
- *Reassessing U.S. Nuclear Strategy* by David W. Kearn, Jr.
- *Deglobalization and International Security* by T. X. Hammes
- *American Foreign Policy and National Security* by Paul R. Viotti

- *Make America First Again: Grand Strategy Analysis and the Trump Administration* by Jacob Shively
- *Learning from Russia's Recent Wars: Why, Where, and When Russia Might Strike Next* by Neal G. Jesse
- *Restoring Thucydides: Testing Familiar Lessons and Deriving New Ones* by Andrew R. Novo and Jay M. Parker
- *Net Assessment and Military Strategy: Retrospective and Prospective Essays* edited by Thomas G. Mahnken, with an introduction by Andrew W. Marshall
- *Deterrence by Denial: Theory and Practice* edited by Alex S. Wilner and Andreas Wenger
- *Negotiating the New START Treaty* by Rose Gottemoeller
- *Party, Politics, and the Post-9/11 Army* by Heidi A. Urben
- *Resourcing the National Security Enterprise: Connecting the Ends and Means of US National Security* edited by Susan Bryant and Mark Troutman
- *Subcontinent Adrift: Strategic Futures of South Asia* by Feroz Hassan Khan
- *The Next Major War: Can the US and its Allies Win Against China?* by Ross Babbage
- *Warrior Diplomats: Civil Affairs Forces on the Front Lines* edited by Arnel David, Sean Acosta, and Nicholas Krohley
- *Russia and the Changing Character of Conflict* by Tracey German

For more information, see **cambriapress.com**.

www.ingramcontent.com/pod-product-compliance
Lightning Source LLC
Chambersburg PA
CBHW050338270326
41926CB00016B/3516